ABBOTSFORD AND SIR WALTER SCOTT
THE IMAGE AND THE INFLUENCE

come and view Conundrum Castle where as you go or come

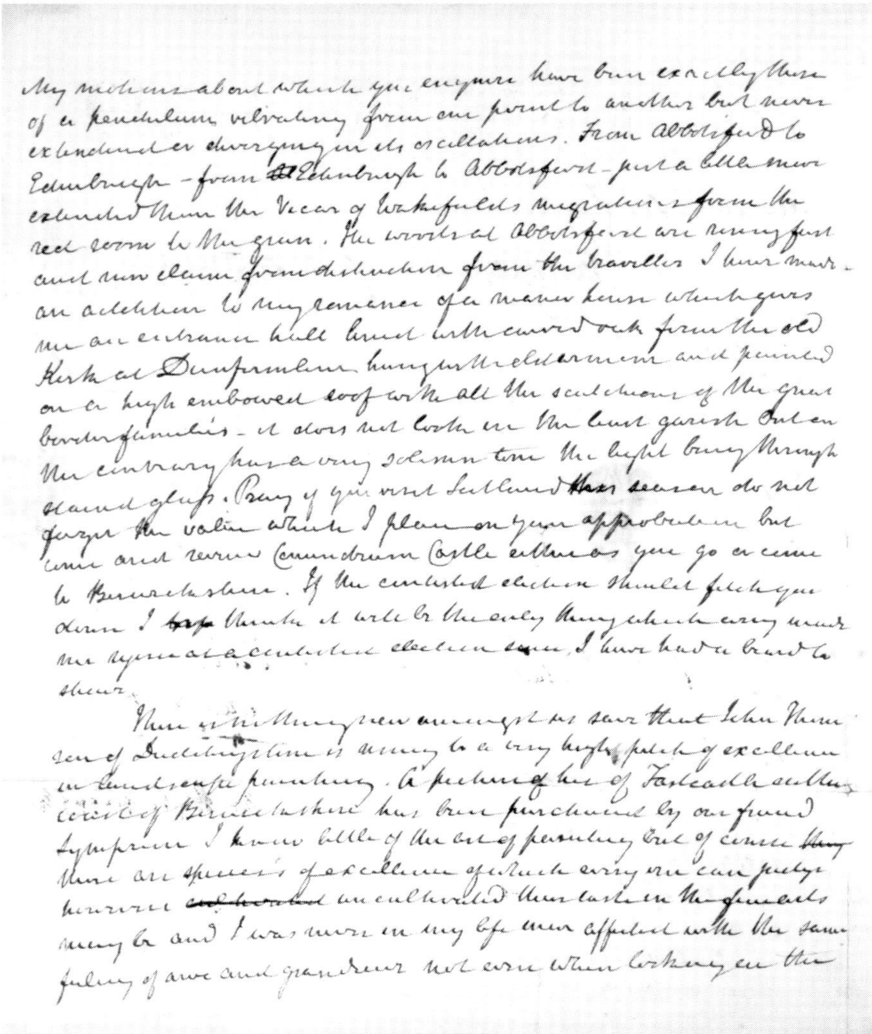

My motions about which you enquire have been exactly those of a pendulum vibrating from one point to another but never extended or diverging in its oscillations. From Abbotsford to Edinburgh — from ~~Ab~~ Edinburgh to Abbotsford — just a little more extended than the Vicar of Wakefield's migrations from the red room to the green. The woods at Abbotsford are rising fast and now claim protection from the traveller. I have made an addition to my romance of a manor house which gives me an entrance hall lined with carved oak from the old Kirk at Dunfermline hung with old armour and painted on a high embowed roof with all the scutcheons of the great border families — it does not look in the least garish but on the contrary has a very solemn tone the light being through stained glass. Pray if you visit Scotland ~~this~~ season do not forget the value which I place on your approbation but come and review Conundrum Castle either as you go or come to Berwickshire. If the contested election should fetch you down I ~~hope~~ think it will be the only thing which could make me rejoice at a contested election since I have had a hand to share.

There is nothing new amongst us save that John Thomson of Duddingstone is rising to a very high pitch of excellence in landscape painting. A picture of his of Fastcastle on the coast of Berwickshire has been purchased by our friend Sympson. I know little of the art of painting but of course there are species of excellence of which every one can judge however ~~untutored~~ uncultivated their taste in the fine arts may be and I was never in my life more affected with the same feeling of awe and grandeur not even when looking on the

FIGURE i

Scott's letter of 7 July 1824 to Sir James Stuart of Allanbank conveys memorably his delight in Abbotsford and its plantations, describes his current decorative schemes for the house with their antiquarian inspiration and invites his correspondent's approbation with a personal visit of inspection to Conundrum Castle.

(National Library of Scotland, MS 23141, f. 146v)

ABBOTSFORD
AND
SIR WALTER SCOTT

The Image and the Influence

Edited by
IAIN GORDON BROWN

Society of Antiquaries of Scotland

Published in 2003 by Society of Antiquaries of Scotland.
Editor: Iain Gordon Brown

Society of Antiquaries of Scotland, Royal Museum of Scotland,
Chambers Street, Edinburgh EH1 1JF.
Tel 0131 247 4115
Fax 0131 247 4163
Email socantscot@nms.ac.uk
Website www.socantscot.org

British Library Cataloguing-in-Publication Data
A catalogue record for this book is available from the British Library

ISBN 0 903903 26 1

Cover image:
Sir Walter Scott by Sir William Allan
(by courtesy of the National Portrait Gallery, London)

Typeset by Waverley Typesetters, Galashiels
Designed by Lawrie Law and Alison Rae
Manufactured in Great Britain by Bookcraft Ltd, Midsomer Norton

CONTENTS

ABBREVIATIONS

INSTITUTIONS

NAS	National Archives of Scotland
NGS	National Galleries of Scotland
NLS	National Library of Scotland
NMAS	National Museum of Antiquities of Scotland
NMRS	National Monuments Record of Scotland
NMS	National Museums of Scotland
RCAHMS	Royal Commission on the Ancient & Historical Monuments of Scotland
SNPG	Scottish National Portrait Gallery

PUBLICATIONS

Letters	*The Letters of Sir Walter Scott*, edited by H. J. C. Grierson, 12 vols, London 1932–7.
Life	John Gibson Lockhart, *The Life of Sir Walter Scott*, Edinburgh edition, 10 vols, Edinburgh 1902–3.
Journal	*The Journal of Sir Walter Scott*, edited by W. E. K. Anderson, Oxford 1972.
Romantic Interior	Clive Wainwright, *The Romantic Interior: the British Collector at Home 1750–1850*, New Haven and London 1989.

CONTRIBUTORS

Dr Iain Gordon Brown is Principal Curator of Manuscripts in the National Library of Scotland and is a Fellow of the Royal Society of Edinburgh and of the Society of Antiquaries of London. His academic work has concentrated on three areas: British antiquarianism and taste; the art and architecture of the eighteenth and early nineteenth centuries; and the literature and culture of the age of Sir Walter Scott. He has published widely in all these fields.

Dr Jeanne Cannizzo was the curator of the exhibition *O Caledonia! Sir Walter Scott and the Creation of Scotland* at the Scottish National Portrait Gallery in 1999. She is an anthropologist teaching in the School of Social and Political Studies at the University of Edinburgh where her field is material culture and museology.

Annette Carruthers is a Senior Lecturer at the University of St Andrews, where she teaches Art History and Museum and Gallery Studies. Her publications include *Edward Barnsley and his Workshop* and an edited volume on *The Scottish Home.* She is currently researching the Arts and Crafts Movement in Scotland.

Hugh Cheape is Curator of Modern Scottish Collections in the National Museums of Scotland, specialising in social and cultural history, in which area he has published widely. He joined the National Museum of Antiquities in 1974 and he has worked on the creation of a number of museums including the Museum of Scotland.

Trevor Cowie is a curator in the Department of Archaeology, National Museums of Scotland, with special responsibility for the Bronze Age collections. His research interests include the Neolithic and Bronze Age periods and focus especially on ceramics and metalwork. He is co-author of *Symbols of Power at the Time of Stonehenge.*

Dr John Frew is a Senior Lecturer at the School of Art History, University of St Andrews. His research interests focus on the Gothic and Mannerist Revivals as well as a wide range of issues relating to Scottish domestic architecture in the nineteenth and twentieth centuries.

Dr Jeremy Howard is a Lecturer at the School of Art History, University of St Andrews. Author and editor of various books and articles on central, east and northern European art 1620–1920. Particular interests include art and cultural transference; Russian art and architecture; and the movements of Romanticism, Realism and Art Nouveau. He was curator of the exhibition *William Allan, Artist Adventurer* (City Art Centre, Edinburgh, 2001).

David Jones lectures in Furniture History at the University of St Andrews. His publications include *The Vernacular Chair in Fife* (1996) and *The Edinburgh Cabinet & Chair Makers' Books of Prices 1805–1825* (2000).

Julie Lawson is a Senior Curator at the Scottish National Portrait Gallery, National Galleries of Scotland, Edinburgh. She read English and History of Art at Cambridge University. She has curated numerous exhibitions including *The Stones of Venice: Ruskin's Venice in Photographs* (1992); *Visions of the Ottoman Empire* (1995); *Prophets and Pilgrims: Ruskin, Proust and Northern Gothic* (1999); and *Thomas Carlyle: A Hero of his Time* (2001).

Dr Stephen Lloyd has been a Senior Curator at the Scottish National Portrait Gallery since 1993. Among his exhibition publications have been a series on portrait miniatures and one in 1999 on the pastellist Archibald Skirving (1749–1819). He received his doctorate – on the Regency artists, Richard and Maria Cosway – from Oxford University in 1997. He is a Fellow of the Societies of Antiquaries of Scotland and London.

Colin Wallace is a post-excavation archaeologist and editor, with special interests in writing and using the history of archaeology. At the time of the Society of Antiquaries of Scotland's Scott Conference and after, he was working in the Department of Archaeology, National Museums of Scotland.

PREFACE

THE conference 'Abbotsford and Sir Walter Scott: the Image and the Influence' was held in the autumn of 2000. It was organised by the Society of Antiquaries of Scotland as a tribute not only to Scott and his achievement at Abbotsford but also to the late Clive Wainwright, whose scholarship did so much to increase our understanding of Scott's house in the context of what Wainwright termed 'the Romantic interior'. The programme of lectures in Edinburgh and the visit to Abbotsford which formed the second part of the event were much enjoyed by participants.

The present book brings together the texts of the conference papers. In every case these have been revised and expanded, sometimes substantially. Also to be found here are essays based upon the more spontaneous 'workshop' presentations which were arranged at Abbotsford to focus on individual items or classes of object in the collection, or to investigate selected pieces of furniture: these now form contributions of enduring value. A special feature of the conference was the so-called 'Scott Trail' in the Royal Museum and the Museum of Scotland. Particular exhibits with a Scott of Abbotsford provenance, or which can be identified with the personal life of Sir Walter, were highlighted for the conference delegates and a short leaflet was produced. Considerable effort went into the devising of the trail, and it was felt that this important aspect of the event deserved more permanent embodiment than the transient currency of an ephemeral hand-list and starred labels in scattered display-cases. The objects in the National Museums' collections which are known to have come from Abbotsford, or which can be classified as Scott memorabilia, now form the subject of a major contribution to the book, in which the research recently devoted to the artefacts is presented in a form which will have lasting importance.

The subject of Scott and Abbotsford offers a rich field for scholarly exploration and debate. As David Daiches, one of the most distinguished literary critics of modern times, has said in his admirable *Sir Walter Scott and his World* (1971), 'The story of Abbotsford would make a book.' It is indeed surprising that no one has yet attempted such a full-scale study. With his unrivalled knowledge Dr James C. Corson, sometime Honorary Librarian of Abbotsford, might have written what would surely have established itself as the standard work on the subject. But there is no evidence that Corson actually began such a study, and he left behind him only extensive notes and a very large accumulation of prints and photographs, all meticulously catalogued in a card-index as an essential contribution towards such an end. This material is today to be found in the vast Corson Sir Walter Scott Collection in Edinburgh University Library. In the 1970s and 1980s Clive Wainwright published a series of valuable articles in *The Connoisseur* (January 1977) and *Country Life* (16 and 23 September 1982, and 8 June 1989) on Scott and his collection, and on Abbotsford; and in 1989 appeared his magisterial study of *The Romantic Interior: the British Collector at Home 1750–1850*. Here Scott's contribution to the design and decoration of his house was set in the context of a comprehensive study of antiquarian interiors ranging from Horace Walpole's Strawberry Hill and William Beckford's Fonthill to the rather less famous Charlecote Park of the Lucy family of Warwickshire, and Sir Samuel Rush Meyrick's Goodrich Court, Herefordshire. But an Abbotsford book does remain to be written. This volume may serve as something of an interim report or as a spur – or rather, perhaps, due to its form as a collection of individual essays, a series of prods – to further investigation. In a short conference every possible aspect of a potentially large topic could not, of course, be covered. No one, surely, would imagine that such would be the case.

If it is felt that the subject of the building of Abbotsford itself in all its vicissitudes has been neglected, the organisers would plead the case that Clive Wainwright's articles and his major book do pay a good deal of attention to the architecture as well as the decoration and furnishing of Abbotsford. An important treatment is accorded to Abbotsford in James Macaulay's excellent study of 1975, *The Gothic Revival, 1745–1845*. Abbotsford will have a long entry in the Kitty Cruft's forthcoming *Borders* volume of the *Buildings of Scotland* series. Some new material relating to William Stark's scheme prepared for Scott soon after he acquired the property has recently come to light, and I plan to discuss this in an article in the near future.

These letters and papers of William Stark formed part of an interesting collection acquired shortly before the conference by the National Library of Scotland (Acc. 11878). Among other documents in this miscellaneous box of Scottiana was the original letter of the Earl of Buchan, founder of the Society of Antiquaries, granting right of interment in an aisle of Dryburgh Abbey to Scott's favourite uncle, Robert Scott of Rosebank. This right, granted in 1791, was exercised by Sir Walter for his wife in 1826. Having attended the burial of Buchan in a nearby part of the ruins in 1829, it was there that Scott himself was laid to rest in September 1832. On the eve of the conference, too, the Library bought a magnificent letter of Scott's that, in so many ways, epitomises what Abbotsford meant to him (MS 23141, f. 146) (Fig. i). He addresses Sir James Stuart of Allanbank in phrases which will be quoted later in the present book but which are lapidary ones for any study of the man and the house:

> My motions about which you enquire have been exactly those of a pendulum vibrating from one point to another but never extended or diverging in its oscillations. From Abbotsford to Edinburgh – from Edinburgh to Abbotsford – just a little more extended than the Vicar of Wakefield's migrations from the red room to the green. The woods at Abbotsford are rising fast and now claim from distinction [*sic*] from the traveller. I have made an addition to my romance of a manor house which gives me an entrance hall lined with carved oak from the old Kirk at Dunfermline hung with old armour and painted on a high embowed roof with all the scutcheons of the great border families – it does not look in the least garish but on the contrary has a very solemn tone the light being through staind glass. Pray if you visit Scotland this season do not forget the value which I place on your approbation but come and review Conundrum Castle as you go or come . . .

The conference was organised by a small committee consisting of Annette Carruthers, Ian Gow, Dr Stephen Lloyd and Dr Jeanne Cannizzo who worked closely with Fionna Ashmore, Director of the Society of Antiquaries of Scotland, in assembling the team of speakers and presenters. Dr J. N. Graham Ritchie, President of the Society, opened proceedings, and outlined the case for consideration of Abbotsford – house, policies, landscape and collections – as a site of world heritage significance. Hugh Cheape, Vice-President, acted as rapporteur.

I must here record our indebtedness to Dame Jean Maxwell-Scott, DCVO, for her interest in our conference (at which she was present), and for her gracious welcome to the house built by her great-great-great-grandfather. Mrs Jane Wainwright, who also attended the conference, subsequently made available to me papers gathered by her late husband on the theme of Scott and Abbotsford. These have now been presented to the National Library (Acc. 12077).

Due to other pressures, two speakers at the conference, both of whom had given memorable lectures, have not chosen to convert their papers to the more permanent form of fully annotated essays in this volume. Of these, Dr Stana Nenadic's talk on Abbotsford as a tourist attraction had been a highlight of the day; and Ian Gow had distilled for delegates his special knowledge of Abbotsford and its decoration in Scott's time and since, coupling this with a tribute to Clive's Wainwright's contributions to scholarship in this field. One further contributor whose efforts are not represented in enduring shape here is Tony Dixon, the architect who has for so long looked after the fabric of Abbotsford, and whose knowledge of the construction and development of the house is probably unrivalled. He gave a most stimulating informal talk on site, and conducted interested persons through some of the more obscure parts of the building.

I was not myself involved with the organisation of the conference, but I was asked to give the opening paper and was thereafter invited to edit this book. I could hardly refuse either commission. As a loyal Antiquary, and as curator of the Scott Collection in the Manuscripts Division of the National Library of Scotland, I needed no convincing of the importance and excitement of the subject. There was the additional impetus provided by the 150th anniversary of the establishment of the Scott Collection. In September 1850 the autograph manuscript of *Waverley* had been presented to the Faculty of Advocates by James Hall; and upon that foundation were developed the enormous and extremely distinguished Scott holdings of the historic Advocates' Library and especially (from 1925) of its successor, the National Library of today. The importance of this vast assemblage of material on Scott and his circle cannot be over-emphasised. As a whole the collection constitutes perhaps the greatest accumulation of any writer's manuscripts, papers and correspondence anywhere in the world. It will always be the foundation upon which serious Scott scholarship must be based. Capitalising upon the sesqicentenary moment, I ended my conference lecture with an exhortation to delegates present, and to literary scholars, historians and historians of art and taste, to make use of this matchless resource. I repeat it here now. I myself, the organising committee, and the authors of the essays in this book all hope that our work may stimulate further research and enquiry.

Our indebtedness to the three great national cultural institutions of Scotland – the National Museums, the National Galleries and the National Library – will be apparent from the individual notes and acknowledgements of the authors. The waiving of photographic reproduction fees is not the least of the many obligations we owe. I must also record our gratitude to the Publications Committee of the Society of Antiquaries of Scotland, under its Convener Alan Saville, which has given every support to this venture. Fionna Ashmore has been a source of great encouragement and an admirable coordinator of our efforts. Duncan McAra has been a patient and perceptive copy-editor; and Alison Rae, Publications Manager for the Society, has had to deal with this book in its last stages as an introduction to her duties. I have been fortunate to work with her, and I appreciate her cooperation and efficiency.

I. G. B.
Edinburgh
21 September 2002

INTRODUCTION

A FLIBBERTIGIBBET OF A HOUSE TO SUIT AN ANTIQUARY

Iain Gordon Brown

WHEN Sir Walter Scott's party reached Frankfurt on its way back to Britain from the journey to the Mediterranean that had been undertaken in the hope of restoring the health and spirits of the exhausted, infirm and ageing writer, the travellers entered a bookseller's shop.[1] Here, in June 1832, in the German city that is now the location of the world's greatest book fair and the major event of the international publishing year, the man who was then the world's most famous author was shown a lithograph of a British country house. The bookseller knew only that this was an English group, and brought out from his stock the one object he was sure would be of interest. It was a print of Abbotsford. Scott, unrecognised, said: 'I know that already, sir.' He was going home to die.

All civilised people once knew of Abbotsford though the extraordinary life and writings of its owner. Following Scott's death some three months after the Frankfurt episode, the house rapidly became one of the most celebrated literary shrines in the world. So it still remains, in an age when its builder is no longer universally read or nationally honoured even in his Scottish homeland. Sir Walter once remarked that his oaks (meaning his plantations at Abbotsford, on which he lavished such loving care) would outlast his laurels.[2] We may, perhaps, adapt this suggestion to apply to his building rather than his arboriculture. It is arguably true that, for antiquaries at any rate, the literary work of Scott is now deemed rather less interesting than his contribution to material culture in the form of his house and its ambience, decoration and collections, these forming his extremely important contribution to what Clive Wainwright termed 'the antiquarian interior' as an aspect of British taste, and to the history of design and the decorative arts in the early nineteenth century. Yet this would be to diminish in a wholly unworthy and ignorant way the essential literary achievement of Scott as poet and novelist, and to forget the vital connection between the varied writing which paid for the architectural and decorative achievement (or indulgence) which was itself a reflection of a literary taste for the romantic. Scott the antiquary was also author of a best-selling work of fiction entitled *The Antiquary*, itself the third in a sequence of novels almost without parallel in the history of world literature. Writing to Charles Kirkpatrick Sharpe, one of the oddest of his antiquarian friends, Scott on one occasion observed that 'you will find yourself quite at home in my new Flibbertigibbet of a house because it will suit none but an antiquary'.[3] Abbotsford was the scene of much antiquarian activity ranging from active, passionate collecting to passive, contemplative reading, everything however being imbued with the most powerful sentimental attitude to the past.

Nothing, perhaps, symbolises the twin characteristics of Abbotsford – on the one hand a scene of pleasure and hospitable entertainment and, on the other, a literary factory given over to intensely hard, often desperate work driven by economic necessity – than the physical arrangements made to connect Scott's new study with his sleeping quarters. Nor is there a better illustration of how the architectural elements of the house reflect the desiderata that a demanding literary life made not only possible (by the money Scott earned) but absolutely essential (on account of the new money he had to make). A concealed, private stair led from the study to the dressing room on the bedroom storey of the house. Scott explained that this arrangement allowed 'the inhabitant of the Study', if 'unwilling to be surprised by visitors' to 'make his retreat unobserved'.[4] Clive Wainwright pointed out that it was equally possible for Scott to make his way thus down again *from* his bedroom: while appearing to retire when his guests did so, he could secretly return to the study to work late into the night.[5] These facts should be borne in mind when we consider the observations of visitors who remarked on Scott's concealment of his literary labours behind a façade of lairdly *bonhomie*.

From early days Scott had matched a literary antiquarianism as a collector and editor of ballads and traditions with a profound interest in the material remains of the past whether in prehistoric Scottish vitrified forts or Roman inscriptions in Northumberland, English medieval abbeys and castles or Jacobite relics. Nothing gave him so much pleasure as to build the past into his own dwelling, a house so modern in other ways with its pneumatic bells and gas lighting.

> I trouble you with these few lines just to say that the stones [from the demolished Tolbooth of Edinburgh] have arrived safe & are of the greatest consequence to me. The downfall of the *crescent* was unlucky but the emblem only regards the Ottoman Empire whereas the Scottish Thistle has arrived uninjured which was a happy omen. It crowns one gable of my building the other being surmounted by the beautiful carved cross from the Auld Kirk of Lindean hence transferred to Galashiels & finally to Abbotsford – so I stand *pro aris et focis* between the emblems of the Kirk and the country.[6]

As owner of Abbotsford, Scott came to see the presence of antiquities of all kinds as assets that made otherwise unproductive land desirable. Thus he told Sharpe that a new purchase of neighbouring ground included 'item butt-end of a Roman camp coverd with broom – the rest untracable' – something, surely, to gladden the heart of the creator of Mr Jonathan Oldbuck, whose wished-for identification of a Roman *praetorium* at the Kaim of Kinprunes is one of the great and enduring jokes of early nineteenth-century fiction[7] – 'item three Roman roads – two of them in bad order . . . item a pair of Roman forceps by the vulgar calld tongs sorely damaged with rust . . .'[8] Of this particular parcel of land (Kaeside) he had told his wife that it was 'supposed a good bargain', but admitted that his friend Charles Erskine, thinking of these various fragments of the past, had been 'so mischievous to allege that they have raised the value of the property greatly in my estimation'.[9] Erskine was probably spot-on. Scott was delighted when other landowners – especially any member of the extended family of his clan chief, the Duke of Buccleuch – found exciting things in their own unproductive bogs. The temptation to become involved and to share vicariously in their pleasure was almost too much to bear for one who had appointed himself 'antiquary in Chief on the [Buccleuch] estate'. Could the limb of the Roman statue found on the farm of Milsington be sent 'provisionally to Abbotsford' for examination? Could he set in train a search for the rest of the statue? Of course he did not want the 'relique' for himself, he assured Lord Montagu. His mind raced ahead: this find might 'be the foundation of a set of Bronzes if stout Lord Walter should turn to vertu'.[10]

Scott saw himself as an antiquarian clearing house, for objects and for information. What others might throw away, alienate, ignore, despise or remain unmoved by were the very things he wanted; and he was far too keen an observer of human nature not to be amused by his own predilections. 'I have been ruining myself,' he told Matthew Weld Hartstonge, shortly before moving from Ashestiel to Abbotsford, 'by the purchase of a small lot of ancient armour and other curiosities (Rob Roy's gun among other things) the stock in trade of a Virtuoso who is leaving off collecting, they are very rare and handsome and I defy any one to say that there is a single article among the two hundred which can be of use to a human being excepting indeed a snuff Box, and that is useless to me as I never take snuff.' And he continued, his imagination taking hold as he described a rather mysterious object which modern authorities regard as having been Roman, possibly, or equally possibly medieval.

> The people who are planting Abbotsford have rejoiced my heart by digging up a brazen utensil much resembling an ill made coffee pot but termed by the learned a sacrificial Vessel for pouring the wine on the brows of the victim. Was this not having great Luck? and does it not bode Corn Wine & Oil in plenty.

The artefact was the gift of the Revd Dr Robert Douglas, from whom Scott had bought the core of what would become Sir Walter's Abbotsford estate. In thanking him, Scott confided that it would be 'to a hobbyhorsical Antiquary omen faustum felixque'.[11] In the tale of this ancient object is epitomised the course of one man's obsession with the past and with his new land and dwelling where he would make that past come alive. Sir Daniel Wilson was right to suggest that 'the impulse which proceeded from Abbotsford' was responsible in some way, and more or less directly, for a zeal for archaeological investigation throughout Europe, and to claim for Scott the primacy in teaching that 'bygone ages of the world were actually filled by living men'.[12]

It is fitting that this book should appear under the auspices of the Society of Antiquaries of Scotland, to which Scott was elected on 13 December 1796, only six weeks after his literary career had begun.[13] Henceforth antiquarianism and literary production were to be very closely interwoven. One of Scott's last letters written before he left Britain for the Mediterranean expedition dealt with the 'original', or prototype, of the character of Jonathan Oldbuck: George Constable of Wallace Craigie. Scott addressed this letter to Captain Basil Hall, who that year had bought at public auction the autograph manuscript of *The Antiquary* even as his younger brother James had bought the manuscript of *Waverley*. Scott had lived long enough to see his himself sold, collected by admirers and valued as some sort of relic. Scott the antiquary had become an antiquity. In his letter he confessed to Basil Hall his own 'particular partiality' for this novel among all his works of fiction and 'the numerous creatures of [his] Imagination'. In so many ways Scott saw his life come full circle.

> And here I am seeking health at the expence of travel just as was the case with me in my tenth [he meant his seventh] year. Well! I am not the first who has ended life as he began and is bound to remember with gratitude those who have been willing to assist him in his voyage whether in youth or age amongst which I must include old George Constable and yourself.[14]

One whom Scott did not remember kindly was David Steuart Erskine, 11th Earl of Buchan, founder of the Society of Antiquaries of Scotland. This is not the place to indulge in a discussion of Buchan, the oddities of his manner and behaviour, or the multiplicity of his concerns. It may well be that Scott's somewhat tenuous connection with the Society over the years was in a measure due to his dislike of things associated with the eccentric Earl. Only in 1827 did Scott assume a position of honour in the Society with the Vice-Presidency conferred in that year, a post he held until 1829, the year of Buchan's death. Scott's own record of his assumption of this office is Laodicean to say the least. 'My course of Composition [of the second series of *Chronicles of the Canongate*] is stopd foolishly enough. I have sent four leaves to London with Lockhart's Review. I am very sorry for this blunder and here is another . . . the Devil tempted me to accept of the office of President [*sic*] of the Antiquarian Society.'[15] In the summer of 1827 Scott made to his *Journal* a strange confession for a man who *lived* in a museum, when he records under 19 June: 'rain forced me into the Antiquarian Musæum. Lounged there till a meeting of the Oil Gas Committee at three o'clock'.[16] Scott was always clear-eyed about the study of the past. He could collect a house full of treasures, yet live there too. He could write about history and antiquities, yet make vast sums of money in so doing. He once commented on 'the usual habit of antiquaries' as tending to neglect 'what is useful for things that are merely curious'.[17] Yet in the dark days of debt and (for a lesser man) despair, he found some comfort in the idle pursuit of the past.

> I do not know any thing which relieves the mind so much from the sullens as trifling discussions about *antiquarian old-womanries* – It is like knitting a stocking, diverting the mind without occupying it, or by our lady, a mill dam which leads the attention gently and imperceptibly out of the channell in which they are chafing and boiling – to be sure it is only conducting them to turn a child's mill – What signifies that? the diversion is a relief though the object is of little importance . . .[18]

And later he wrote:

> I like the muddling work of antiquities . . . No one who has not labourd as I have done on imaginary topics can judge the comfort afforded by walking on all fours and being grave and dull. I dare say when the clown of the pantomime escapes from his nightly task of vivacity it is his especial com[fort] to smoke a pipe and be prosy with some goodnatured fellow the dullest of his acquaintance . . . This muddling among old books has the quality of a sedative and saves the tear and wear of an over-wrought brain.[19]

NOTES

1 *Life*, X, p. 176 retails the anecdote.
2 Quoted in Hesketh Pearson, *Sir Walter Scott: His Life and Personality* (London 1954), p. 149.
3 *Letters*, IV, p. 539, 11 October 1817.
4 *Romantic Interior*, p. 197, quoting from Scott's fragmentary and unfinished 'Reliquiae Trottcosienses, or the Gabions of Jonathan Oldbuck', his projected catalogue *raisonné* of his collections.
5 'Abbotsford House, Roxburghshire', *Country Life*, 8 June 1989, p. 267.
6 I conflate *Letters*, IV, p. 538, to Robert Johnston, 11 October 1817 (with an emendation of the text printed by Grierson to read correctly 'cross' rather than 'crop') and that quoted above to Charles Kirkpatrick Sharpe of the same date which uses similar but rather more expressive phrasing to describe the same event.
7 See Stuart Piggott, 'The Roman Camp and Four Authors', in *Ruins in a Landscape. Essays in Antiquarianism* (Edinburgh 1976), pp. 161–70, and Iain Gordon Brown, *The Hobby-Horsical Antiquary. A Scottish Character 1640–1830* (Edinburgh 1980), pp. 18–19.
8 *Letters*, IV, pp. 539–40.
9 *Letters*, XII, p. 153, 11 November 1815.
10 *Letters*, p. 139, 22 February 1820.
11 *Letters*, III, pp. 45–46, 22 December 1811 and XII, p. 409, 2 December 1811. The second passage quoted gave me the title for my essay *The Hobby-Horsical Antiquary*: see page 6 of that work for the find in the context of the Scottish antiquarian tradition. Scott may actually have been referring to and describing two separate finds made at about the same time in the same general area. On this point the reader is referred to the chapter by Cheape, Cowie and Wallace in the present book.
12 *The Archaeology and Prehistoric Annals of Scotland* (Edinburgh 1851), Preface, p. xi. Wilson quotes from Thomas Carlyle, *Miscellanies*, 2nd edn, V, p. 301.
13 Scott's translations of *The Chase* and *William and Helen* from the German of Gottfried Bürger were published on 1 November 1796: see William B. Todd and Ann Bowden, *Sir Walter Scott. A Bibliographical History 1796–1832* (New Castle, Delaware 1998), p. 9.
14 *Letters*, XII, pp. 36–8, 27 October 1831.
15 *Journal*, pp. 385–6, 29 November 1827. Scott refers to his review-essay 'On Landscape Gardening', published in the *Quarterly Review,* the periodical edited by his son-in-law John Gibson Lockhart, in March 1828.
16 *Journal*, p. 317.
17 *Journal*, p. 170, 9 July 1826.
18 *Journal*, p. 441, 9 March 1828.
19 *Journal*, p. 540, 28 and 29 March 1829.

CLIVE WAINWRIGHT AND ABBOTSFORD

Annette Carruthers

CLIVE WAINWRIGHT was invited to lecture to the Society of Antiquaries of Scotland on the strength of his major work, *The Romantic Interior: the British Collector at Home 1750–1850*.[1] The product of twenty years of research, this magisterial book defined the 'Romantic interior' of this period as one created by the collector of medieval and Renaissance objects to express a passion for the past or a renewed interest in national identity. Scott as an antiquary was placed in the wider context of the burgeoning of historical studies in the late eighteenth and early nineteenth centuries, and the densely packed interiors of Abbotsford itself were set at the heart of the book, partly because of the wealth of surviving documentation about the house but also in acknowledgement of the extraordinary influence of Scott's writings.

In his lecture in June 1998 Clive summarised the substance of his argument that 'Abbotsford . . . is the most influential and highly developed of the suites of Romantic interiors' that he studied.[2] Scott's view of the past is embodied in the stones and atmosphere of Abbotsford, as much as it is revealed in his literary creations, and like them the house received admiration and imitation from abroad, particularly in Germany, Bohemia and Russia. Clive's suggestion that this wider field deserved more attention inspired the conference held by the Society in October 2000. In initial discussions with the Society's Director, Fionna Ashmore, Clive agreed to contribute, but after his sudden death in July 1999 the event was organised in his memory.

Clive Wainwright was born in Somerset in 1942 and attended Huish's Grammar School in Taunton, where he was pushed into studying science. He was practical as a boy and built his own small boat, and on leaving school he worked as a research chemist for ICI in Welwyn Garden City. He was also a great reader, however, and a lover of books. While in his first job he attended evening classes and joined the Victorian Society and in 1966 he was appointed Museum Assistant at the Victoria and Albert Museum, where his encyclopaedic knowledge of nineteenth-century decorative arts, and particularly of furniture, was largely acquired.

Two years in the National Art Library at the V&A gave him a thorough knowledge of the museum's bibliographic resources before he transferred to the Department of Furniture and Woodwork, then led by Peter Thornton. There he worked with Simon Jervis, Elizabeth Aslin and others re-evaluating the furniture and decorative arts of the Victorian period. Clive took a special interest in the Gothic Revival and his greatest hero was A. W. N. Pugin, a passion that came to fruition in the V&A exhibition and comprehensive catalogue of 1994.

By this time Clive was based in the Research Department of the museum and was actively involved in the postgraduate course on the history of design jointly run by the V&A and the Royal College of Art. As a curator in Furniture and Woodwork he had built up an archive that was available to researchers, though as Charles Saumarez Smith wrote in an obituary, 'in some ways the greatest research resource was Wainwright himself'.[3] He was always extremely helpful to enquirers from local and regional museums, as I know from personal experience, and his encouragement, enthusiasm and willingness to travel long distances to advise on historic interiors (and increase his own knowledge) were a model for the staff of national museums. These qualities also made him a very successful teacher and lecturer. As in Edinburgh, his lectures always appeared easy; he never lost his comfortable Somerset burr and his direct conversational style disguised his hours of preparation and careful selection of slides. After gaining a PhD for his work on the Romantic interior he enjoyed an exchange at Sussex University, contributed regularly at the RCA, and became a Visiting Professor at Birkbeck College, University of London.

Clive Wainwright was elected a Fellow of the Society of Antiquaries of London in 1973 and FSA Scot in 1982. Although he cultivated the traditional image of an antiquarian scholar, with his abundant beard and tweedy suit and waistcoat adorned with a watch chain, Clive followed his hero's enthusiasm for innovation as well as for history. While Scott was a pioneer in the use of household gas, Clive was known for his love of kitchen gadgets and his early adoption of the mobile phone. Like Scott and Pugin he worked energetically and productively, contributing articles and essays to many books, catalogues and journals, and his death at only 57 was a great loss to the world of museums, design and decorative art studies. The RCA was about to award him an Honorary Fellowship and has inaugurated a memorial scholarship in his name, and several books have already been dedicated to him. The conference in Edinburgh and visit to Abbotsford, attended by his widow Jane, provided the Society's tribute to a scholar who illuminated an important part of Scotland's history and cultural influence.

NOTES

1 New Haven and London 1989.
2 *Romantic Interior*, p. 207.
3 *The Independent*, 5 July 1999.

Clive Wainwright
(Source: Victoria & Albert Museum Picture Library)

SCOTT, LITERATURE AND ABBOTSFORD

Iain Gordon Brown

LATE in October 1832 David Wilkie wrote to his fellow painter Andrew Wilson in Rome. He described the effect of Sir Walter Scott's death upon his friends and the nation in general, and went on to discuss the possibility of some suitable commemoration in architecture and sculpture of the writer's life and achievement. Wilkie's was only one of many such letters emanating from Scotland in the weeks after Scott's passing. There was a profound sense of national loss such as is difficult for us now to comprehend, and this widely held feeling that a monument of some kind should be undertaken was to lead ultimately to the Gothic space-rocket in Princes Street. Scott himself had, of course, already constructed his own monument in stone and lime, bright heraldic paint and carved wood, elaborate furnishings and antiquarian re-use of the salvaged fragments of older buildings. That monument was Abbotsford; and it reflects, almost as does no other house, the mind and appetites of its creator. In his letter to Wilson, Wilkie had gone on to suggest that an alternative to an architectural and sculptural memorial might be a more practical one: the redressing (as he put it) and settling of Abbotsford on Scott's family 'as the most appropriate monument'. 'Why might not Abbotsford,' Wilkie concluded, 'be made the Blenheim of literature? No such claim upon a nation's gratitude can ever occur again.'[1]

This letter, and the feeling that lay behind it, was provoked by the disaster that had befallen Scott in January 1826 when he was ruined by the financial crash of his publisher, Archibald Constable & Co., and his printer, James Ballantyne & Co., in which last firm he was a partner. Henry Cockburn would recall the circumstances and their effect on Scott's circle.

> The opening of the year 1826 will ever be sad to those who remember the thunderbolt which then fell on Edinburgh in the utterly unexpected bankruptcy of Scott . . . If an earthquake had swallowed half the town, it would not have produced greater astonishment, sorrow, and dismay. Ballantyne and Constable were merchants, and their fall, had it reached no further, might have been lamented merely as a casualty of commerce. But Sir Walter! The idea that his practical sense had so far left him as to have permitted him to dabble in trade, had never crossed our imagination. How humbled we felt when we saw him – the pride of us all, dashed from his lofty and honourable station, and all the fruits of his well-worked talents gone . . . Well do I remember his first appearance after this calamity was divulged, when he walked into Court one day in January 1826. There was no affectation,

> and no reality, of *facing it*; no look of indifference or defiance; but the manly and modest air of a gentleman conscious of some folly, but of perfect rectitude, and of most heroic and honourable resolutions.[2]

Yet Cockburn was also to confess to a telling caveat. In setting down his memories of Scott's manner of living in his last years, with an unremitting daily regimen of hard work being fitted into a pattern of sociability and lairdly pursuits, Cockburn reflected: 'Would that his money and his care had been given to a better subject than Abbotsford.'[3] The link is immediately established between Scott's vast literary effort and huge success, the catastrophic failure of his fortune, and the totemic nature of the house to which he was in thrall.

Scott's heroism in clearing the enormous debt is one of the finest tales in literature. 'My own right hand shall do it'[4] was the famous boast which he honoured to the last in an almost superhuman effort to earn sufficient by his pen to pay his creditors and to save not only his reputation and his place in history, but also his beloved Abbotsford. The strict facts are that Abbotsford had been settled on his son and heir, Walter, on the latter's marriage not long before the crash. Furthermore, Scott's trustees and creditors had treated him leniently as far as his own life-rent of the house went. They had awarded him the use of his 'furniture, plate, linens, paintings, library and curiosities of every description' in grateful recognition of his literary efforts on their behalf – 'his most honourable conduct . . . and unparalleled and most successful exertions'.[5] Nevertheless it also remains the fact that a man who had made more money by his pen than practically anyone else before him in literary history had seen those riches disappear overnight. The whole edifice of life at Abbotsford was supported upon the flimsiest of financial structures. Scott's life as Laird of Abbotsford was to a very great extent dependent upon his past, present and – most risky of all – *future* literary achievement, and therefore earning-power. Scott used to like to call Abbotsford 'Conundrum Castle'. So indeed it was: and it was many other things. Abbotsford, despite its relatively modest size – and we do not need to go as far as A. N. Wilson, who observes that many of its suburban imitators were larger and flashier[6] – remains perhaps the most celebrated monument to literary glory. Abbotsford, one might say, is the *Waverley* novels in stone. Abbotsford is more than a great house, for it has always the quality of an idea.

To be asked to discuss the subject of 'Scott, Literature and Abbotsford' is indeed to be asked a good deal. Who, after all, wrote more than Walter Scott, in verse or prose, either under his own name or that of the 'Great Unknown', the author of *Waverley*, or under those of a dozen aliases and *noms de plume*? There is verse of all kinds, from the short lyric to the narrative epic in many cantos that made him (until Byron arose, first to rival and then to surpass him) the most famous poet in Europe. There is the great sequence of novels, products of an almost unmatched creativity and a fertility of genius that turned him into the most famous writer of prose fiction in the world. Nor should one forget the complex mass of annotation and prolix prefacing that Scott readily spun around his own literary production, so as to cocoon his novel texts in a web of extensive commentary and a tangle of many-layered deception aimed at half-concealment of authorship. For him, the editorial role was almost more natural than original composition itself; but, ironically, it was this task which has, to a degree, conspired to make some, at least, of his novels, in the eyes of later generations, formidably ponderous and even downright dull. The fresh approach and meticulous scholarship of the Edinburgh Edition, now in progress, may go a long way to correct a view of Scott which still associates him too much with huge sets of unread works in the darker corners of second-hand bookshops. Then there are the shorter prose tales, and the poetical dramas. There is historical writing, whether in the form of narrative histories of Scotland for adults and for children, or the editorial work of publishing and commenting upon historical texts as primary sources. There is biography on a grand scale: *The Life of Napoleon Buonaparte* extended to nine volumes. There is literary criticism, and there are the large editions of the works of others. There are, of course, the great collections of Border ballads. There is the journalism; quantities of reviews; encyclopedia articles; political pamphlets; even sermons. Finally, and by no means least, there survive upwards of some 7,000 letters, the invaluable memorials of a lifetime of inveterate communication on every conceivable subject with hundreds of correspondents at home and abroad. Indeed is the clerihew 'Sir Walter Scott/Wrote a lot . . .' literally and indisputably true.[7]

The story of the building and furnishing of Abbotsford is a fascinating one. When thinking about how I might approach the rather large topic of the present paper I looked under the heading 'Abbotsford' in James C. Corson's invaluable index to Sir Herbert Grierson's twelve-volume edition of Scott's *Letters,* a work containing only some 3,400 letters and thus an edition very far from complete.[8] There are eleven columns of entries ranged over six pages. These are organised in six sections, one of which has two subsections and one four, two of these being themselves subdivided. There are fifteen separate references to Scott announcing to friends his purchase of Abbotsford. For the house itself entries are arranged under the first New Cottage proposed but not built, 1811–14; then under 'alterations to the Old Cottage' from 1812 on; then under the heading of the present house, first portion (1817–19) and the second portion (1822–5). For both periods of building one also has to look at the large entry for William Atkinson, the architect, and also at the entries for Edward Blore and Daniel Terry, which last itself runs to three columns. In the entry for the first portion there are forty-seven references to the Dining Room with separate entries for 'planning of', carpet, chairs, curtains, fireplace and grate, pictures for, sideboard, table (and the wood for it), wallpaper and stained glass window (abandoned). There are thirty-four references to the Armoury. Under the second portion one finds thirty-two references to the Library on everything from Scott's looking for oak timber for the panelling, to the design and procurement of his consulting desk. If interested in the curios, furniture, and the like, one has to look also beyond Section V of Corson's 'Abbotsford' index entry (with its miscellaneous entries on subjects ranging from chamois horns, Covenanters' flag, Borghese chairs, and the improbable 'Grecian marbles') to search under the separate headings of: 'Armour and Weapons', 'Brooches', 'Clock', 'Coins', 'Hair' (i.e. that of Charles I and Napoleon), 'Inkstand', 'Purses', 'Forceps', 'Quaichs', 'Rings', 'Roman' (figurines, paterae, pots and forceps), 'Seals', 'Silver', 'Skulls' (of Scottish wild bulls, of animals from South

Africa, a cast of Robert Bruce and that of Trooper Shaw of the Life Guards, killed at Waterloo), and finally under 'Snuffboxes'. Yes, Abbotsford is a large topic; that of Scott's life and art is enormous; literature bigger than both. And a mere conference paper with an allocated title not of my own making in which to sum it all up! Yet, what a subject. Arguably I was both fortunate and cursed in being allotted the opening slot of the conference, and this first essay of the published proceedings. I console myself by remembering an anecdote of Scott's watching the demolition of the Old Tolbooth of Edinburgh, the infamous Heart of Mid-Lothian. The painter Alexander Nasmyth and his son James, and the English artist John Linnell, were with him as they witnessed the crash of the condemned cell. Linnell rushed forward to rake for a souvenir and came away with the mummified corpse of a rat, whereas Scott did rather better by securing for his antiquarian treasure-chest of Abbotsford the door and lock of the prison itself.[9]

Abbotsford is a romance of a house (Fig. 1). It represents a romance of an idea. The very name is a romance. Before Scott's purchase, the existing farm on the boggy riparian

FIGURE 1

The fantasy of Abbotsford reduced to a drawing-room pursuit. An engraved view of the house, with a peacock as well as the essential dogs, decorates the title page of an Edinburgh stationer's album, made for the use of ladies as a scrap- or commonplace-book. The ornamental binding bears a repoussé profile portrait of Scott.

(National Library of Scotland, MS 1625)

spot had been known as Cartley or more expressively Clarty Hole. There was a ford on the Tweed below it, and the land had once belonged to the abbots of Melrose: Scott's invention did the rest. There is the romance of the Laird's life there, a world created by his imagination and paid for by the profits of the exercise of that same imagination. Washington Irving, remembering what Abbotsford had been in earlier days and thinking of what it would become at its zenith, analysed well the peculiar nature of the house. 'As yet, however,' Irving reminisced, 'all was in embryo and perspective, and Scott pleased himself with picturing out his future residence, as he would one of the fanciful creations of his own romances. "It was one of his air castles," he said, "which he was reducing to solid stone and mortar."'[10] It was, too, the scene of factual as opposed to fictional literary romance, with the famous episode of Scott's alleged chancing upon the incomplete and forgotten manuscript of *Waverley* when looking in an old writing-desk for fishing tackle for the use of a friend – that providential moment which turned the most famous poet of the day into the world's most famous novelist. As I have hinted, there was the romance of the dangerously precarious underpinning of it all, and to this I shall return. Finally, Abbotsford was the scene of romance of another kind, that of heroic labour in adversity when Scott's own noble efforts exceeded those of any of his *Waverley* novel heroes.

Whatever else it was or would become, Abbotsford was certainly the obsession of its creator. The critics have tried to analyse the nature of this. Here, for example, is A. N. Wilson:

> . . . some obsession created Abbotsford, extending it, cultivating it, rebuilding the house and knocking it down again, filling the estates with tame gillies, and shepherds and gamekeepers. The cottage ornée swelled in his mind into a castle of gothic romance into which all his fortunes were poured. No bit of bog on its borders could come on the market without his wanting to buy it. No historical fake or relic of Scotland's past could appear in the salerooms but Scott would want it for the library. No modern invention was too costly or too elaborate for this palace of art . . . One can never explain the consuming passion some men feel for their houses. Scott was not unique in wanting to live handsomely or establish an estate. Nor is the house grandiose. But his obsessive devotion to Abbotsford seems at times to contrast with his common sense and his fundamental decency. When it came to his estates and his house, he was like a gambler held to the tables by an inescapable addiction.[11]

This perceived obsession leads the critics themselves – as, indeed, was the case with people of the time seeking to explain one of the great mysteries of the day – to become obsessed with finding a reason for Scott's inexplicable preoccupation. Early on, Lord Macaulay condemned Scott for his 'profuse and ostentatious expense; agitated with the hopes and fears of a gambler . . . extravagant waste or rapacious speculation'.[12] Many of Macaulay's contemporaries shared this view, some reluctantly others less so. Seeing Abbotsford, once 'merely a cottage', being transformed into a 'castle', Frances Lady Shelley concluded that 'the money which Scott received through his writings created wants which in past years he had never felt'.[13] William Macready, the actor, visiting the house in 1846, branded it the 'suicidal instrument of [Scott's] fate, and monument of his vanity and indiscretion', a place redolent of 'extravagance or precipitation'. These comments were in contrast to Macready's recollections of his pleasure in the fact that Scott, dangerously ill in 1819, had been spared 'to swell still further the amount of his contributions to the world's entertainment and instruction', and to his diary entry when Scott's passing was announced: 'Whatever his defects, a very great man, whose death brings sorrow with it.'[14] Elizabeth Grant of Rothiemurchus, more cutting still, excoriated Abbotsford as 'that monument of vanity, human absurdity, or madness', and confided that even Scott's greatest friend of his youth, William Clerk, 'used to speak of this melancholy act of folly almost with tears.'[15]

Yet, in an effort to understand, some have tended to make the house either too grand and feudal, as if – and Eric Anderson does well to point this out – no other well-doing Scottish lawyer with ancestral roots in a district and a need to live both in Edinburgh and within his sheriffdom would *not* want to buy an estate once he had prospered;[16] or else they demean or minimise the house by calling it (as does Wilson) 'the dwelling not of a medieval baron, but of a successful bourgeois'.[17] Scott's obsession with Abbotsford was merely a national tendency writ larger than normal: 'Whenever a Scotsman gets his head above *water,*' Scott himself had written, 'he immediately turns it to *land.*'[18]

A kinder critic than Macaulay, Sir Herbert Grierson, declared in 1932 that the chief pleasure Scott derived from his wealth was 'the ability to help others, if he did also delight to surround himself with all that appealed to his imagination – land and trees and furniture and antiquities and bric-à-brac, tenants and work people whom he could befriend, animals to love and be loved by'.[19] In his analysis of Scott's motivation in creating the dream that was Abbotsford, with the tension apparent in the story between surrender to money values and the cultivation of altruistic paternalism, Grierson followed the reasoning of Scott's contemporary, Mrs Eliza Fletcher, a woman more charitable by far than 'The Highland Lady', who had written:

> Sir Walter was one of those great men who had an undue estimate of the 'pride of life'. He did not care for money, but he cared much for baronial towers and aristocratical distinction; and yet this taste was unaccompanied by haughtiness of disposition or manners. It was rather the romance of his character that had led him to add acre to acre and to found the dynasty of Scott of Abbotsford; for there was nothing sordid in his nature; he was frank and kind-hearted, as much beloved by his poor neighbours as he was admired and courted by the great.[20]

This is an important point. In concentrating on Scott's expenditure on his house, estate and collections, we should not forget his generosity to all in less fortunate circumstances. No matter how preoccupied he was with multifarious literary undertakings of his own, and regardless of his overwhelming financial commitment to Abbotsford, he still found energies to encourage others in ways both intellectual and practical. In sending James Bailey a cheque for £20, for example, Scott balances his own obsessional devotion to

Abbotsford with genuine concern for the struggling Cambridge classicist, a 'young man of Genius in temporary distress': 'The sum is small for I have been something of an unthrift lately with whims of planting and building and it shall be reinforced hereafter as circumstances may require.'[21] While recognising the inescapable fact that Scott was 'a most reckless spender' at and on his house and estate, A. O. J. Cockshut goes on to link the Abbotsford episode with the most marked characteristics of Scott's life as a whole. As Abbotsford (at once his greatest delight and his most destructive infatuation) demonstrates,

> he had a peculiar kind of materialistic imaginativeness that was in practice much more damaging to his prospects than any ordinary extravagance could have been. His mind moved, wildly but not altogether selfishly, through images of great towers, of wildernesses become fertile land, of forests, of generously treated and contented peasants. His hospitality combined in an unusual way the magnificent with the homely and personal.[22]

Cockshut's judgment appeared in the year after another scholar had published his tellingly effective demolition job on Scott's methods as a man of business, of literature and even of friendship. Eric Quayle's is a study of paradox, failings and fatal temptation, in which Scott, the enigma commanding alternately respect and condemnation, was coolly assessed as 'a genius in many aspects of his work as a novelist, and as a weakling beset with traits of character that allowed a consuming self-interest to dictate modes of conduct that finally brought ruin on himself and many lesser men'.[23] Although the fact is known to all, Quayle expressed the matter memorably: Scott was driven by 'the whips of financial necessity' to write ceaselessly. The reason, this writer argues, was essentially because Scott had been 'consumed with financial ambitions' from an early age, a characteristic outlook born of 'inate [*sic*] greed'.[24] But if Quayle was able to show that Scott's dealings with the Ballantynes were less than candid and irreproachable, and that the young publisher Robert Cadell, worried that the audaciously grasping Mr Scott was 'not like his poems – immortal', and that he might be 'summoned to the other world' with paid-for work unwritten and still in debt,[25] neither should we forget Cadell's own later treatment of Scott in his final years, when Sir Walter served his last publisher like some literary milch cow grazing on the broad acres of Abbotsford.[26]

In his novel *The Ragged Lion*, Allan Massie gives us what purports to be Scott's lost autobiography. Here we find what we are asked to accept as Scott's own defence of his mock-medievalism at Abbotsford, which is to be considered within the context of the fictional portrayal of the Middle Ages to be found in a novel such as *Ivanhoe*. That book is, of course, set in a period of which Scott had no personal knowledge, and for which he was dependent on historical reading and upon the deployment of his own imagination. Massie's Scott wrote:

> No doubt as scholarship progresses, more inaccuracies will be discovered, and poor *Ivanhoe* be denounced as a tissue of fancies. The time will come when scholars will undoubtedly know far more about the Middle Ages than I have been able to learn, for true historical

> scholarship has scarcely penetrated that period. Yet I may boast that I have done things which bring me into a closer kinship with medieval man than a scholar immured in a library may ever attain. I have, after all, ridden in a cavalry troop. I have hunted the fox and the hare, flown a hawk, and speared a salmon. I have employed my own piper and chaplain, and lack only a jester or Fool, though Lockhart, whose tongue is sharper than mine, has been known to observe that certain of my guests at Abbotsford have played that role well enough. Indeed the mention of the dear place prompts me to add that if I have not built a Gothic castle, I have at least built a fine house with some Gothic decoration and appurtenances, and have therein an armoury that any Norman baron might envy.[27]

The modern in Abbotsford has fascinated commentators. Here was a faery realm, echoing far-off chivalric days of yore, yet one with pneumatic bells and the celebrated gas lighting. Virginia Woolf is said to have described Scott as 'the last minstrel and the first chairman of the Edinburgh oil gas company'.[28] The old and the new, the practical and the hobby-horsical, inhabited the house together, much as in the best of his novels – those set in the Scotland of his own day or the immediately preceding generations, a world which he knew from observation, experience or personal reminiscence – the glamour of Scotland's violent and heroic past could be shown to be subsumed now into a peaceful present of Enlightenment and Union.[29]

What is certain is that Scott's literary career was driven by his desire for money; and his desire for money was provoked and intensified by his obsession with Abbotsford. The price Scott paid for the original farm was huge for the time: £4,000. This was effected by borrowing half the price from his elder brother and half from the Ballantyne firm 'on the security of a poem' (as John Buchan noted)[30] of which Scott 'had not written a line'. Try that with a building society today! This was the fatal step, as Buchan elegantly observed: 'For the first time he put Pegasus between the shafts, and counted upon literature to meet the normal expenses of his life.'[31]

It may be interesting now to look at what Abbotsford and his land meant to him. The intimate connection between his lairdly ambition and his present and future literary activity will be strikingly apparent. We shall also be able to see how, gradually, the dream that was Abbotsford consumed much of his thinking. There are the early letters of expectation, around 1811, when he announced to all and sundry his purchase of the original farm and modest house. There are the letters written during the period of the building and elaboration of Abbotsford, of the expansion of its policies and of the accumulation of its idiosyncratic collections, which rush of activity and heady enthusiasm he shared with friends who were prepared to indulge his whims and join in his evident excitement. And there are the late letters of near-despair of the year 1826, when he faced the loss of his beloved house and grounds, his library and worldly possessions. This seemingly inescapable disaster gave rise to supremely great and noble writing in his superb *Journal*, with his thoughts ever on Abbotsford and its people.

From the very outset, then, Abbotsford was tied to literary production and the financial risk of heavy borrowing against future intellectual productivity. Thus Scott wrote to James Ballantyne:

> My lease of Ashestiel is out and I now sit a tenant at will under a heavy rent and at all the inconveniences of one who is in the house of another. I have therefore resolved to purchase a piece of ground sufficient for a cottage and a few fields . . . and I must have recourse to my pen to make the matter easy. The worst is the difficulty which John [Ballantyne] might find in advancing so large a sum as the copy-right of a new poem, supposing it to be made payable in the course of a year at farthest from the work going to press would be essential to my purpose. Yet the Lady of the Lake came soon home. I have a letter this morning from Mr. Dundas giving me good hope of my treasury business being carried through [that is, his Clerkship of the Court of Session]; if this appointment take place I will buy both the little farms which will give me a mile of the beautiful turn of Tweed above Gala-foot, if not I will confine my purchase to one. As my income in the event supposd will be very considerable it will afford a sinking fund to clear off what debt I may incur in making the purchase. It is proper John & you should be as soon as possible apprised of these my intentions, which I believe you will think reasonable in my situation & at my age, while I may yet hope to sit under the shade of a tree of my own planting.'[32] (Figs 2a and 2b.)

The turning of his mind and attentions to land had, as he admitted to Robert Surtees, 'interfered with [his] literary labours or amusements'. But these circumstances 'are now like to impel me toward them'. He continued: 'For if I build I must have money, and I know none will give me any but the booksellers; so I must get up into my wheel, like a turnspit, or lose the pleasant prospect of one day placing roast mutton before you at Abbotsford.'[33]

The poem Scott was banking on was *Rokeby*. Writing excitedly to Mrs Clephane of his 'planting and enclosing', he admitted that his new diversons would probably mean postponement of a hoped-for visit to Mull. Furthermore he had 'the prettiest plan you ever saw'; 'everything in short, expecting a great pouch full of money, which is the most necessary thing of all. I am terribly afraid I must call in the aid of Amphion and his harp, not indeed to found a city, but if it can rear a cottage it will be very fair for a modern lyre. If I fairly set to writing I must be stationary for this year . . .'[34] But for the new poem he was offered 3,000 guineas. 'My work *Rokeby*,' he told J. B. S. Morritt, the owner of the eponymous Yorkshire estate, 'does and must go forward or my trees and inclosures might perchance stand still.' What he referred to as the 'affairs of Abbotsford *on earth* were intimately connected with those of Rokeby *on paper*'.[35] 'As for the house and the poem, there are twelve masons hammering at the one, and one poor noddle at the other.'[36] He even compared the construction of the poem to the building of the house; to Matthew Weld Hartstonge, whose assistance in laying the literary foundations of this particular work he was here acknowledging, he asserted that his own part had been but that 'of the Painter or Plasterer to the Mansion already built'.[37]

The purchase financed and the link to literature established, Scott began to describe the cottage and ground to his friends. 'It would do,' he said, 'till the Muse and the Masons have made me a better', and,

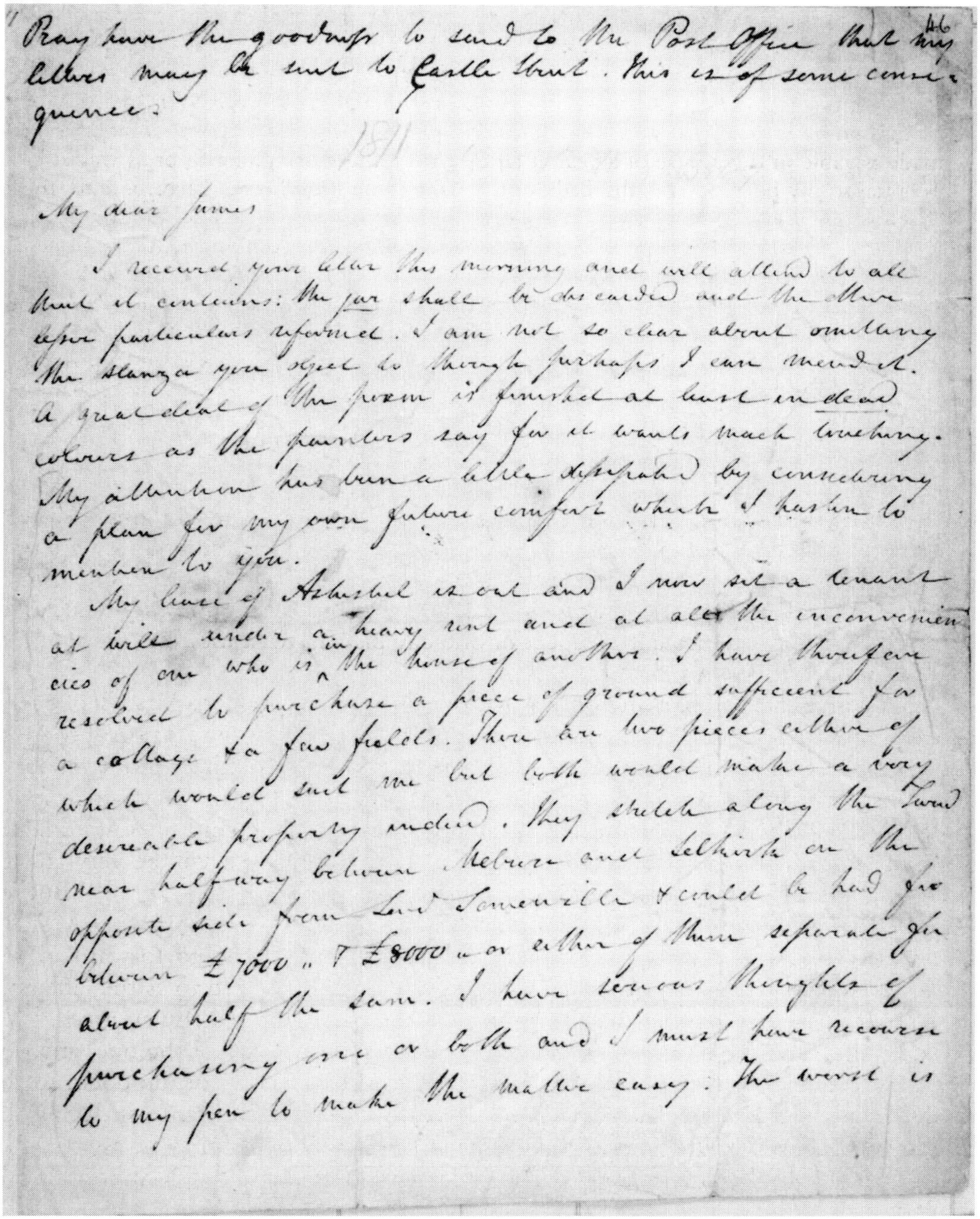
Pray have the goodness to send to the Post Office that my letters may be sent to Castle Street. This is of some consequence. 46

1811

My dear James

I received your letter this morning and will attend to all that it contains: the jar shall be discarded and the other particulars reformed. I am not so clear about omitting the stanza you object to though perhaps I can mend it. A great deal of the poem is finished at least in dead colours as the painters say for it wants much touching. My attention has been a little dissipated by considering a plan for my own future comfort which I hasten to mention to you.

My lease of Ashestiel is out and I now sit a tenant at will under a heavy rent and at all the inconveniencies of one who is in the house of another. I have therefore resolved to purchase a piece of ground sufficient for a cottage & a few fields. There are two pieces either of which would suit me but both would make a very desireable property indeed. They stretch along the Tweed near halfway between Melrose and Selkirk on the opposite side from Lord Somerville & could be had for between £7000 & £8000 or either of them separate for about half the sum. I have serious thoughts of purchasing one or both and I must have recourse to my pen to make the matter easy. The worst is

FIGURE 2a

Scott confides in James Ballantyne his dream of landed proprietorship on Tweedside.

(National Library of Scotland, MS 2525, ff. 46–46v)

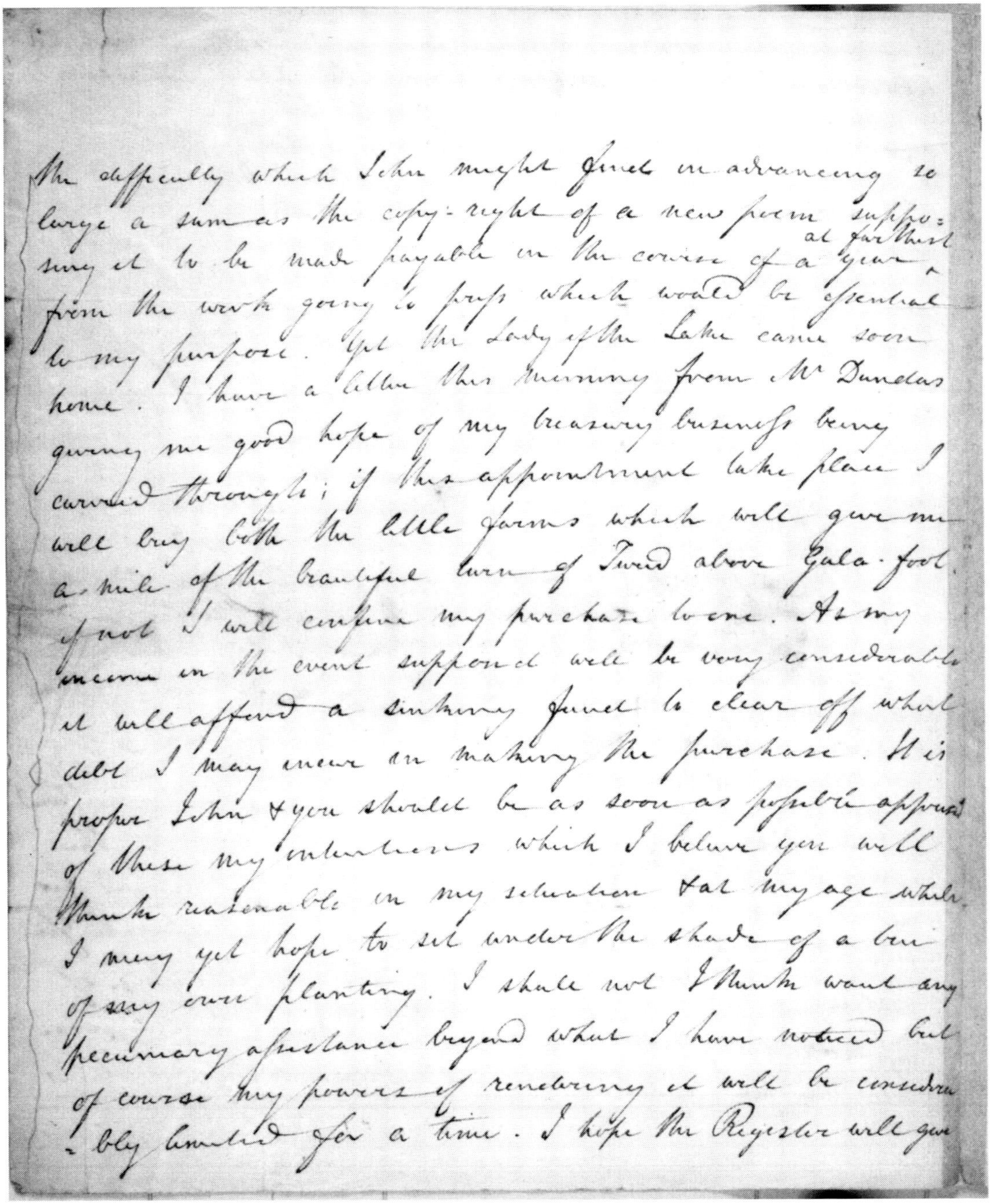

the difficulty which John might find in advancing so
large a sum as the copy-right of a new poem suppo=
sing it to be made payable in the course of a year at furthest
from the work going to press which would be essential
to my purpose. Yet the Lady of the Lake came soon
home. I have a letter this morning from Mr Dundas
giving me good hope of my treasury business being
carried through; if this appointment take place I
will buy both the little farms which will give me
a mile of the beautiful turn of Tweed above Gala-foot.
if not I will confine my purchase to one. As my
income in the event supposed will be very considerable
it will afford a sinking fund to clear off what
debt I may incur in making the purchase. It is
proper John & you should be as soon as possible apprised
of these my intentions which I believe you will
think reasonable in my situation & at my age while
I may yet hope to sit under the shade of a tree
of my own planting. I shall not I think want any
pecuniary assistance beyond what I have noticed but
of course my powers of rendering it will be considera
-bly limited for a time. I hope the Register will give

FIGURE 2b
Scott confides in James Ballantyne his dream of landed proprietorship on Tweedside.
(National Library of Scotland, MS 2525, ff. 46–46v)

> This place is just better than a Scotch inn though only in the article of cleanliness . . . It is at present terribly bare but has a fine reach of the Tweed wandering round it so I hope by dint of planting and time to make it tolerable . . . my thoughts are running on nothing at present but woods and groves all of which are as yet in the clouds and not one stick of them in the earth their proper element.[38]

To Joanna Baillie he declared that his

> principal occupation at present is building not castles but cottages in the air, and that not for lack of earthly foundation for if there be faith in lawyer's parchment I may style myself Laird of Abbotsford . . . It is not *very* beautiful and the plantations are young; but they are thriving and shall be increased please Heaven fivefold . . . Next season if we all be spared we enter our own fairy land and bigg our bower after the fashion of the olden time.[39] (Fig. 3)

His perceptive correspondent, apparently aware even then of what Scott's initial investment was likely to come to mean to him, replied:

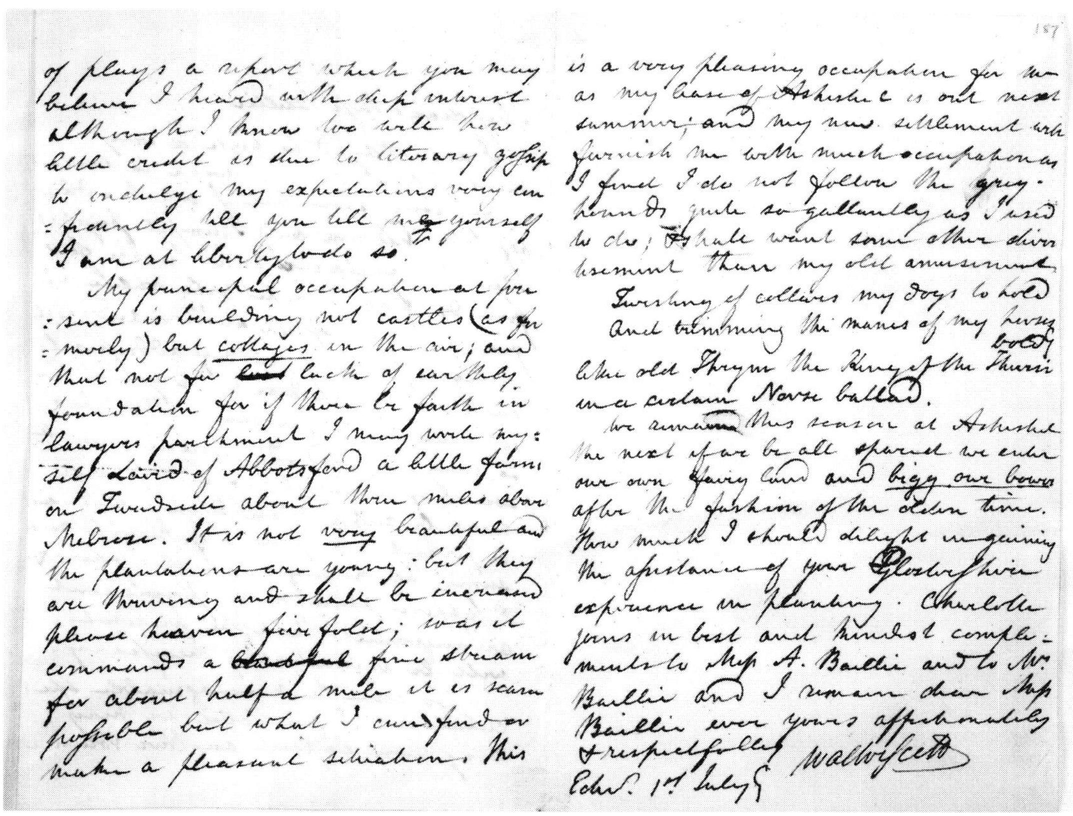

of plays a report which you may believe I heard with deep interest although I know too well how little credit is due to literary gossip to indulge my expectations very confidently till you tell me yourself I am at liberty to do so.

My principal occupation at present is building not castles (as formerly) but cottages in the air; and that not for lack of earthly foundation for if there be faith in lawyers parchment I may write myself Laird of Abbotsford a little farm on Tweedside about three miles above Melrose. It is not very beautiful and the plantations are young: but they are thriving and shall be increased please heaven fivefold; was it commands a fine stream for about half a mile it is scarce possible but what I can find or make a pleasant situation. This is a very pleasing occupation for me as my lease of Ashestiel is out next summer; and my new settlement will furnish me with much occupation as I find I do not follow the greyhounds quite so gallantly as I used to do; I shall want some other divertisement than my old amusement

Twisting of collars my dogs to hold
And trimming the manes of my horses bold
like old Thrym the King of the Thursi in a certain Norse ballad.

We remain this season at Ashestiel the next if we be all spared we enter our own fairy land and bigg our bower after the fashion of the olden time. How much I should delight in gaining the assistance of your Glostershire experience in planting. Charlotte joins in best and kindest compliments to Miss A. Baillie and to Mrs Baillie and I remain dear Miss Baillie ever yours affectionately & respectfully Walter Scott

Edinr. 1st July

FIGURE 3

Scott styles himself 'Laird of Abbotsford' in a letter to Joanna Baillie, 1811.

(National Library of Scotland, MS 23118, ff. 186v–187)

> So you have become the Laird of Abbotsford. A respectable sounding name this; and would become a large estate fully as well as a little farm; and I hope it will be the name of a good estate with a good house upon it too, in which your prosperous descendants, ages after this, will proudly point out the picture of the first Laird. With all my ambition on your behalf, however, I like the thoughts of your Cottage & your plantations & your streams exceedingly . . .[40]

And Scott, for his part, confessed tellingly to Baillie: 'I fear I shall want a great deal of money to make my cottage what I should like it.'[41] He assured her, nevertheless, that (despite temptation to press on with the enticing designs solicited from the brilliant young William Stark) he would 'keep the lee-side of prudence in [his] proceedings'.[42] But at the same time his earliest ventures into planting and improvement, let alone into building, convinced him of a basic fact: 'while my trees grow, and my fountain fills, my purse, in an inverse ratio, sinks to zero'.[43] Temptation did beckon: 'in draining my land I drain my purse . . .'[44]

At first Scott considered this ur-Abbotsford merely a 'whimsical, gay, odd cabin'. 'We are attempting,' he told Lord Montagu, 'no castelleted conundrums to rival those Lord Napier used to have executed in sugar . . . and no cottage neither but an irregular somewhat like an old English hall in which your Squire of £500 a year used to drink his ale in days of yore'.[45] Lady Shelley entered fully into this dream-world, with its culinary overtones. The former cottage, she recorded

> has now been transformed into a tiny castle. As one approaches by a road halfway up the opposite hill one looks down upon its loftiest turret, which is a copy of that of Melrose in miniature. It does not require a giant, but only an elfin page, to take it up and run away with it. Abbotsford has the appearance of a castle built of pastry – something like those we see on a supper table. But one must not quiz the castle or criticise the whims of such a genius.[46]

Gradually, and then more rapidly, and at length with breathless, pressing urgency the fantasy took hold and took over.

Literature, its financial reward and the obsessional dream of Abbotsford were intimately connected. In 1815 Scott wrote to J. B. S. Morritt of the result of two recent poetical ventures:

> these matters have answered well; for since I acquired possession of some of my copyrights, and adhered to the plan of retaining the property in the new publications, money has tumbled in upon me very fast, and I am enabled to make a very nice little purchase adjoining to Abbotsford which will cost about £3,000. I know it will do your kind heart good to know I am increasing my territories on Tweedside, and at so easy a rate. You who gave me so kind a shove when I was pinched with my long-dated bills, will I know rejoice that your friendship has not been throwing water into a sieve. The place is at present a sort of Kamtschatka [a bleak peninsula in Eastern Siberia], but marches along with my own, and has capabilities especially for planting and forming grass parks, which let here very high.[47]

Sir Arthur S. MacNalty, who talked architectural nonsense about the house of Abbotsford, and who failed to understand that what he thought excessive was actually what Scott himself liked, is nevertheless memorable on the essential connection between the estate in general and Scott's literary achievement.

> So, as wealth flowed in from the *Waverley* novels, field was added to field, moor to moor and wood to wood to make the noble estate on which the Laird of Abbotsford could ride and hunt and entertain his hosts of friends. Not entirely an ignoble ambition; concrete evidence of the toil of the slave of the lamp. A wood here represents *Guy Mannering*, a homestead there *The Antiquary*, that tract of moorland *Rob Roy* or *Old Mortality*, and so on. One can picture the 'Wizard of the North' drawing rein as he rode over his domain on his sure-footed pony to survey hill and copse and hough and to reflect proudly that he had conjured them into his own hands through the flights of his imagination.[48]

Less charitably, indeed with an ill-disguised sneer at the 'great novelist', Elizabeth Grant, the 'Highland Lady', looking back on events some fifteen or twenty years after Scott's death, mocked what she saw only as the extravagance, ostentation and sheer folly of Abbotsford. It was all swaggering show built on the profits of a popular pen she despised and an author, unoriginal and derivative, whom she disliked. Of *Waverley* she wrote that the 'determined mystery as to the Authour added much to its vogue' and further elaborated:

> I did not like it . . . intolerably dull, so lengthy, and so prosy, and the persons introduced so uninteresting, the hero contemptible, the two heroines unnatural and disagreeable, and the whole idea given of the highlands so utterly at variance with the truth . . . Then burst out *Guy Mannering*, carrying all the world before it, in spite of the very pitiful setting . . . Here again is the copyist . . . People now began to feel these works could come but from one Authour, particularly as a few acres began to be added to the recent purchase of the old tower of Abbotsford, and Mrs Scott set up in a carriage, a Barouche landau built in London, and which from the time she got it she was seldom out of, appearing indeed to spend her life in driving about the streets all day. I forget which came next, the Baronetcy or *the Antiquary* – the one very quickly succeeded the other – and were followed by the *Castle* at Abbotsford.[49]

In time the woods of Abbotsford became Scott's particular comfort and delight. One almost feels that the Shirra's pleasure in arboriculture on his estate was greater even than his devotion to literature and to his achievement of an enduring place among the immortals. 'I promise you,' he once wrote, 'my oaks will outlast my laurels, and I pique myself more on my composition for manure than on any other compositions whatsoever to which I was ever accessory.'[50] The attraction of a particular piece of ground, whether improvable by Scott through planting and cultivation or satisfactory enough in its existing state, sometimes lay in its literary associations or even would-be associations. Buying land was buying the poetry and romantic past of Scotland. Scott told John Richardson, a Scotsman exiled in London:

> I have enlarged my dominions here not greatly in extent but infinitely in point of beauty, as my boundary is now a strange secluded ravine full of old thorn trees, hazels, guelder roses & so forth, with a dashing rivulet & and certain large stones which in England your cocknies would call rocks. I call it the Rhymer's Glen as it makes part of the scene where Thomas the Rhymer is said to have met the Queen of the fairies. Vulgarly it is called Dick's Cleuch – a fico for the phrase.[51] (Fig. 4)

As for the house itself, the original cottage became a much more magnificent dwelling: as John Buchan put it, the new Abbotsford 'was growing piece-meal round the core of the old farm with the irregularity of the British Constitution'.[52] Scott liked to think that Don Quixote would have taken Abbotsford for 'an absolute Castle', though he confessed that he himself considered it a 'good deal more of an inn', but one which brought the landlord no profit.[53] In this he candidly admitted the drain on his resources which Abbotsford constituted. At other times, however, he, too, took the Quixotic view and, seduced by the grandeur of his folly, referred to his house as 'Conundrum Castle'.[54]

> It is a kind of Conundrum Castle to be sure, and I have great pleasure in it, for while it pleases a fantastic person in the stile and manner of its architecture and decoration it has all the comforts of a commodious habitation.[55]

But even more did Scott delight to refer to his dream and his real achievement as 'my romance of a house'.[56] Three times in 1822 he calls it this, or variants of this expression. 'I have been busied all this season in finishing a sort of a Romance of a house here, built in imitation of an old Scottish manor house and I think I have attained not unsuccessfully the scrambling stile of these venerable edifices . . .'[57] He tells Lord Montagu that

> It is worth while to come were it but to see what a romance of a house I am making which is neither to be castle nor abbey (God forbid) [was Scott here thinking of the awful example of William Beckford and Fonthill, both in terms of prodigal, self-indulgent extravagance and of shoddy building?] but an old Scottish manor house. I believe Atkinson [his architect] is in despair with my whims for he cries out Yes-Yes-Yes – in a tone which exactly signifies no-no-no . . .'[58]

Certainly Scott and his literary achievement helped in very large measure to put Scotland on the international tourist trail. The Border country of the ballads was much visited. Scott's narrative poems and *Waverley* novels, and his physical and cerebral existence at Abbotsford, made Scotland fashionable, and prepared the way for the Victorian love-affair with the Highlands.

Scott wanted his friends to see his house as it developed and share his pleasure as it swelled within him: for both the house and the pleasure grew in equal measure. He wrote to John Richardson in 1823:

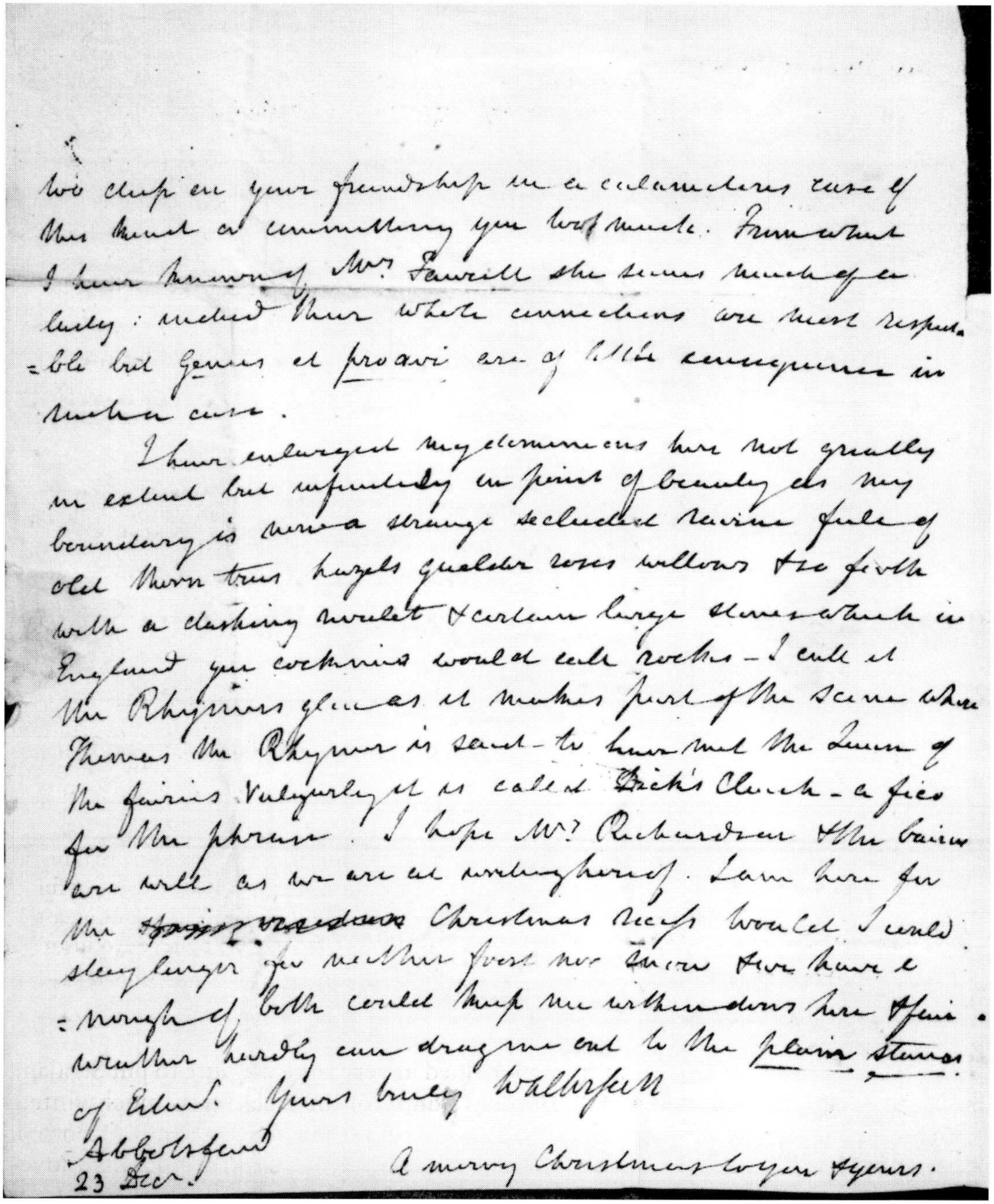

to clap in your friendship in a circumstance of
this kind as committing you but much. From what
I have known of Mr. Fawcett she seems much of a
lady: indeed their whole connections are most respect-
=ble but Genus et proavi are of little consequence in
such a case.

I have enlarged my dominions here not greatly
in extent but infinitely in point of beauty as my
boundary is now a strange secluded ravine full of
old thorn trees hazels guelder roses willows & so forth
with a dashing rivulet & certain large stones which in
England you cockneys would call rocks — I call it
the Rhymers glen as it makes part of the scene where
Thomas the Rhymer is said to have met the Queen of
the fairies. Vulgarly it is called Dick's Cleuch — a fico
for the phrase. I hope Mrs. Richardson & the bairns
are well as we are all [illegible]. I am here for
the ~~Spring vacation~~ Christmas recess would I could
stay longer for neither frost nor snow & we have e
=nough of both could keep me within doors here & fine
weather hardly can drag me out to the plain stones
of Edinr. Yours truly Walter Scott

Abbotsford
23 Decr.

A merry Christmas to you & yours.

FIGURE 4

Scott describes the literary appeal of buying land in a letter to John Richardson, 1816.
(National Library of Scotland, MS 23141, f. 94v)

> Abbotsford has cost me a mint of money, without much return as yet. But after all it is the surest way of settling a family if one can do without borrowing money or receiving interest. Said Abbotsford has thrust its lofty turrets into the skies since you saw it & I will scarce forgive you unless you make it a comfortable visit next season. It is from the unusual combination of the garden & courtyard with the manor house a sort of romance in Architecture.
>
> *A place to dream of not to tell.*
>
> In fact I have at last nearly completed a sort of vision which I always had in my mind. All our rooms are moderate in size except the Library which is forty feet by eighteen yet will not hold my books without assistance of my private room.[59]

And the next year Scott told Matthew Weld Hartstonge that he

> should come and see Abbotsford which as Augustus said of Rome (I love magnificent comparisons) I found of Brick and have left of marble. It is really a very handsome old manorial looking place both without and within, with a fine library, a Gothick hall of entrance and what not. But in truth it does not brook description any more than it is amenable to the ordinary rules of architecture.

He went on to quote that line of Coleridge yet again (and incorrectly yet again, for in *Christabel* Coleridge actually says 'sight'): 'A thing to dream of not to tell.'[60] Abbotsford was, as even its begetter realised, something almost beyond description: it belonged in the realm of 'experience'. It is worth noting, in passing, that when Scott actually saw Rome and the sights of the Grand Tour in his last wretched year of life it was of his native Scotland and of Abbotsford that he constantly thought and with which he made comparisons.

While there were not many days when he could afford the luxury of idleness Scott confided to his *Journal* in November 1826.

> I idled away the rest of the day happy to find myself at home, which is home though never so homely, and mine is not so homely neither – on the contrary I have seen in my travels none I liked so well – fantastic in architecture and decoration if you please – but no real comfort sacrificed to fantasy.[61]

On another occasion he declared that the hall, with its surfeit of heraldry, 'does not look in the least garish but on the contrary has a very solemn tone'.[62] (See Fig. i in *Preface*.) It is touching to note Scott's transparent and innocently vain satisfaction with his 'Dalilah': amongst all his other literary undertakings he might well have found a vocation as a writer of blurbs for the property agents of the day.

No man in Scotland, it has been said, with some truth, knew more people than did Scott, nor more kinds of people.[63] This aspect of Scott's place in the world is well represented by Sir William Allan's oil sketch *Gala Day at Abbotsford* (Scottish National Portrait Gallery) in which 'the Shirra' appears almost in the guise of an Eastern potentate under an umbrella with his friends and staff about him (Fig. 5). It is a graphic equivalent

FIGURE 5
Gala Day at Abbotsford *by Sir William Allan. Oil on panel.*
(Scottish National Portrait Gallery, SNPG 1193)

of John Buchan's verbal description of Scott's 'feudal retinue' and his 'feudal hospitality'.[64] Maria Edgeworth made the direct link between Scott's literary efforts and his wish to live this kind of life at Abbotsford. 'Dean Swift said he had written his books in order that people might learn to treat him as a great lord. Sir Walter Scott writes his that he may be able to treat his people as a great lord ought to do.'[65] That is a nineteenth-century novelist's view of a contemporary's achievement. Allan Massie, in our time, has put these words into Scott's mouth in the memoir purporting to be Scott's own:

> If I have done anything good in my life, Abbotsford is at the heart of it. My writings have, I am aware, given pleasure to many, and may continue to do so; it would be foolish to pretend otherwise. Yet this sort of pleasure is an easy business, and for my part, there has been no merit in the achievement. Writing has been as natural to me as breathing. But at Abbotsford I believe I have set an example . . . I have been fortunate to have had the opportunity to make of Abbotsford what I thought life should be . . . When I was but a bairn at Sandyknowe, I knew the reality of Eden; and it is the restoration of the sense of fitness which that knowledge insensibly secured for me that I have attempted in everything which I have done and made at Abbotsford.[66]

Yet another novelist, John Buchan, put the matter thus: Scott, he said

> realized his romance far less in the pepper-box turrets of Abbotsford and the plaster copies of the Melrose gargoyles than in his re-creation of a fragment of what seemed to him an older and happier world. He was living in his ancestral countryside as a little king, with all the felicities and some of the burdens of kingship . . . He had restored, though only in a corner, the liberal and kindly customs of more spacious days, mellowed, indeed, and civilized, but preserving intact their freedom and manliness and courtesy. If the dream was baseless it was assuredly not ignoble.[67]

When in 1831 Scott's trustees were attempting to justify to his creditors his intention to keep certain literary profits for himself rather than surrendering them to the Trust they spoke of his expensive domestic establishment and of how he was compelled to receive and entertain at Abbotsford 'every stranger who can procure an introduction to him . . . many of them people of rank'.[68] Abbotsford, and the curiosity of personal and literary life there, was a national institution; Scott's standing that of a representative of his country, certainly ambassadorial-plenipotentiary and almost regal. This is hardly exaggeration. In 1822, when Scott welcomed George IV in Leith roads, the King declared that *this* was the man in Scotland whom he most wished to see. The sovereign of Great Britain met on equal terms the king of literature and romance. In his very person 'King' Walter embodied the spirit of Scotland, past and present.

But, on occasion, Scott could and did take a different view of his duties, as seen in this extract from his *Journal* in 1825.

> Abbotsford begins to be haunted by too much company of every kind. But especially foreigners. I do not like them. I hate fine waistcoats and breast pins upon dirty shirts. I hate the impudence that pays a stranger compliments and harangues about his works in the Author's house, which is usually ill breeding. Moreover they are seldom long in making it evident that they know nothing about what they are talking of excepting having seen the *Lady of the Lake* at the opera.[69]

Joanna Baillie had early recognised the danger, in terms of his time and his resources, that the combination of literary fame and a striking house in a picturesque landscape might hold for Scott as possessor of all three. As early as 1811 she had warned,

> Many happy days may you & Mrs Scott & the children have in your new habitation! but don't let all the idle Travellers, who come to visit the country & the ruins which you have made famous, make an Inn of your house, for their own convenience and that they may boast in their stupid Tours afterwards of the great attentions they received from their *Friend* Mr Scott.[70]

Again, in 1819, she alluded to the threat of life at Abbotsford, where 'as Poet, Host, country Laird & Sheriff, you are like to be torn to pieces by clients & neighbours & travellers from all parts of the earth & of all degrees'.[71] Now, in the time of Sir Walter's financial undoing, she gave vent to her full feelings on the way that the Wizard of the

North had been exploited on account of the celebrity of his person and the concomitant fame of his house. What made her, as she said, 'grumble & growl like an evil spirit' was the thought of

> the multitude of impudent Travellers with letters of introduction from their as impudent friends who have abused your hospitable nature & made Abbotsford for so many summers an Inn & a Tavern for way faring Idlers of all sexs [*sic*] and ages. I have no charity for such people . . . and that you should have been their prey to such a degree provokes me . . .[72]

It is significant that in seeking a metaphor for Scott's hospitality at Abbotsford Joanna Baillie, poet and playwright, could only compare Scott, the inveterate maker of characters, with one of his own literary creations: 'you are a good humoured, open handed, open hearted Dandy Dinmount [Dinmont] kind of a man'.[73] Henry Cockburn, who spent some time with John Richardson at Abbotsford in September 1828, had 'the rare good fortune to find [Scott] nearly alone'. Cockburn's portrait of the Laird, his opponent in politics, is as delightful as it is sincere in its affection:

> His simplicity and naturalness after all his fame are absolutely incredible. I remember him when he was famous for almost nothing except imitating Eskgrove (a power which fortunately he has never lost), and his manners are the same now as they were then. No bad idea will be formed of Scott's conversation by supposing one of his Scotch novels to be cut into talk. It is not so much conversation as a joyous flow of anecdote, story, character and scene, mostly humorous, always graphic, and never personal or ill-natured.[74]

Cockburn (as I have already said) recalled how Scott's punishing schedule of literary labour at Abbotsford in his last years was accomplished with no loss of attention to the demands of gentlemanly sociability. In earlier days, when living was easier and when money from the great poems and the early novels was plentiful, David Wilkie, a guest at Abbotsford while he painted a picture of the writer with his wife, children and retainers in their landscape, found difficulty in understanding how work and play could be so easily united. The former element seemed, indeed, suppressed to the point of invisibility. Days with Scott were spent 'quite in the ancient style of Border conviviality' with a laird rather than a littérateur. Wilkie recorded the rustic idyll in his *The Abbotsford Family* (Scottish National Portrait Gallery) (Fig. 6). He told his sister of a life and a world paid for in a mysterious way.

> I have never been in any place where there is so much real good-humour and merriment. There is nothing but amusement from morning till night; and if Mr Scott is really writing 'Rob Roy', it must be while we are sleeping. He is either out planting trees, superintending the masons, or erecting fences, the whole of the day. He goes frequently out hunting, and this morning there was a whole cavalcade of us out with Mr and Miss Scott, hunting hares. The family here are equally in the dark about whether Mr Scott is the author of the Novels. They are quite perplexed about it: they hope he is the author, and would be

FIGURE 6

The Abbotsford Family *by David Wilkie. Oil on panel. Scott sits surrounded by (on his right) his daughters Sophia and Anne, and his wife, and (on his left) his sons Walter and Charles with (in the background) an elderly shepherd called Thomas Scott and (with his hands in his waistcoat pockets) Sir Adam Ferguson.*
(Scottish National Portrait Gallery, SNPG 1303)

> greatly mortified if it were to turn out that he was not. He has frequently talked about the different characters himself to us, and the young ladies express themselves greatly provoked with the sort of unconcern he affects towards them. He has denied the Novels, however, to various people that I know; and though the family used to tease him at first about them, yet they dare not do it now.[75]

Two years later, Frances Lady Shelley described how the 'Scotch Novels' were discussed during dinner at Abbotsford. Her host calmly heard her – wholly unaware of his authorship – say that she found the heroes and heroines insipid. Scott played his game magnificently, offering possible explanations and excuses for the author's technique. He praised the way that Lady Shelley rode when he had seen her at Paris, and added that he was quite sure the author of the 'Scottish novels' must have seen his guest's horsemanship ere he described Diana Vernon in *Rob Roy*![76]

It was left to a fictional character, the creation and *alter ego* of John Gibson Lockart, to describe better than anyone else the impression made on visitors by Scott in his dual personae of territorial magnate and literary magnet. In *Peter's Letters to his Kinsfolk*, Lockhart put into the mouth of Dr Peter Morris, an inquisitive and observant visitor to Scotland equally interested in arts and letters, a wonderfully memorable evocation of Abbotsford and its laird. Morris's account of his sojourn at Abbotsford and his travels in the vicinity occupy several long letters in the second volume of Lockhart's work. Together these form a tremendous – even overblown – portrait of a writer's place in the literary tradition of his country and as the living symbol of its soul. Morris praises Scott as poet and as novelist, for Lockhart makes him perceptive enough to realise, even in 1819, that Scott is the true author of the tales. Scott, at his house which recreates the past, is master of that past.

> The grave loses half its potency when he calls. His own imagination is one majestic sepulchre, where the wizard lamp burns in never-dying splendour, and the charmed blood glows for ever in the cheeks of the embalmed, and every long-sheathed sword is ready to leap from its scabbard . . . His works are altogether the most remarkable phenomenon in this age of wonders – produced among a people, whose taste had been well nigh weaned from all those ranges of feeling, on which their main inspiration and main power depend – they have of themselves been sufficient to create a more than passionate return of faith and homage to those deserted elements of greatness, in all the better part of his countrymen. I consider him, and his countrymen should do so, as having been sole saviour of all the richer and warmer spirit of literature in Scotland. He is, indeed, the *Facillime Princeps* of all her poets, past and present, and I more than question the likelihood of his having hereafter any 'Brother near the throne'.[77]

After Scott's death, Abbotsford would continue to be besieged by visitors drawn by the magic combination of Scott the man, his literary reputation and the renown of the place where everything in this magical world had been epitomised. Abbotsford became a shrine, unique in its power to attract pilgrims. Thomas Frognall Dibdin described in 1838 his recent visit.

> If I have been brief in my account of Melrose Abbey, I must be yet briefer in that of Abbotsford – for, in the first place, all the world has been there: though not stirring from their fire-sides. What Shakespeare and Stratford-upon-Avon have been, such Scott and Abbotsford now are. Upon the stage – off the stage – in the banquetting-room [*sic*] of the rich, and in the cottage of the poor – *there* is Abbotsford, or its late master: or both together. I can present no new feature; even to the man whose migrations have been exclusively confined from Cripplegate to Austin Friars ... But the hall door is opened – and here breathed, and for a while lived, the greatest of intellectual mortals in this country, after Shakespeare, Bacon, Milton, and Newton . . .[78]

If Dibdin's view of Abbotsford as a literary shrine was the one that largely prevailed, we must remember that there were dissenting voices. One might love Scott the man and Scott the writer, yet be disappointed by or even actively dislike his dwelling and his landscape. Nathaniel Hawthorne is an example of this attitude. He hated the Abbotsford countryside – 'cold, dreary, disheartening' – where the woods which had been Scott's delight appeared to him to lie on the hilltops like tightly fitting wigs. The house was adapted to the tourist trade, with a sign-posted visitor route through the rooms. In the Study Hawthorne saw Scott's clothes, 'and remarked how his old green coat was worn at the cuff, – a minute circumstance that seemed to bring Sir Walter very near me'. But Scott's collection of curiosities, his beloved 'gabions', left this visitor unmoved and even repelled:

> The feeling in visiting Abbotsford is not that of awe; it is little more than going to a museum. I do abhor this mode of making pilgrimages to the shrines of departed great men. There is certainly something wrong in it, for it seldom or never produces (in me, at least) the right feeling. It is an odd truth, too, that a house is for ever after spoiled and ruined as a home, by having been the abode of a great man. His spirit haunts it, as it were, with a malevolent effect, and takes hearth and hall away from the nominal possessors, giving all the world the right to enter here, because he had such intimate relations with all the world.[79]

Theodor Fontane, the father of the modern German novel, is an example of a rather different aspect of unfavourable reaction to Abbotsford as place of earnest literary pilgrimage. From youth he had been devoted to Scott as poet, storyteller and historian. On his tour of Scotland in 1858 Abbotsford had been one of the principal attractions. His responses to what he saw are fascinating, and his observations worth quoting at some length. Fontane argued that Scott's supreme exercise of the literary imagination was not necessarily something that could be extended with success into the architecture of imagination, or at least not so as to make that transformation appeal to others or to succeeding generations:

> Willy-nilly the whole building proves that what suits one set of circumstances does not suit all, and that the revival of the past, the embellishment of a modern creation with the rich poetic details from the Middle Ages, may bewitch and enchant us in one context while in another it can become something little better than an oddity and a joke. This romance in stone and mortar, if I am to maintain the metaphor on which the poet himself was so intent, affects one very much as though he had taken from a drawer of his desk a hundred pretty passages from all kinds of old ballads, in the firm hope that by patching such fragments together he would be able to achieve the perfect romance. There has been no flash of inspiration sufficiently strong to weld the hostile elements into a unity.
>
> There is a rhyming party game in which the participants write a line, then turn the paper down save for the last word, so that there can be no possible connection between what the next man writes and what has been written before him.
>
> Abbotsford is very like that. It has all been built for the sake of some forty or fifty catchwords . . .[80]

Fontane, indeed, fought to stop himself dismissing the house merely as 'an ill-built job' by keeping in mind its begetter and the circumstances of its creation. Outside and in, it seemed to him (as to Hawthorne the year before) but a mass of assorted curiosities verging on the ugly, the clumsy and the jocular. He left the house-shrine with relief, his duty paid and his only regret that he had not been able to see this monument of literature quite as its creator had done, or as he had evidently wished others to do. 'We breathed again in the fresh air,' wrote Fontane, 'and felt as though a kind of pressure upon us had been eased . . . While the writer was himself still alive for whom these things had real significance, for whom they were really a matter of the heart, they were endowed with life under the influence of the living word which proceeded from him . . . Now, however, when these notes can no longer be heard, the stones are stone again, and even one who is familiar with Scottish history and song walks through these rooms as though they were a waxwork show.' Nevertheless, Fontane concluded, the house had a resonance beyond its mere ability to appeal to later visitors with all the fervour that it had done to its begetter. In this, surely, he perceptively analysed the essence of Abbotsford's true historical significance.

> What fame would Scotland have, had it not been for this same Walter Scott? He collected the songs of his country and has immortalized its history in his writing. I now experience a full pure satisfaction at having wandered through that strange house with its gables and tiles, that house which was also the creation of his poetic genius and which, though it may lag far behind the other creations of his spirit, will always remain the place where this miracle tree of the romantic movement put forth its fairest and above all its *healthiest* blossoms.[81]

The dream of Abbotsford as a magical realm built by the Wizard of the North out of almost measureless and continuing wealth had crashed about Sir Walter in the winter of 1825–6. Not many months before, in a spirit of theoretical moralising, he had told his sister-in-law that 'the real road to ruin is . . . to have an improveable estate with a taste for building . . . you will find the bottom of the purse with a vengeance. But there is always balm in Gilead for Clerks of Session whose quarterday is always coming round in its due time'.[82] An improvable estate and a taste for building: both were his undoing. Years before, in 1813, Scott had delighted to tell Morritt of the success of *Rokeby*, specifically undertaken, of course, to make money for the new laird and would-be builder.

> The book has gone off here very bobbishly for the impression of 3000 and upwards is within two or three score of being exhausted and the demand for these continuing faster than they can be boarded [that is, bound in boards]. I am heartily glad of this for now I can have nothing to fear but a bankruptcy in the gazette of Parnassus.[83]

Now, in November 1825, he resolved on 'No more Building. No purchases of Land till times are quite safe. No buying books or expensive trifles. And Clearing off encumbrances with the returns of this year's labour'.[84] But it was all to no avail. Scott's borrowings had almost no capital to support them but Abbotsford itself; and Abbotsford was supported by the very insecure scaffolding on which his literary and financial life was itself supported: borrowing in a system of interdependence, with accommodation bills set off by counter-bills.[85] As Allan Massie (writing in the persona of Scott in the dark days of 1826) memorably puts it, 'it is my debts and my dreams that have brought me to my present pass'.[86] Washington Irving, writing within three years of Scott's death and recalling with sadness his visit to the house in 1816, hinted at the fatal flaw that was Abbotsford, the dream that devoured the dreamer. Irving remembered:

> He talked about his proposed plans of Abbotsford: happy would it have been for him could he have contented himself with his delightful little vine covered cottage, and the simple, yet hearty and hospitable style, in which he lived at the time of my visit. The great pile of Abbotsford, with the huge expense it entailed upon him, of servants, retainers, guests, and baronial style, was a drain upon his purse, a task upon his exertions, and a weight upon his mind, that finally crushed him.[87]

Lockhart's shrewd analysis was that there was an element of the gambler in his father-in-law. All subsequent biographers have agreed, and echo Lockhart on this point. Lockhart indeed, taking this as the inevitable corollary of Scott's genius, attributed his huge achievement to this character trait. He lived by risk. The retired literary life was not enough: he must live it to the full, on one occasion even being prepared to fight a duel with a French general over a remark in his *Life of Napoleon Buonaparte* – using Napoleon's own pistols, indeed, which he just happened to possess.[88] Scott's life was always more than that of the mere lawyer or the mere writer. As Massie's Scott declares, 'a man who is only an author is in general a puir cratur'.[89]

The dream-world of Scott's fiction and the dream-world of his life at Abbotsford coalesced in the years following the crash when, with a heroism worthy of a fictional character, he worked to pay his debts and preserve his house and land. The folly of his extravagance, which required ceaseless literary effort to support it, gave rise to a literary triumph in the creation of his *Journal*, the greatest thing, I believe, that ever he wrote, and in which he shows us a figure nobler by far than any in his novels or poetry. It will be relevant to see how Abbotsford figures in this particular literary achievement. The following *Journal* entry, quoted here in a much condensed form, must rank as perhaps the finest facing-up to adversity recorded in the English language.

> 18 December 1825. Ballantyne calld on me this morning. My extremity is come . . . I suppose it will involve my all . . . I have been rash in anticipating funds to buy land. But then I made from £5,000 to £10,000 a year, and land was my temptation . . . Men will think pride has had a fall. Let them indulge their own pride in thinking that my fall makes them higher or seem so at least. I have the satisfaction to recollect that my prosperity has been of advantage to many and that some at least will forgive my transient wealth on account of the innocence of my intentions and my real wish to do good to the poor. This news will make sad hearts at Darnick and in the cottages of Abbotsford which I do not nourish the least hope of preserving . . . It has been my Dalilah and so I have often termd it – and now – the recollection of the extensive woods I have planted and the walks I have formed from which strangers must derive both the pleasure and profit will excite feelings likely to sober my gayest moments. I have half resolved never to see the place again – how

could I tread my hall with such a dimishd crest? How live a poor indebted man where I was once the wealthy – the honourd? My children are provided – thank God for that. I was to have gone there on Saturday in joy and prosperity to receive my friends – my dogs will wait for me in vain – it is foolish – but the thoughts of parting from these dumb creatures have moved me more than any of the painful reflections I have put down – poor things I must get them kind masters. There may be yet those who loving me may love my dog because it has been mine. I must end this or lose the tone of mind with which men should meet distress. I find my dogs' feet on my knees – I hear them whining and seeking me everywhere – this is nonsense but it is what they would do could they know how things are – poor Will Laidlaw – poor Tom Purdie – this will be news to wring your heart and many a poor fellow's besides to whom my prosperity was daily bread . . .

For myself the magic wand of the Unknown is shiverd in his grasp. He must henceforth be termd the Too well Known. The feast of fancy is over with the feeling of independence. I can no longer have the delight of waking in the morning with bright ideas in my head, haste to commit them to paper, and count them monthly as the means of planting such groves and purchasing such wastes . . . It is a bitter thought, but if tears start at it let them flow. I am so much of this mind that if any one would now offer to relieve all my embarrassments on condition I would continue the exertions which brought it there, dear as the place is to me, I hardly think I could undertake the labour on which I enterd with my usual alacrity only this morning; though not without a boding feeling of my exertions proving useless. Yet to save Abbotsford I would attempt all that was possible. My heart clings to the place I have created. There is scarce a tree on it that does not owe its being to me and the pain of leaving it is greater than I can tell . . . An odd thought strikes me. When I die will the journal of these day[s] be taken out of the Ebony cabinet at Abbotsford and read as the transient pout of a man worth £60,000 with wonder that the well seeming Baronet should ever have experienced such a hitch? Or will it be found in some obscure lodginghouse where the decayd son of chivalry has hung up his scutcheon for some 20/- a week and where one or two old friends will look grave and whisper to each other, 'poor gentleman' – 'a well meaning man' – 'nobody's enemy but his own' – 'thought his parts could never wear out' – 'family poorly left', 'pity he took that foolish title'? Who can answer this question?

What a life mine has been. Half educated, almost wholly neglected or left to myself – stuffing my head with nonsensical trash and undervalued in society for a time by most of my companions – getting forward and held a bold and clever fellow, contrary to the opinion of all who thought me a mere dreamer – Broken-hearted for two years – My heart handsomely pieced again – but the crack will remain till my dying day – Rich and poor four or five times – Once at the verge of ruin yet opend new sources of wealth almost overflowing – now taken in my pitch of pride and nearly winged (unless the good news hold) becaue London chuses to be in an uproar and in the tumult of bulls and bears a poor inoffensive lion like myself is pushd to the wall – And what is to be the end of it? God knows and so ends the catechism.[90]

Yet the thought of the next visit to Abbotsford, at Christmas 1825, cheered him: 'We are for Abbotsford today with a light heart.' There he threw himself into work on

Christmas Day itself. 'Arrived here last night at seven. Our halls are silent compared to last year but let us be thankful when we think how near the chance appeared but a week since that these halls would have been ours no longer . . . There shall be no lack of wisdom.'[91]

But with the turn of the year the news worsened, and the debt deepened. 'I apprehend I shall neither save Abbotsford nor any thing else – Naked we enterd the world and naked we leave it. Blessed be the name of the Lord.'[92]

So Scott prepared to make the best of adversity:

> I feel neither dishonoured nor broken down by the bad – miserably bad news I have received. I have walkd my last on the domains I have planted, sate the last time in the halls I have built. But death would have taken them from me if misfortune had spared them. My poor people whom I loved so well! There is another dye to turn up against me in this run of ill luck – i.e. If I should break my magic wand in a fall from this elephant and lose my popularity along with my fortune. Then *Woodstock* and *Boney* may both go to the paper-maker and I may take to smoking cigars and drinking grog or turn devotee and intoxicate the brain another way. In prospect of absolute ruin I wonder if they would let me leave the Court of Session. I should like methinks to go abroad
>
> And lay my banes far from the Tweed.
>
> But I find my eyes moistening and that will not do. I will not yield without a fight for it. It is odd, when I set myself to work *doggedly* as Dr. Johnson would say, I am exactly the same man that I ever was – neither low spirited nor *distrait*. In prosperous times I have sometimes let my fancy and powers of language flag – but adversity is to me at least a tonic and bracer – the fountain is awakend from its inmost recesses as if the spirit of afliction had troubled it in his passage . . . I will involve no friend either rich or poor – My own right hand shall do it – Else I will be *done* in the slang language and *undone* in common parlance . . . If I am hard pressd and measures used against me I must use all measures of legal defence and subscribe myself bankrupt in a petition for sequestration. It is the course I would have advised a client to take and would have the effect of saving my land, which is secured by my son's contract of marriage. I might save my library etc. by assistance of friends and bid my creditors defiance. But for this I would in a court of Honour deserve to lose my spurs for – No, if they permit me, I will be their vassal for life and dig in the mine of my imagination to find diamonds (or what may sell for such) to make good my engagements, not to enrich myself. And this from no reluctance to allow myself to be calld the Insolvent which I probably am but because I will not put out of reach of my creditors the resources mental or literary which yet remain to me . . .[93]

We may take up the story in three letters of Scott, all of them sent on 26 January 1826, to Willie Laidlaw, to his son Walter and to his son-in-law, Lockhart. In his letter to Willie Laidlaw he wrote:

> Lady Scott's spirits were affected at first, but she is getting better. For myself, I feel like the Eildon Hills – quite firm, though a little cloudy. I do not dislike the path which lies before me. I have seen all that society can shew, and enjoyed all that wealth can give me, and am satisfied much is vanity.[94]

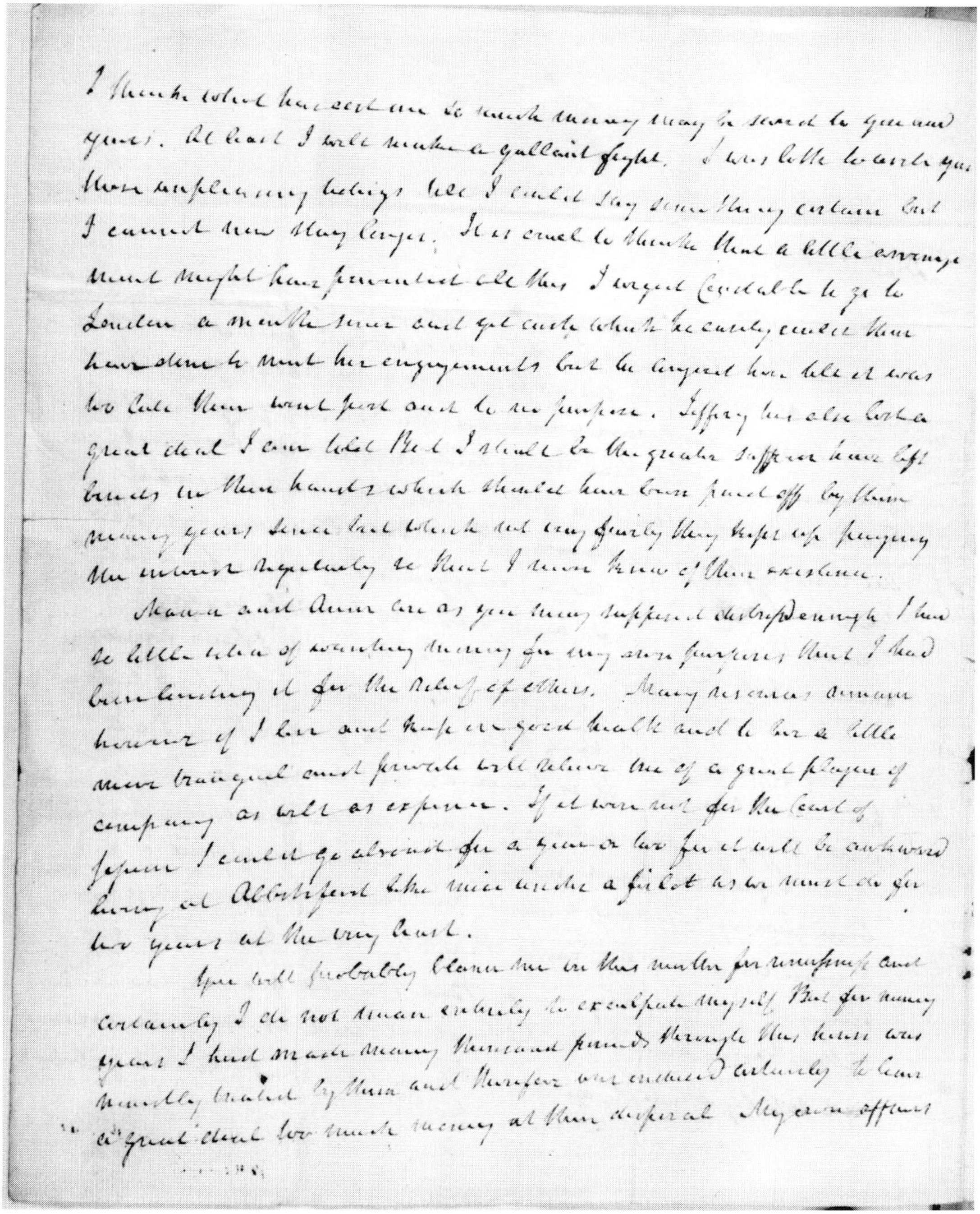
I think what has cost me so much money may be saved to you and
yours. At least I will make a gallant fight. I was loth to write you
these unpleasing tidings till I could say something certain but
I cannot now stay longer. It is cruel to think that a little arrange-
ment might have prevented all this. I urged Constable to go to
London a month since and get cash which he easily could then
have done to meet his engagements but he lingered here till it was
too late then went post and to no purpose. Jeffrey has also lost a
great deal I am told But I shall be the greater sufferer having left
bonds in their hands which should have been paid off by them
many years since but which not very fairly they kept up paying
the interest regularly so that I never knew of their existence.
Mama and Anne are as you may suppose distressed enough I had
so little idea of wanting money for my own purposes that I had
been lending it for the relief of others. Many resources remain
however if I live and keep in good health and to be a little
more tranquil and private will relieve me of a great plague of
company as well as expense. If it were not for the look of
[illegible] I could go abroad for a year or two for it will be awkward
living at Abbotsford like men under a pilot as we must do for
two years at the very least.
You will probably blame me in this matter for imprudence and
certainly I do not mean entirely to exculpate myself But for many
years I had made many thousand pounds through this house was
[illegible] treated by them and therefore was inclined certainly to leave
a great deal too much money at their disposal. My own affairs

FIGURE 7
Scott breaks the news of his ruin to his eldest son, 1826.
(National Library of Scotland, MS 139, f. 121v)

And to his son, Walter:

> I would give up much rather than part with Abbotsford . . . I think what has cost me so much money may be saved to you and yours, At least I will make a gallant fight . . . Many resources remain, however, if I live and keep in good health and to live a little more tranquil and private will relieve me of a great plague of company as well as expence. If it were not for the Court of Session I could go abroad for a year or two for it will be awkward living at Abbotsford like mice under a firlot . . .[95] (Fig. 7)

And to his son-in-law, Lockhart:

> I look with perfect firmness and calmness on the life before me . . . I shall get rid of company from Dukes to canvas daubers, for when the kitchen and the cellar fail there will and shall be an end of the hospitalities of Abbotsford . . . study must be at once my amusement and my business, as indeed it always has been. For I never knew that day that I would have given up literature for ten times my late income. The success of my efforts I must consider as more precarious than my friends are willing to admit. The public are apt to desert folks when their back is at the wall. If I succeed in my labours I shall in time recover all that I have lost – if not bread I shall eat or white or brown and I trust I will at least leave no debt behind me.[96]

Later that year, the Trustees indicated that better times might indeed lie ahead and they conveyed their

> very high admiration of the astounding exertions which you have made and are still making for the benefit of the Trust. In common with other men we admire the inexhaustible fertility of that genius which has so often delighted us; but as your Trustees we have opportunities which others do not enjoy of observing and duly appreciating the energy and magnanimity with which you have met the distressing exigencies of your situation.[97]

In 1830, when he retired from the Clerkship of the Court of Session – in his letter of resignation inviting the Lord President to visit him at Abbotsford to see that 'the old rat is not quite starved in his hollow tree'[98] (Fig. 8) – he received the Library and plenishings of the house from the trust. Looking forward one day at Abbotsford in December 1830 Scott reckoned that by 1832 his debts would be well nigh cleared. 'This view cannot be absolutely certain but it is highly probable and it is calculatented [*sic*] in the manner in which one builds schemes and not visions. The year 1833 may probably see me again in possession of my estate.'[99]

But, as we know, life is not always a romance, like a *Waverley* novel, with a happy ending. This moment of release from overwhelming debt was a blessed time Scott was fated never to see, for he died at Abbotsford on 21 September 1832. Having endured a last wretched journey home from Italy, he had lingered for weeks between semi-conscious existence and inevitable but kindly death. In his great biography Lockhart turned these last sad episodes of the Laird of Abbotsford's extraordinary life at his beloved 'Conundrum Castle' into literature worthy of the subject, and movingly described the death-bed

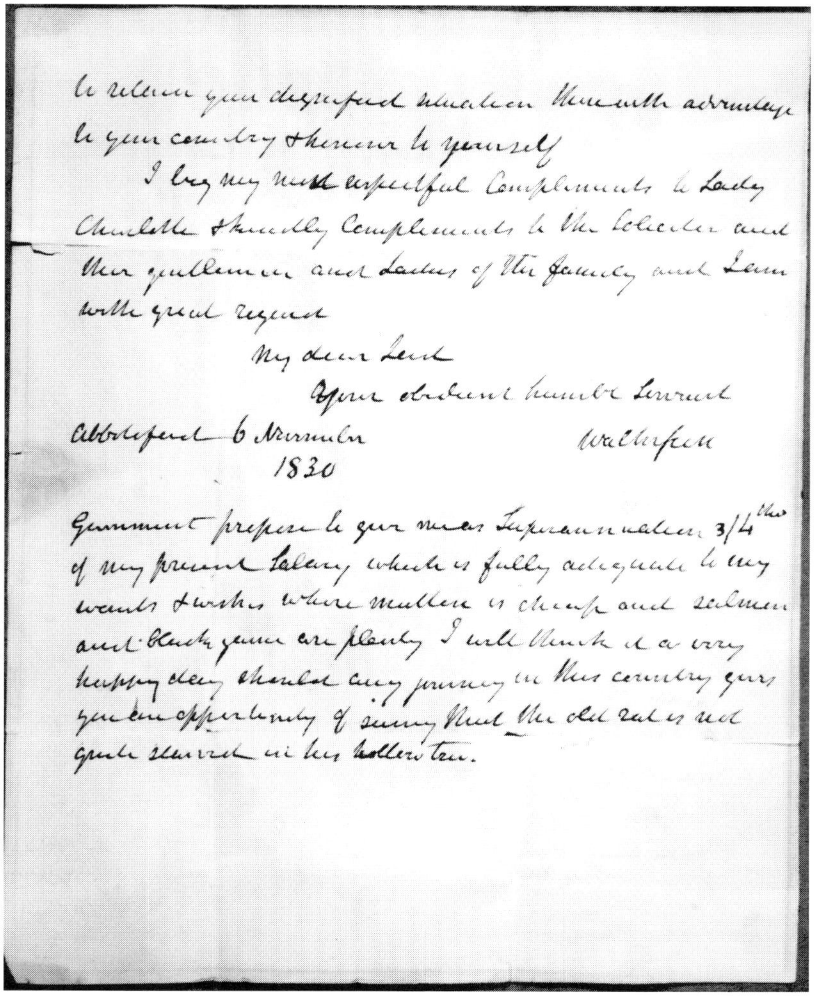

to return your dignified situation there with advantage to your country & honour to yourself

I beg my most respectful Compliments to Lady Charlotte & kindly Compliments to the Collector and other gentlemen and Ladies of the family and I am with great regard

My dear Lord

Your obedient humble Servant

Abbotsford 6 November 1830 Walter Scott

Government propose to give me as Superannuation 3/4ths of my present Salary which is fully adequate to my wants & wishes where mutton is cheap and salmon and black game are plenty I will think it a very happy day should any journey in this country give you an opportunity of seeing that the old rat is not quite starved in his hollow tree.

FIGURE 8

Scott expresses optimism about continued existence at Abbotsford, albeit in reduced circumstances, 1830.

(National Library of Scotland, Adv. MS 20.3.16)

scene. With less artifice, but no less true feeling for an old friend, Henry Cockburn, the keenest observer of the age, wrote in his *Journal* the next day:

> Scott is dead . . . I had been on a visit at Kirklands . . . and on coming home to-day I saw Abbotsford reposing beside its gentle Tweed, and amidst its fading woods, in the calm splendour of a sweet autumnal day. I was not aware till I reached Edinburgh that all that it then contained of him was his memory and his remains. Scotland never owed so much to one man.[100]

NOTES

1 National Library of Scotland [NLS], MS 3812, f. 47, 25 October 1832; printed in Allan Cunningham, *The Life of Sir David Wilkie*, 3 vols (London 1843), III, p. 62.
2 Henry Cockburn, *Memorials of his Time*, new edn by Harry C. Cockburn (Edinburgh 1909), pp. 402–3.
3 Ibid., p. 424.
4 *Journal*, p. 65, 22 January 1826.
5 NLS, MS 113, Sederunt Book of the Trustees of James Ballantyne & Co., p. 177.
6 A. N. Wilson, *The Laird of Abbotsford: A View of Sir Walter Scott* (Oxford 1980), p. 8.
7 For Scott's literary production both the serious scholar and interested general reader will find William B. Todd and Ann Bowden, *Sir Walter Scott: A Bibliographical History 1796–1832* (New Castle, Delaware 1998) an invaluable guide.
8 James C. Corson, *Notes and Index to Sir Herbert Grierson's Edition of the Letters of Sir Walter Scott* (Oxford 1979).
9 James Nasmyth, *Autobiography*, edited by Samuel Smiles (London 1897), p. 84. Scott alluded to the demolition of the Tolbooth – 'a sort of Bastile in the centre of the principal street [of Edinburgh]' – in a letter to Robert Surtees, 12 November 1816 (*Letters*, IV, p. 286). He continues with an almost prophetic aside to the effect that architectural desire could lead a man into trouble: 'Building has procured many a man a niche in the jail; but I shall be the first who reverses that order of things and brings a niche *from* the jail.'
10 Washington Irving, *The Crayon Miscellany. No. 2: Abbotsford and Newstead Abbey* (Philadelphia 1835), p. 43.
11 *Laird of Abbotsford*, p. 59.
12 Quoted in Grierson, 'Sir Walter Scott in his Letters': Introduction to *The Letters of Sir Walter Scott*, 12 vols (London 1932–7), I, p. xxx.
13 *The Diary of Frances Lady Shelley 1818–1873*, edited by Richard Edgcumbe, 2 vols (London 1913), II, pp. 45–6.
14 *Macready's Reminiscences, and Selections from his Diaries and Letters*, edited by Sir Frederick Pollock, 2 vols (London 1875), II, p. 276; I, pp. 181, 345.
15 *Memoirs of a Highland Lady*, edited by Andrew Tod, 2 vols (Edinburgh 1988), II, p. 73.
16 W. E. K. Anderson, Introduction to *The Journal of Sir Walter Scott* (Oxford 1972), p. xxii.
17 *Laird of Abbotsford*, p. 8.
18 *Letters*, V, p. 184, to J. B. S. Morritt, 10 September 1818.
19 Grierson, Introduction to *Letters*, I, pp. xxx–xxxi.
20 *Autobiography of Mrs Eliza Fletcher*, ed. by Lady Richardson (Edinburgh 1875), p. 168; cf. H. J. C. Grierson, *Sir Walter Scott, Bart.* (London 1938), p. 259.
21 *Letters*, IV, p. 138.
22 A. O. J. Cockshut, *The Achievement of Walter Scott* (London 1969), p. 17.
23 *The Ruin of Sir Walter Scott* (London 1968), p. 11 and *passim*.
24 Ibid., pp. 97, 24.
25 Ibid., p. 66.
26 On this topic see Jane Millgate, *Scott's Last Edition. A Study in Publishing History* (Edinburgh 1987), especially Chapter 4; and Iain Gordon Brown (ed.) *Scott's Interleaved Waverley Novels. An Introduction and Commentary* (Aberdeen 1987), especially p. 47.
27 *The Ragged Lion* (London 1995, pb edn), p. 153.
28 The assertion is made, and then half withdrawn, by Paul Henderson Scott, *Walter Scott and Scotland* (Edinburgh 1981), pp. 18, 24. The apophthegm does not occur in Virginia Woolf's

essay 'Gas at Abbotsford', reprinted in *The Moment and other essays* (London 1947), pp. 50–5.

29 On this point see David Daiches, *Sir Walter Scott and his World* (London 1971), p. 83.
30 John Buchan, *Sir Walter Scott* (London 1932), p. 102.
31 Ibid.
32 *Letters*, II, pp. 492–3, 12 May 1811.
33 *Letters*, III, p. 30, 10 December 1811.
34 *Letters*, III, pp. 68–9, 18 January 1812.
35 *Letters*, III, pp. 88–9, 2 March 1812.
36 Quoted in Wilfred Partington (ed.), *The Private Letter-Books of Sir Walter Scott* (London 1930), p. 183n, to Morritt, April 1812.
37 *Letters*, III, p. 105, 20 April 1812.
38 NLS, MS 23118, f. 80, to Lady Charlotte Rawdon, 14 August 1811.
39 NLS, MS 23118, f. 186, 1 July 1811.
40 *The Collected Letters of Joanna Baillie*, ed. by Judith Bailey Slagle, 2 vols (Cranbury, NJ and London 1999), I, p. 282.
41 Quoted in Daiches, *Sir Walter Scott*, p. 86.
42 *Letters*, III, p. 34, 12 December 1811. Scott referred to Stark's plan for Abbotsford as 'this great adventure', but had to relinquish it as too expensive: see *Letters*, III, p. 65, n. 1.
43 *Letters*, III, p. 154, to Daniel Terry, September 1812.
44 *Letters*, IV, p. 286, to Robert Surtees, 12 November 1816.
45 *Letters*, IV, p. 464, 8 June 1817.
46 *Diary of Frances Lady Shelley*, II, p. 46.
47 *Letters*, IV, pp. 111–12, 2 November 1815.
48 Sir Arthur S. MacNalty, *Sir Walter Scott: The Wounded Falcon* (London 1969), p. 58.
49 *Memoirs of a Highland Lady*, II, p. 72.
50 Quoted in Hesketh Pearson, *Walter Scott: His Life and Personality* (London 1954), p. 149.
51 *Letters*, IV, p. 326, 23 December 1816, the text corrected from the manuscript in NLS, MS 23141, f. 94v. See also Scott's letter to Charles Kirkpatrick Sharpe, 11 October 1817, *Letters*, IV, p. 539.
52 *Sir Walter Scott*, p. 148.
53 *Letters*, VIII, p. 117, to Richard Heber, 12 November 1823.
54 See, for example, Scott's letter to Sir James Stuart of Allanbank, 7 July 1824, NLS MS 23141, f. 146.
55 *Journal*, p. 411, 7 January 1828.
56 *Letters*, VII, p. 100, to Lord Montagu, 14–15 March 1822.
57 *Letters*, VII, p. 282, to Mrs Hughes, 14 November 1822.
58 *Letters*, VII, p. 111, to Lord Montagu, 27 March 1822.
59 *Letters*, VIII, p. 129, November–December 1823.
60 *Letters*, VIII, p. 289, 27 May 1824.
61 *Journal*, p. 246.
62 NLS, MS 23141, f. 146v, to Sir James Stuart of Allanbank, 7 July 1824.
63 NLS exhibition catalogue *Sir Walter Scott* (1971), p. 17.
64 *Sir Walter Scott*, p. 176.
65 Quoted in Buchan, *Sir Walter Scott*, p. 223.
66 *The Ragged Lion*, p. 255.
67 *Sir Walter Scott*, p. 223.

68 NLS, Acc. 11878, Report of Trustees to the Committee of Creditors, February 1831.
69 *Journal*, p. 10, 23 November 1825.
70 *Collected Letters of Joanna Baillie*, I, pp. 282–3.
71 Ibid., p. 391.
72 Ibid., p. 435.
73 Ibid., p. 435.
74 Cockburn, *Memorials of his Time*, p. 423. The elderly judge Sir David Rae, Lord Eskgrove, was much mocked and his manners imitated by young advocates. Scott held the palm for such mimicry.
75 Allan Cunningham, *The Life of Sir David Wilkie*, 3 vols (London 1843), I, pp. 481–3.
76 *The Diary of Frances Lady Shelley*, II, p. 48. The reference to this character is to her appearance in a scene in Chapter 5 of *Rob Roy*.
77 John Gibson Lockhart, *Peter's Letters to his Kinsfolk*, 3 vols (Edinburgh 1819), I, p. 314 (Letter LI) and p. 361 (Letter LV).
78 T. F. Dibdin, *A Bibliographical Antiquarian and Picturesque Tour in the Northern Counties of England and in Scotland*, 2 vols (London 1838), II, pp. 1008–12.
79 Nathaniel Hawthorne, *English Notebooks* (London 1870), pp. 339–40.
80 Theodor Fontane, *Beyond the Tweed: A Tour in Scotland in 1858*, translated by Brian Battershaw with an introduction by Charlotte Jolles (London 1998), p. 214.
81 Ibid., pp. 217–18, 223.
82 *Letters*, IX, p. 123, to Mrs Thomas Scott, 21 May 1825.
83 *Letters*, III, pp. 224–5, 12 January 1813.
84 *Journal*, p. 14, 25 November 1825.
85 On this, see the convenient summary by W. E. K. Anderson in his Introduction to his edition of the *Journal*, pp. xxiii–xxv.
86 *The Ragged Lion*, p. 5.
87 *The Crayon Miscellany. No. 2: Abbotsford and Newstead Abbey*, pp. 42–3.
88 *Journal*, pp. 343–4.
89 *The Ragged Lion*, p. 60.
90 *Journal*, pp. 38–42.
91 *Journal*, p. 48.
92 *Journal*, p. 64, 21 January 1826.
93 *Journal*, pp. 64–6, 22–24 January 1826.
94 *Letters*, IX, p. 378.
95 *Letters*, IX, pp. 379–80.
96 *Letters*, IX, p. 384.
97 NLS, MS 3903, f. 127, John Gibson, WS, to Scott, 9 October 1826; cf. NLS, Acc. 11878 and MS 113, Sederunt Book, p. 177.
98 NLS, Adv. MS 20.3.16.
99 *Journal*, p. 614.
100 Henry Cockburn, *The Journal of Henry Cockburn*, 2 vols (Edinburgh 1874), I, p. 37. After the words 'sweet autumnal day' Cockburn added a footnote with a quotation from *The Lay of the Last Minstrel*:

> Call it not vain; they do not err
> Who say that when the poet dies
> Mute nature mourns her worshipper
> And celebrates his obsequies.

SCOTT, ABBOTSFORD AND THE ANTIQUARIES

John Frew

THE building history of Abbotsford is now pretty well understood.[1] Following a modest enlargement of the original 'farmhouse' in 1811–12, the structure was aggrandised in two phases, between 1816–19 and 1822–4. Both phases provided focus for the deliberations of a latter-day Committee of Taste, encouraging parallels with the experiments of Horace Walpole at Strawberry Hill, near Twickenham, and (less plausibly) William Beckford at Fonthill Abbey, Wiltshire.[2] Three architects are documented as contributing to the development of Abbotsford during Scott's lifetime: William Stark (involved in the initial 'farmhouse' alterations only) and, more importantly, William Atkinson and Edward Blore. Although the relationship between these last two has long been a source of some confusion, it is now generally agreed that it was Atkinson who fulfilled the more conventional role, as lead architect.[3] Blore's position as, effectively, architectural adviser, was nevertheless of very considerable significance, not least because he is generally assumed to have been more sympathetic than Atkinson to the fostering of 'the old-fashioned Scotch style', signalled by the introduction of 'all manner of bartizans' and 'notch'd Gable ends', as well as the incorporation of fragments cannibalised from an assortment of original Scottish medieval sources, including Melrose Abbey and Dunfermline Abbey.[4]

Virtually from the very outset, therefore, the intention was clear. It aimed at a degree of historical authenticity that would immediately distinguish Abbotsford from the non-specific medievalism that had characterised the great majority of country-house experiments produced in an earlier phase of the Gothic Revival, many of which had identified with the Adam 'Castle Style'. As such, Abbotsford has come to assume a watershed significance, reflected in James Macaulay's assessment of it as the 'unsung prototype of Scots-Baronial architecture', an appraisal subsequently reinforced by Clive Wainwright, who considered it to be 'crucial' to the development of the same revival.[5]

This paper aims to refine these assessments, and focuses on the period immediately preceding the start of work at Abbotsford. It relates Scott's decision to adopt an overtly Scottish style to a wider contemporary context, arguing in the process that the 'isolation' of the experiment – and its pioneering significance – should, at the very least, be subject to significant qualification. It finds a starting point in Scott's confessed 'madness' for the Picturesque, and, as a further reflection of this, his interest in the writings of Uvedale Price (the Picturesque movement's greatest theorist) and Humphry Repton (its most distinguished exponent in terms of landscape design).[6] Of the two, it was Repton who had the more obvious relevance to architectural developments at Abbotsford. As early as 1795, in *Sketches and Hints on Landscape Gardening*, he had defended the merits of the Gothic style, remarking that it was 'calculated for additions and repairs' and allowed the introduction of a degree of compositional informality that was inseparable from 'picturesque effect'. In his own words, 'we may add a room to any part of the building without injuring the picturesque outside, because an exact symmetry, so far from being necessary, is rather to be avoided in a Gothic building'.[7] Eight years later, in the enormously influential *Observations on the Theory and Practice of Landscape Gardening* (1803) he returned to the same theme, defending the merits of the 'irregular' or 'modern Gothic' style (the latter a description subsequently favoured by Scott when discussing Atkinson's plans for Abbotsford)[8] on the basis of its flexibility, this facilitating the development of a convenient country-house format that was responsive to the revolution that had taken place in landscape design.[9]

Observations nevertheless differed from *Sketches and Hints* in one important respect. In 1795 Repton had been openly indifferent to the demands of historicism. But in 1803 we find him taking what at first sight appears to be a firmly antiquarian stance, confessing that *Sketches and Hints* had been written 'before I became better acquainted with subjects of antiquity', warning against the unnecessary destruction of old buildings, censuring 'fanciful' interpretations of Gothic, and encouraging the principle of 'imitation': '. . . in designing any Gothic building, it is presumed that some fragments exist of the style we propose to imitate; otherwise it ceases to be an imitation'.[10] As an example he cited the north front of Corsham Court, Wiltshire, as recently remodelled by John Nash and John Adey Repton (1797–8), and incorporating features inspired by Hampton Court and Westminster Abbey.[11]

Repton, therefore, provides clear evidence of what, by the last decade of the eighteenth century, was a well-established drift in the direction of historicism, which he identified with experiments south of the border, and, in particular, the various Gothic country-houses associated with James Wyatt. Although obscured by his short-lived, if highly productive, working 'partnership' with Nash, Repton's promotion of the Wyatt Gothic style may well have held far-reaching consequences for Abbotsford. Not the least significant of these is a possible explanation for Scott's choice of Atkinson, who, as a former assistant within the Wyatt office, was as well placed as anyone to exploit the opportunities provided by his former master's death in 1813, having already secured two major Gothic commissions north of the border, for Scone Palace, Perthshire (1803–12) and Rossie Priory, Perthshire (1807–15).[12]

In contrast to this, Repton's Scottish interests were restricted to a single commission, for Valleyfield in Fife, secured in c. 1799.[13] The hostile response the resulting transformation of the landscape provoked, as expressed in John Claudius Loudon's *Observations on Planting* (1804) and *Treatise on Country Residences* (1806), is what most concerns us here. This stemmed not simply from Repton's failure to visit the Valleyfield site but also from his alleged indifference to the geography of Scotland, with results that 'counteracted' nature and 'deformed' the estate.[14] Loudon's almost exactly contemporary proposals for Barnbarroch, Wigtownshire (1804) confirm, indeed, that at this early stage of his career he should be identified as an extreme exponent of the 'natural' style, the promotion of which he clearly viewed as vital to his strategy of resistance to further encroachments from the Repton firm (John Adey and George Repton had supervised the execution of the Valleyfield alterations), and, in particular, 'the wholesale application of English solutions to Scottish problems'.[15]

> I hope the proprietors of that lovely country will never again admit such a formidable foe. If they do, I conjure all my countrymen to unite in declaiming against their taste; and if they will not then refrain, let the poets enrol their names among the enemies of nature.[16]

The relevance of this to any notion of a national revival hardly needs emphasising, and it was afforded additional significance by Loudon's advice on country-house architecture, as outlined in part three of *Country Residences*. Although the core recommendations this contained were far from original – the various arguments advanced on behalf of the 'Irregular or Mixed Gothic Style' derived almost exclusively, and without obvious embarrassment, from building categories contained in Repton's *Observations*[17] – it is worth noting that *Country Residences* also provided Loudon with an opportunity to promote an appropriate architectural counterpart to the 'natural' landscape, in the form of buildings in the 'Turret Style'. His description of this category of building is revealing, and points – eight years before the publication of Scott's description of the fictional mansion of Tully-Veolan in *Waverley* ('which seemed to consist of two or three, narrow and steep-roofed buildings, projecting one from the other at right angles')[18] and a full decade before work began on the main building programme at Abbotsford – to a precociously early effort to revive features associated with the Scottish fortified house format.

> . . . characterized by projecting turrets at most of the corners; by very high roofs both on the turrets and principal masses; by attic windows, and windows in the eaves, terminated by triangular pediments. The windows in the turrets are few and very small, generally only *arrow* holes. The ground-plan of the whole is commonly in the form of an L. A square tower, containing the staircase, is generally placed in the angle, carried up nearly as high as the roof, and terminated by a rude balustrade enclosing a lead roof or bastion.[19]

Reinforcing the point, the accompanying engraving (Fig. 1) illustrated 'a House in a Style peculiar to Scotland & common in the Highlands' and, drawing on his familiarity with Gogar House, Coates House and Saughton Hall, an elevation of 'a variety of the Turret Style common in the neighbourhood of Edinburgh'.

In the preamble to the same chapter we find Loudon making reference to a wide range of medieval buildings (Glasgow Cathedral, Jedburgh, Dunfermline, Holyrood, Kelso and Melrose abbeys are all cited, as well as Durham Cathedral and Westminster Abbey)[20] suggesting that his antiquarian credentials should, at the very least, be accorded a degree of credibility. All the more frustrating, therefore, is the fact that there is no

FIGURE 1

Two versions of the 'Turret Style', comprising a 'house in a Style peculiar to Scotland and common in the Highlands' and (below) 'a variety . . . common in the neighbourhood of Edinburgh'; from J. C. Loudon, Treatise on Forming, Improving and Managing Country Residences *(London 1806).*

evidence in the *Letters* for personal contact between Loudon and Scott, presumably reflecting the fact that from 1803 Loudon was domiciled in London where he operated more or less independently of the Edinburgh establishment.

The situation regarding Scott and the remaining two figures this paper examines in relation to the development of Abbotsford – Sir James Hall, 4th Baronet of Dunglass, and George Gordon, 4th Earl of Aberdeen – was significantly different. Scott and Hall, for example, shared membership of the Society of Antiquaries of Scotland. Furthermore, Scott succeeded Hall as President of the Royal Society of Edinburgh in 1820. Although it is only at this date that Hall first figures in Scott's correspondence, when his sons Basil and James (the former of whom would forge a close friendship with Scott) are recorded as guests at Abbotsford,[21] Scott was certainly familiar with Hall's research rather earlier as a reflection of their shared interest in Gothic architecture. It was in 1785, when carrying out geological surveys in France, that Hall had been 'struck with the beauty of Gothic edifices' and found himself drawn to investigate the origins of the Gothic style, which he traced to wooden prototypes.[22] The unusual determination with which he pursued this idea subsequently (1792) resulted in the construction by a local cooper, John White, of a wickerwork 'cathedral' in the grounds of Hall's own house, Dunglass, East Lothian (Fig. 2). The apparent evidence this experiment provided in support of the theory (the sprouting of ash and willow staves in 1793 gave a source for crockets and finials, while the curling of dried bark in 1796 suggested an origin for tracery cusps) was given wider exposure by Hall's paper on 'the origin and principles of Gothic architecture', delivered to the Royal Society of Edinburgh on 6 April 1797 and published as part of its 1798 *Transactions*, and, later (1813), as an independent, much-expanded volume illustrated by Blore.[23]

It is now difficult to determine the seriousness with which Hall's theory was taken by his fellow antiquaries. The modern tendency to dismiss his contribution out of hand – 'naïve' and 'fantastical' are some recent assessments[24] – certainly underestimates its contemporary appeal. Scott, at least, found the image of a petrified willow structure irresistible, and evoked it when describing Melrose Abbey by moonlight in *The Lay of the Last Minstrel* (1805):

> Thou wouldst have thought some fairy's hand
> Twixt poplars straight the ozier wand
> In many a freakish knot had twined;
> Then framed a spell, when the work was done
> And changed the willow wreathes to stone.[25]

Of equal importance is the fact that, in arguing his case, Hall revealed an impressive grasp of the late eighteenth-century antiquarian achievement, as evidenced by his familiarity with Murphy's *Plans, Elevations, Sections etc. of the Portuguese Church of Batalha* (1792–5) and Halfpenny's *Gothic Ornaments in the Cathedral Church of York* (1795–1800), and, developing from these sources, his generally sensible observations on the stylistic evolution of Gothic architecture.[26]

The value of this to our understanding of Scott is that it provides a reliable start date – 1805 – for his own 'serious' interest in medieval antiquities. This is perhaps slightly later than might have been expected, but it is significant that further supporting evidence dates from this and a later period. With the exception of Francis Grose's *The Antiquities of England and Wales* (1783–7) and *The Antiquities of Scotland* (1789–91), there is little in the contents of the Abbotsford Library to suggest Scott's familiarity with the remarkable spate of publications (the majority of which emanated from the Society of Antiquaries of London) that had transformed Gothic research in the second half of the eighteenth century. It was only, indeed, in 1811 (at the earliest) that Scott appears to have made his first significant additional purchase in this field, in the form of John Britton's *Essay towards an History and Description of Roslyn Chapel, Scotland*, published as an offprint from the same author's *Architectural Antiquities of Great Britain*.[27] Tantalising glimpses of Scott's own further reading in this area are, however, provided by his wider literary output. His convincing description of Tully-Veolan, already touched on, was first highlighted by Wainwright. It is nevertheless *The Antiquary* (published in

FIGURE 2
Frontispiece from Sir J. Hall, Essay on the Origin, History and Principles of Gothic Architecture *(Edinburgh and London 1813).*

May 1816, well in advance of Blore's arrival in November of the same year)[28] and the lecture the mysterious Mr Lovel receives from Jonathan Oldbuck 'upon monastic architecture, in all its styles' ('from the massive Saxon to the florid Gothic . . . [and] from that time, to the mixed and composite architecture of James the First's time')[29] that provides the single most revealing insight, to the extent it identified with the nomenclature adopted by Thomas Warton in the footnote on the stylistic development of Gothic architecture contained in his *Observations on the Faerie Queene of Spenser.* This had appeared in 1762 and distinguished between 'Saxon', 'Absolute Gothic', 'Ornamental Gothic' and 'Florid Gothic'.[30] Although it is referred to in the preface of Grose's *The Antiquities of England and Wales* it is tempting to speculate that it was in 1800 that the full text first became familiar to Scott, as part of the enormously popular *Four Essays on Gothic Architecture* (further editions were published in 1802 and 1808). This was a source that would also have introduced him to James Bentham's influential essay on Saxon, Norman and Gothic architecture (originally published as part of *The History of Ely Cathedral*, 1771) and John Milner's observations 'on the rise and progress of the pointed arch', taken from the same author's introduction to *The Antiquities of Winchester* (1798–1801).[31]

Scott's first encounter with Lord Aberdeen was in 1807, when he was visited by him at The Priory. On that occasion Scott described the future Foreign Secretary and Prime Minister, with some prescience, as 'a very accomplish'd young man who promises to make a figure'.[32] Subsequent references in Scott's correspondence[33] hint, indeed, at a friendship that would result in a number of modest collaborative research ventures, and which would prove close enough for Scott to consider staying with Aberdeen when planning a visit to the Continent in 1813. This followed Aberdeen's appointment as Ambassador Extraordinary to Vienna, a year after his acceptance of the Presidency of the Society of Antiquaries of London.

Throughout this early part of his career Aberdeen had identified with the cause of the Greek Revival. His nickname, 'Athenian Aberdeen', reflected this and commemorated the key part he played in founding the Athenian Society in 1803 as well as his contribution to a succession of progressively more weighty publications on Greek antiquities. These included his observations on Gell's *Topography of Troy* (published in the *Edinburgh Review* for 1805) and his major work, comprising an *Historical View of the Rise and Progress of Architecture amongst the Greeks*, prefixed to William Wilkins' translation of *The Civil Architecture of Vitruvius* (1812), and published separately as *An Inquiry into the Principles of Beauty in Grecian Architecture*. Largely as a consequence of this overt classicism the extraordinary importance of his contribution to the course of the Gothic Revival has too frequently been overlooked. In 1802 and 1803, as part of an extended Grand Tour that took him to Greece, he had travelled in France and Italy in the company of George Downing Whittington.[34] Whittington died in 1807, leaving Aberdeen to complete for publication his account of discoveries made in the course of the French part of the tour, eventually brought out in 1809 under Whittington's name (but with a lengthy preface by Aberdeen) as *An Historical Survey of the Ecclesiastical Antiquities of France*.

Developing a theory first afforded prominence by Wren, and now elaborated upon by Aberdeen, this traced the origins of Gothic to the Near East. More importantly, it also argued that the fully developed Gothic style had first emerged in northern France, leading to the claim that Suger's work at Saint Denis had predated comparable experiments in England.

> The abbey of St Denis as it now stands, contains examples of three aeras of French Gothic Architecture . . . When it is remembered that the works of Suger were all executed before the middle of the 12th century, and that the Chevet of St Denis was indisputably finished in the year 1144, our belief that the English artists were prior to those of other nations in the use of the pointed arch, must be considerably shaken. No certain instances can be brought forward amongst the anterior or contemporary buildings of this country, in which the pointed arch was decidedly introduced. All authorities concur in fixing the reign of Henry II (that is, after the year 1154), as the earliest era of the introduction into England of the mixed style of round and pointed arches, which we see practised in Suger's works in France before that period. The first work in which the pointed arch decidedly occurs in this country . . . are the vaults of Archbishop Roger, at York, begun in 1171; the vestibule of the Temple Church, built in 1184; the great western tower of Ely, finished in 1189; the choir at Canterbury, carried out between 1175 and 1180; and the two western towers of Durham which are almost exactly in the same style as Suger's front of St Denis, erected 1233.[35]

Why is this of relevance to Scott and Abbotsford? First, because the appearance of the *Ecclesiastical Antiquities of France* exactly coincided with Aberdeen's early contact with Scott, who could not have ignored the uproar its publication caused within antiquarian circles on account of the head-on challenge its advocacy of the 'prior excellence of the French style' posed to orthodox accounts of the development of Gothic architecture, and, in particular, the notion that this should be viewed as an essentially English achievement. Here note should be taken, not simply of the advances in late eighteenth-century antiquarianism, inasmuch as these resulted in the unravelling of the mysteries surrounding medieval architecture, but of the fact that this identified with the achievement of a comparatively small number of scholars, most of whom were closely associated with the Society of Antiquaries of London.[36] One less positive outcome of this is to be found in the narrow geographical scope of their research base. This drew heavily on the evidence of antiquities in the southern half of England; witness the skewed range of buildings selected for inclusion in the *Cathedral Series*, a prestige venture initiated by the Society of Antiquaries of London, which focused on Westminster Abbey, Exeter Cathedral, Bath Abbey, Norwich Cathedral and (as a single northern example, introduced as a concession to the mid-1790s restoration debate) Durham Cathedral.[37]

Compounding this was the tendency, hugely reinforced by the spirit of isolationism engendered by the French Revolutionary and Napoleonic wars, to ignore the wider European achievement. This was given particularly strident expression in the numerous publications associated with John Carter, whose campaign – still celebrated by the usage of the stylistic category 'Early English'– was to substitute 'English' for 'Gothic', on the basis of the argument that the Gothic style had originated and found most perfect expression in England.[38] Not surprisingly, therefore, the appearance of the *Ecclesiastical Antiquities of France* met with a furious response, Carter denouncing it in *The Gentleman's Magazine* as the product of a 'mania of travelled prejudice', which had resulted in 'blind delusion' and 'dark deviation', and a volume poisoned by 'Gallic scientific presumption'.[39] Earlier in the same decade he had challenged the very basis of the Grand Tour, exposing this as a keystone of a 'plan of anti-nationalism': 'Eternal self-reproof may those patrons feel, who send abroad our youth for Architectural Improvement, where, sucking in the poison of foreign prejudice, they disgorge their venom on our native architecture at home.'[40]

Whittington and Aberdeen's research itinerary prompted an equally scathing response:

> They [i.e. Aberdeen and Whittington] fly, when landed on the shores they pant to idolise, from town to town, from city to city, glancing at this building or that, taking superficial notes and trifling sketches . . . listening with a willing ear to national historical prejudices . . . return fully qualified in their own and friends' opinions, to give all praise to foreign Artists, and to cry down the merits of their countrymen . . . France has their enthusiastic admiration![41]

Acceptance of the correctness of the Whittington/Aberdeen argument could only, however, be delayed, and was implicitly recognised with Aberdeen's appointment as President of the Society of Antiquaries of London in 1812. From this date the status of the *Ecclesiastical Antiquities of France* as a milestone publication in the history of what was now properly recognised as a pan-European movement was more or less assured. David Watkin's assessment of it in this respect is revealing, and identifies the volume as one of the earliest examples of a recognisably 'modern' architectural history, based on a 'detached and scholarly investigation into a past style in a country other than his own'.

> He [Whittington] has no special non-architectural axe to grind: he is not a topographer recording the history of his own country or church; he is not a Romantic seeking experiences of the Infinite; he is not a nationalist arguing that his own country must have given birth to the style of his choice; nor is he an ecclesiologist studying Gothic as the basis for a revival of mediaeval design or liturgy in the modern church. Indeed, his brief account of the adoption of Renaissance forms in sixteenth-century France, though written without enthusiasm, has a carefully impartial air.[42]

Viewed from this standpoint, the relevance of the *Ecclesiastical Antiquities of France* to Abbotsford quickly becomes apparent through its contribution to a process that, if it did not quite 'de-Anglicise' Gothic, established the style as an appropriate vehicle for nationalist sentiment across Europe, whether in England, France, Germany, Russia, or, no less certainly, Scotland.[43] Appropriately, therefore, it was at precisely this point that Sir James Hall financed the independent publication (1813) of his *Essay . . . on Gothic Architecture*, expanded to include observations on the early manifestation of Gothic at Melrose, Dryburgh and Kelso abbeys, and the contention that 'of the two nations' (i.e.

Scotland and England) the style 'seems to have appeared earliest in Scotland'.[44] Britton's interpretation (1826) of this, implying that the pointed arch had originated in Scotland,[45] nevertheless overstated Hall's case. However, at the very least, it highlighted an emerging confidence in the inherent interest of Scottish Gothic, inconceivable less than a generation earlier, that must, surely, be seen as relevant to subsequent revivalist ambitions.

This, then, is my 'widened context' for Abbotsford: one that provides evidence, in advance of the involvement of Atkinson and Blore, of Scott's developed interest in Gothic and, of equal importance, the existence of an intellectual climate that was increasingly receptive to the notion of a Scottish revival. Contemporary expectations in this latter respect should not, however, be overstated, a point reinforced by the fact that it was Scotland rather than England that provided a platform for the emergence of a fully developed Tudor revival, signalled by William Wilkins' revised proposals (1814) for Dalmeny House, West Lothian.[46] Any misgivings Scott may have had about this turn in events – and it is tempting to view the only very slightly later remodelling of Abbotsford in terms of a corrective to what he might reasonably have identified as inappropriate historicism – would, surely, have been compounded by a recognition that it had derived impetus from a sustained programme of research. Culminating in 1811 with John Adey Repton's meticulously illustrated survey of Wolterton Manor House, East Barsham,[47] this had failed to prompt a convincing research response in Scotland. Astonishingly, it would take a further two decades to rectify the situation,[48] a time-lapse that did little to lessen the eventual extraordinary impact of the Scottish Baronial Revival, but which undoubtedly contributed to obscure the origins of a movement that had found early, but not sole, expression in the Abbotsford experiment.

NOTES

1 The fullest accounts are provided in *Romantic Interior*, pp. 147–79; and J. Macaulay, *The Gothic Revival 1745–1845* (Glasgow and London, 1975), pp. 223–8.
2 Wainwright, op. cit., pp. 147, 323–4; Macaulay, op. cit., pp. 223–4.
3 Macaulay, op. cit., p. 226.
4 *Letters*, IV, pp. 333–4; Wainwright, op. cit., pp. 149, 155, 157; Macaulay, op. cit., pp. 225–6.
5 Wainwright, op. cit., p. 155; Macaulay, op. cit., p. 227.
6 *Letters*, III, pp. 237, 240; IV, p. 292.
7 H. Repton, *Sketches and Hints on Landscape Gardening* (London 1795), p. 59.
8 Wainwright, op. cit., p. 157.
9 H. Repton, *Some Observations on the Theory and Practice of Landscape Gardening* (London 1803), pp. 302, 307, 310.
10 Ibid., p. 289.
11 Ibid., pp. 286–8.
12 Macaulay, op. cit., pp. 210–14. The same source details Atkinson's later Scottish commissions in the Gothic style, notably Biel, East Lothian (1814–18), Tullialan Castle, Fife (1817–20), and the west wing of Taymouth Castle, Perthshire (1818–21, 1827–8).
13 A. A. Tait, *The Landscape Garden in Scotland 1735–1835* (Edinburgh 1980), pp. 83–4, 87–8, 180–4, 242–9.

14 J. C. Loudon, *Treatise on Forming, Improving and Managing Country Residences* (London 1806), ii, p. 438; Tait, op. cit., pp. 179–84.
15 Tait, op. cit., p. 179.
16 Loudon, *Country Residences*, ii, p. 439; Tait, op. cit., p. 183.
17 Repton distinguished between 'Castle', 'Church' and 'House Gothic', with a compromise being found in a 'mixture' of all three categories. H. Repton, *Some Observations on the Theory and Practice of Landscape Gardening* (London 1803), pp. 277, 288–9. Loudon's elaboration on this identified the 'Cathedral', 'Castle', 'Quadrangular', 'Tower', 'Turret' and 'Irregular or Mixed Gothic' styles; see *Treatise on Country Residences*, i, pp. 105–13.
18 Scott, *Waverley* (Edinburgh 1814), pp. 93–4; Wainwright, op. cit., pp. 157–9.
19 Loudon, op. cit., i, p. 111.
20 Ibid., pp. 103–4.
21 *Letters*, V, p. 377.
22 Sir J. Hall, 'An Essay on the Origin and Principles of Gothic Architecture', *Transactions of the Royal Society of Edinburgh*, iv, Part ii, 1798, pp. 3–27; J. Rykwert, *On Adam's House in Paradise: The Idea of the Primitive Hut in Architectural History* (New York 1972), pp. 82–7; D. Watkin, *The Rise of Architectural History* (London 1980), pp. 55–6; I. G. Brown, 'Intimacy & Immediacy: James Hall's Journals in Italy and Germany, 1821–2', in C. Richardson and G. Smith (eds), *Britannia Italia Germania: Taste & Travel in the Nineteenth Century* (Edinburgh 2001), pp. 24–5.
23 Sir J. Hall, *Essay on the Origin, History and Principles of Gothic Architecture* (Edinburgh and London 1813).
24 P. Breman, *The Gothic of Gothick* (London 1969), p. 29.
25 O. Smeaton (ed.), *The Poems of Sir Walter Scott* (London n.d.), p. 13.
26 Hall, *Essay* (1798), pp. 14–16 (i.e. noting the significance of the pointed arch when related to the problem of vaulting irregularly spaced bay widths). See also Hall, *Essay* (1813), pp. 21–8 and (for his 'History of Gothic in successive ages'), pp. 103–14.
27 *Catalogue of the Library at Abbotsford* (Edinburgh 1838), pp. 177, 270.
28 Scott's first reference to Blore is in a letter to Robert Surtees of 12 November 1816. *Letters*, IV, pp. 285–6. Atkinson was involved by December of the same year (ibid., pp. 333–4).
29 Scott, *The Antiquary*, ed. by D. Hewitt (Edinburgh 1995), p. 148.
30 T. Warton, *Observations on the Faerie Queene of Spenser* (2nd edn, vol. ii, London 1762), pp. 186–94.
31 For further analysis see J. Frew, 'James Bentham's *History of Ely Cathedral*: a forgotten classic of the Gothic Revival', *Art Bulletin*, lxiii, 1980, pp. 290–3.
32 *Letters*, XII, p. 100.
33 *Letters*, II, p. 69; III, pp. 217, 389, 395; V, p. 279; VII, p. 380; VIII, p. 440.
34 J. D. Whittington, *An Historical Survey of the Ecclesiastical Antiquities of France* (London 1809), p. iii.
35 Ibid., pp. 107, 109–11.
36 For further analysis see J. Frew, 'An aspect of the early Gothic Revival: the transformation of medievalist research 1770–1800', *Journal of the Warburg and Courtauld Institutes*, lxiii, 1980, pp. 174–85.
37 Ibid., pp. 183–4.
38 J. Frew, 'Gothic is English: John Carter and the revival of Gothic as England's national style', *Art Bulletin*, lxiv, 1982, pp. 315–20.
39 *Gentleman's Magazine*, lxxix, 1809, pp. 523–6, 627–9, 929–31.
40 Ibid., lxxii, 1802, pp. 300–1; lxx, 1800, p. 838.
41 Ibid., lxxix, 1809, p. 524.

42 Watkin, op. cit., p. 58.

43 For spread of the revival in the second, third and fourth decades of the nineteenth century see G. Germann, *Gothic Revival in Europe and Britain: Sources, Influences and Ideas* (London 1972).

44 *Essay* (1813), pp. 88, 93, 95, 105, 124–5 and Pl. 55.

45 J. Britton, *The Architectural Antiquities of Great Britain*, v, 1826, Preface and p. 52.

46 Macaulay, op. cit., pp. 318–22.

47 A. Repton, *An Account of Wolterton Manor House at East Barsham, Norfolk* (London 1811; republished in *Vetusta Monumenta*, iv, 1815).

48 Note especially the impact of R. W. Billings, *The Baronial and Ecclesiastical Antiquities of Scotland*, 4 vols (Edinburgh 1845–52), examined in V. Fiddes and A. Rowan, *David Bryce* (Edinburgh 1976), pp. 60–6; M. Glendinning, R. MacInnes and A. MacKechnie, *A History of Scottish Architecture from the Renaissance to the Present Day* (Edinburgh 1996), pp. 274–80.

SIR WALTER SCOTT, THE ABBOTSFORD COLLECTION AND THE NATIONAL MUSEUMS OF SCOTLAND

Hugh Cheape, Trevor Cowie and Colin Wallace

INTRODUCTION

SIR Walter Scott was elected to the Society of Antiquaries of Scotland in December 1796, when he was 25. He was certainly familiar with the earliest of the present-day National Museums' collections – that begun by the Society in 1781 – and he was to be inspired directly by it. As a keen collector himself he was not, in his lifetime, a significant contributor to the Antiquaries' Museum, but his own collecting zeal left its mark thereon. The nature of collections in a 'museum of culture' evolving since the late eighteenth century is such that the man himself is also now represented in the collections of the National Museums of Scotland. Whereas the imperative has been the systematic assembling of Scotland's prehistoric and historic record and the accumulation of proper archaeological collections, the temptation is always to perceive national importance in objects which are linked, perhaps sensationally, to hero and incident, personality and event. Scott has been an obvious focus of such an interest.

Scott was as much alive to the significance of material culture to the historian as he was to that of conventional sources. This is well seen in the building and finishing of Abbotsford, in the enthusiastic and detailed description of costume and artefacts in his novels, and in his appetite for collecting objects as well as facts. Daniel Wilson (1816–92), the English-speaking world's first modern archaeologist, was moved to comment:

> The zeal for Archaeological investigation, which has recently manifested itself in nearly every country of Europe, has been traced, not without reason, to the impulse which proceeded from Abbotsford.[1]

In this survey, we have assembled some details of the Scottish archaeological finds that once belonged to Scott or with which he was associated, and in their light we offer some discussion of Scott's role as antiquary and archaeologist. We also draw attention to several historic artefacts, then in the collections of the Society of Antiquaries of Scotland, from which he drew inspiration and to which he made direct reference in his writings. Indeed, by way of introduction, quotations from Scott's works serve not only to illustrate his view of his own collecting activities but also to provide examples of a novelist's inspiration and literary imagination put at the service of history.

The richly detailed description in *Waverley* (1814) of the venerable mansion-house of Tully-Veolan is often quoted as an example of Scott's handling of detail, although the sense of humour may often be elided: '. . . built at a period when castles were no longer necessary, and when the Scottish architects had not yet acquired the art of designing a domestic residence'.[2] Having been entertained at the Baron of Bradwardine's board, and after toasts had been drunk from an ancestral tankard (the 'Bear of Bradwardine'), the party repaired to the Change-house to take the 'deoch an doruis, a stirrup-cup, to the honour of the Baron's roof-tree'.[3] We are referred to the author's Note V on the 'stirrup-cup' where Scott shares in detail his source of information and inspiration with his readers:

> The Poculum Potatorium of the valiant Baron, his blessed Bear, has a prototype at the fine old castle of Glammis, so rich in memorials of ancient times; it is a massive beaker of silver, double gilt, moulded into the shape of a lion, and holding about an English pint of wine. The form alludes to the family name of Strathmore, which is Lyon, and when exhibited, the cup must necessarily be emptied to the earl's health.[4]

Observation was increasingly matched by collection as the adornment of his own baronial mansion-house of Abbotsford proceeded and he came to create his own weapon-hung baronial hall. His entertaining account of a precious acquisition holds a mirror to his antiquarianism:

> On the hearth before the grate is placed a bronze pot of the largest size, which was found about twenty years since in the domain of Riddle, in Roxburghshire. It happened that the housemaid, with unnecessary prodigality of domestic labour, had bestowed on the bronze pot several coatings of black-lead when she was burnishing the utensils of the kitchen with that substance. It chanced at a sale of household goods by auction that the present proprietor [i.e. Scott] and a gentleman of rank in the neighbourhood were contending with emulation for the possession of what they well knew, especially from its size, was a gabion of great merit. This produced no little amazement among the uninitiated, of whom there were a considerable number present, when an old woman, after a long look at the countenance first of one bidder and then of the other, at length ejaculated with a sigh, when the contest was over: 'Heigh, sirs, the foundry wark must be sair up in Edinburgh, to see the great folk bidding that gait about a kale pot!' 'Aweel,' she added, in a tone of submission, 'its needless for me to wait for the frying-pan if the kale pot is gaun to gae off for a' thae guineas.' With which declaration the good lady left the auction.[5]

Typical of the novelist's imagination and his zeal for words was Scott's coining of 'gabion' as cachet for his acquisitions. The *Oxford English Dictionary* specifically notes

Scott's whimsical 'gabion' as a revival from a work about the Gowrie Conspiracy of 1600, the *Muses Threnodie* of 1638.[6] It becomes a key word for the descriptive catalogue of his collections, the *Reliquiae Trottcosienses* (see further below). The collector's motive and purpose was the 'quest' and the prize was the 'gabion'. The generally understood meaning of this word has been that of the basket filled with earth and stones used in fortification – deriving presumably from a term of the Italian Renaissance – but this figurative meaning of the small curiosity seems to have been given a new definition by Scott himself: '. . . curiosities of small intrinsic value, whether rare books, antiquities, or small articles of the fine or of the useful arts.'[7]

The 'Abbotsford Museum' was the entertaining and instructive product of these 'quests', or 'raids' as Scott called his own expeditions into Liddesdale and the traditionally fierce territory of the western Border.[8] With his eye on the Border landscape and history and his mind on the ballad tradition, he described (for example) the Border war-horn as a 'trophy' of a raid into Liddesdale.[9] Other prizes were Montrose's sword, described as the most precious 'gabion' in his collection, Claverhouse's pistol, Bonnie Prince Charlie's quaich, Rob Roy's gun, sword and sgian dubh, and Rob Roy's 'purse', the irony of which few would appreciate.

Lockhart described the gift of this last, and how Scott's fame as a writer attracted treasures such as these:

> The generous supervisor [i.e. Joseph Train], visited him in Edinburgh in May 1816, a few days after the publication of the Antiquary, carrying with him several relics which he wished to present to his collection; among others a Purse that had belonged to Rob Roy.[10]

A distinct group of 'modern' material such as swords and cuirasses was acquired when Scott visited the battlefield of Waterloo but this contemporaneity did not compromise historical authenticity for the recreation of the baronial hall; the context of warfare and battle answered the need for the romantic décor. More poignant and more exciting were the personal items of Napoleon: his pistols, pen-case and blotting book as found in the Emperor's carriage, and a lock of the Emperor's hair. Other gabions are more strictly or satisfyingly 'antiquarian', and chime with the eccentric enthusiasm of his literary creation, Jonathan Oldbuck. Pre-eminent is the 'Wallace Chair', made from wood of the house at Robroyston in which, it was said, William Wallace was betrayed; it was presented to Scott by the loyal and admiring Joseph Train in 1822. The intrinsic value of such an item for the antiquary, but especially for Scott, was enormously enhanced by the folk tradition of curious circumstantial evidence that came with it:

> It is generally said that he was made prisoner at Robroyston, near Glasgow, and the tradition of the country bears that the signal for rushing upon him and taking him unawares was when one of his pretended friends who betrayed him should turn a loaf, which was posed upon the table.[11]

OBJECTS RELATING TO SCOTT'S LIFE AND WRITINGS

As material culture offers a context of the past and one which Scott himself could describe with such relish, objects also bring us closer to our subject and the circumstances of his own life. Well-known facts of Scott's life such as the circumstances of his birth in August 1771 in Edinburgh, and his lameness, are commemorated touchingly in the collections. There is a baby-basket beautifully woven with white willow and lined with satin, said to have been owned by Sir Walter Scott's mother, Anne Rutherford (NMS: W.QP 19), and a walking stick which he used (NMS: H.UH 2). Such is the 'pull' of personal association that curatorial judgement may be adversely influenced. What must be, or must have been made as, a silver toddy-ladle is described according to the tradition of the owner, as the 'pap' or feeding-cup used by Scott as a baby and presented by his mother to a Mrs Mackenzie (NMS: H.MEQ 118).

In the way that biographers might summarise Scott's career, the objects in this section of the paper, surviving perhaps by chance in different hands, have been regrouped within the Museum of Scotland to provide a vivid summary of the changes and chances of his life. The relatively short episode of the writer as warrior-hero is commemorated in the helmet which he wore in the Midlothian Volunteer Yeomanry, gifted to the Museum of Antiquities by a family friend, William Trotter, in 1833 (NMS: H.NC 2). The financial failure of his publishers in January 1826 may be recalled with irony in a cheque for £35 signed at Abbotsford on 12 April 1825 (NMS: H.OA 77), and the bitter consequences of Ballantyne's bankruptcy and Scott's reaction to it indicated in the half-hour glass (Fig. 1) used by him to time his literary output when he had undertaken to pay off his liabilities in full (NMS: H.NL 71).

FIGURE 1

Half-hour glass used to time his literary output, when Scott had set himself the challenge of writing himself out of debt after his bankruptcy. (Copyright Trustees of the National Museums of Scotland)

Nineteenth-century perceptions of Scott and his influence are significantly reflected in the silver centrepiece of Sir Walter Scott, decorated with three emblematic figures of History, Poetry and Music, presented to David Laing in 1861 as Secretary of the Bannatyne Club (Fig. 2). Designed and modelled by Peter Slater, it was made by Walter Crichton of Edinburgh in 1858–9 (NMS: H.MEQ 1606 A–F). The Edinburgh scholar and antiquary, David Laing (1793–1878), was one of the most important figures in the intellectual community in which Scott shared. He was appointed Secretary of the Bannatyne Club by Scott and remained as editor and secretary for

FIGURE 2

Engraving by R. Anderson, from the painting by W. Fettes Douglas RSA, c. 1863, of David Laing with the Bannatyne Club centrepiece. This silver centrepiece by Peter Slater, in the form of a statuette of Sir Walter Scott seated on a column, with emblematic figures of History, Poetry and Music, was presented by the Bannatyne Club to their Secretary, the bookseller, antiquary and bibliophile David Laing, at its termination in 1860 (from Archaeologia Scotica *V, 1890, facing page 1).*

almost forty years, a length of service acknowledged by the presentation in 1861. This, the first of the Scottish historical publishing clubs founded in the nineteenth century, was set up in 1823 by Scott, Archibald Constable, Robert Pitcairn, Thomas Thomson and David Laing himself to print the sources of the nation's history. During the nine years alone that Scott was its President, the Bannatyne Club published forty-three volumes on historical and literary subjects.[12]

The sculpting of the centrepiece reflects how 'the impulse which proceeded from Abbotsford', as Daniel Wilson characterised it, continued to reverberate. The statue of Scott in homely and contemplative seated pose is symbolically placed as a presiding genius supported by Poetry, Music and History. The composition evokes Renaissance ideals and significantly classifies History firmly with the imaginative and creative faculties of Literature.

SCOTT AND ARCHAEOLOGY

Scott's passion for antiquities may have started in his adolescence. There is a tradition that, upon the discovery of a fourteenth-century grave-cover at Roxburgh in 1788, the young Scott was the first to decipher it.[13] Certainly his active interest in Scotland's ancient past can be traced back at least as far as the 1790s, when he made a brief foray into field archaeology while courting Miss Williamina Belsches, of Fettercairn House in what was Kincardineshire.[14] In 1796 he undertook excavations at the site of 'Lady Fenella's Castle', a prehistoric fort near Fettercairn. One of Scott's letters refers to his otherwise unpublished work at the site, which is now known as Green Cairn (Fig. 3). Scott wrote:

> I had plenty of time on my hands – which I employed in causing two labourers begin at the ring or vallum immediately without the main rampart and cut down till they came decisively to the original soil . . . we then continued opening our trench still digging down to the soil, till we came to the very foundation of the main and innermost Bulwark – You may guess my satisfaction when on laying this bare I found the most unequivocal marks of human industry . . . upon all this mass the effect of fire was very visible and at the bottom I found quantities of charcoal, but these effects were much less remarkable below and appeared more and more strong upon the higher stones till you came to the top where the mass was completely vitrified.[15]

Excavations in the 1970s confirmed that this was indeed a 'vitrified fort', one of a number of distinctive Iron Age forts where the timber-laced construction of the defensive walls appears to have promoted the formation of large masses of fused stone as a result of destruction by fire. The construction and use of such forts spans the period from the first millennium BC to the first millennium AD.[16]

Scott's career as an archaeological fieldworker and his courtship of Miss Belsches were both relatively short-lived.[17] However, he certainly continued to take a close interest in Borders discoveries, and was obviously considered as someone to whose attention local finds should be brought. He was, for example, a member of the group which followed up the early nineteenth-century discovery of the Early Christian Yarrow Stone.[18]

Two other significant Borders discoveries can serve as examples of Scott as an enquirer and recorder. The 1806 find of an Iron Age gold hoard from Shaw Hill, New Cairnmuir (now Netherurd), Peeblesshire was described in a letter to Scott the year after the discovery; this was subsequently read to the Society in 1828.[19] The surviving objects were donated that same year to the Society by Scott's correspondent John Lawson. Another, less celebrated discovery was the 1820 find of the foot and part of the lower right leg of a gilt bronze Roman statue (just over life-size) at Milsington, Roberton, Roxburghshire. This having been reported to Scott, he added to a letter to Lord Montagu the request that 'I wish your Lordship would permit it to be sent provisionally to Abbotsford and also allow me if it shall seem really curious to make search for the rest of the statue . . . I do not of course desire to have anything more than the opportunity of examining the relique'.[20] It is not known if any of this happened, since the leg appears

FIGURE 3
Aerial view of the vitrified fort at Green Cairn, near Fettercairn, Kincardineshire, 1989.
(Reproduced by permission of the Royal Commission on the Ancient and Historical Monuments of Scotland)

to have remained in the possession of the Buccleuch family (Lord Montagu [1776–1845] was a younger son of the 3rd Duke) until loaned to the national collections in 1920.

After the partial destruction in 1814 of the Roman carved figure at Parkhead, near the Roman fort of Risingham in Northumberland[21] (called Rob of Risingham), Scott was told of this by his correspondent James Ellis (1763–1830) of Otterburn.[22] Scott felt partly responsible: he later wrote 'it was mentioned in the notes to a certain poem called *Rokeby* [published by Scott in 1813] and acquired such celebrity that the Boor on whose ground it stood teazed with the number of visitors broke it to pieces. I wish the fragments were in his bladder with all my heart.'[23]

As noted above, Scott was elected to the Society of Antiquaries of Scotland in 1796. He had joined at a time when the Society had run into financial and administrative troubles. Already called to the Bar in 1792, Scott may have been more closely involved with the aspirations of the Faculty of Advocates, which (as the Society of Antiquaries of Scotland was to find out) took seriously its status as preserver of the archaeological record.[24] Indeed, his later involvement in historical publication societies (the Bannatyne, Maitland and Roxburghe Clubs) has to some extent eclipsed Scott's concern for archaeological investigation. At the time of his Green Cairn excavations and early membership of the Society of Antiquaries of Scotland, the major effort in this field involved the compilation of the *Statistical Account of Scotland* by parish ministers between 1791 and 1799. By contrast, Scott, whose literary career began in 1796, was directly involved in the work of making available the written sources of Scotland's history.[25] Yet Scott had obviously absorbed enough of the atmosphere of the antiquarian world to draw on this for the character and conduct of Jonathan Oldbuck in *The Antiquary* (1816).[26] He could synthesise trends in current knowledge very well too, as his Introduction to *Border Antiquities* (1814) demonstrates.

Scott's interest in the objects in the nascent national collections, though no doubt considerable, may have been tempered by the presence of David Steuart Erskine, 11th Earl of Buchan, the founder of the Society. An often-quoted observation in Scott's *Journal* following the funeral of Buchan at Dryburgh in April 1829 reveals the ambivalent feelings of the author towards that quixotic nobleman: 'Lord Buchan is dead, a person whose immense vanity, bordering upon insanity, obscured, or rather eclipsed, very considerable talents.'[27] Also to be considered was the 'enthusiastical' Sir John Sinclair: 'Cavaliero Jackasso' in Scott's *Journal*.[28] It does look likely that Scott's affinity with the past was limited to certain fields – not those of Lord Buchan's Caledonian triumphalism, nor the statistical appreciation of the past. In a way, this distaste is illustrated by the paucity of references to the Antiquaries' meetings in Scott's published *Journal*, compared with those involving the Royal Society of Edinburgh, which Scott evidently found more congenial, and of which he served as President. Nevertheless, he became active in the affairs of the Society of Antiquaries of Scotland in the 1820s, towards the end of his life: he was a Vice-President in 1827–9,[29] addressed the Antiquaries on three occasions,[30] and presented some items to the Society.[31]

Much of his collection of Scottish artefacts was to remain at Abbotsford until the 1920s when the then National Museum of Antiquities of Scotland acquired two of the more significant finds: the Torrs Chamfrein by purchase and the Woodwray Pictish cross-slab by donation (see below). A further disposal of his archaeological collections took place in 1934–5 with the result that, just over a century after Scott's death, most of the Scottish antiquities formerly housed at Abbotsford had, after all, become part of the national collections.[32]

OBJECTS COLLECTED BY SCOTT THE ANTIQUARY

'The most celebrated antiquarian ambience was, of course, Abbotsford, a museum for living in.'[33]

Scott moved to Abbotsford in 1812, all the while amassing a large collection of books and objects for reference and display. Among his collections was a range of prehistoric and Roman artefacts, known or likely to be from Scotland (Appendix 1).[34] As noted above, most if not all of the Scottish archaeological material that was at the house came into the national collections in the 1920s and 1930s at the same time as the National Library of Scotland was acquiring manuscript material from Abbotsford.[35] Little attention appears to have been paid to the original circumstances of discovery and acquisition of most of these artefacts. Scott's own account of the house and library, left in manuscript and called *Reliquiae Trottcosienses – or the Gabions of the late Jonathan Oldbuck, Esq*, was published by one of his descendants in 1889 and 1905.[36] However, it makes no reference to any of his prehistoric and Roman objects and only the Torrs pony cap and a medieval vessel appear in the *Personal Relics and Antiquarian Treasures* volume.[37] With few exceptions, the artefacts that came to the museum in 1935 appear in its register as having no localities or, at best, as coming 'from the Scottish side of the Border'.[38] However, alongside the better-known names of those responsible for the furnishing of Abbotsford, there emerge strong hints of a network of antiquarian and archaeological contacts. In at least two instances shared, literary interests provided the initial impetus for meeting. For example, Scott and the Irish antiquary and author T. Crofton Croker (1798–1854) were brought together by their mutual interest in fairy legends. This led to the gift from Croker to Scott of a hoard of Bronze Age gold from the south of Ireland.[39]

Chief among Scott's archaeological correspondents was the Ayrshire-born exciseman and man of letters Joseph Train (1779–1852).[40] Train attracted Scott's attention in 1814 following the publication of his *Strains of the Mountain Muse*. Thereafter he supplied Scott with ballads, stories and antiquarian information, as well as a wide range of objects principally found in Kirkcudbrightshire but also from further afield. Train was clearly both an eclectic and an assiduous collector of antiquities[41] (see Appendix 2). Robert De Bruce Trotter printed an amusing story of Train's unsuccessful attempt to obtain for Scott the stone called St John's Chair from Dalry, Kirkcudbrightshire:

> . . . he stoppit the gig, an jumpit oot, an liftit the chair intae't, an in efter't, an doon the Clachan as hard as he could drive. Some o' the natives notice't him liftin something inta the gig, but thocht little o't, but Jenny Mounsey saw whut it wus, an roar't oot – 'Eh, the villain! He haes stown the chair!' . . . The gig wusna worth a croon whun they wur dune wi't, an the Gauger wud a' been worth less could they 'a gotten a haud o' him, but he hid in a garret at the Inns, an had tae slip awa through the nicht, an gang hame a' the wey on his fit . . . he try't tae bribe different gangrels tae pit St John's Chair in their cuddy-cairts an bring't tae him; but it's no at Abbotsford yet.[42]

A visitor in the last year of Train's life noted that 'the room was full of antiquities, – here a rude weapon of the aboriginal Celt, or one of the conquering Roman; there is a baptismal font from Wigton monastery'.[43]

It was Train who was instrumental in bringing to Scott's notice the discovery of the famous bronze pony cap found at Torrs, Kirkcudbrightshire – one of the most significant pieces of Iron Age art to have been discovered in Scotland (see below). Whereas the Torrs pony cap survives, only some of the other objects sent by him to Scott can now be traced. Among the prehistoric material sent by Train were some human bones, said to have been of a very large size (and thus reminiscent of a common folklore motif), which were found in 1819 along with the antlers of a large deer at least 12ft below the surface, in the bank of the Water of Cree; a 'Roman battle-axe' (i.e. a prehistoric bronze axe) from the Moss of Cree; a stone axe said to be of granite and weighing 7lb 9oz, which had been found at least 8ft below the surface on the moor of Knockbrax (now known as Knockbrex Moor, Penninghame); the 'entire head and horns' of an auroch (*urus*) from a 'marl-pit on the estate of Castlewig [*sic*], in Wigtownshire'; prehistoric pottery from a cist burial in Minnigaff parish; a flint implement (one of three or four) from another burial at Milton near Kirkcudbright; a 'Roman javelin' from a peat-moss at Auchengibbert in Urr parish, Kirkcudbrightshire; and a flint arrowhead and Roman coin found at/near the Repentance Tower by Hoddom in Dumfriesshire.[44] Other artefacts of archaeological interest came from Kirkintilloch and Castlecary, along with two medieval three-legged vessels. The full list of objects of all periods sent to Scott by Train runs to some thirty-three items.

Scott was also acquiring material much more locally: a 'very broad-headed metal javelin or spear' is said to have been found near Friarshaugh, Melrose, and was given to Scott by the owner, Mr John Tod.[45] In *Border Antiquities*,[46] Scott refers to 'some bronze vessels and Roman antiquities found by the author in improving that part of his property through which these lines [i.e. the linear earthworks of the 'Military Way' and the Bowden Moor group] run'. In a letter of 1817, Scott lists among his possessions at Abbotsford 'a pair of Roman forceps by the vulgar calld tongs sorely damaged with rust' from Kaeside.[47] A 'camp-kettle' (in this case a medieval three-legged cooking vessel) from Edgerston, Jedburgh parish, was said to have been presented to Scott about 1824.[48]

Doubtless, as his fame spread, material was also given to Scott from much further afield. Mention may be made here of the 'most superb collection of the stone axes (or adzes, or whatever they are), called celts' which was presented to Scott during his visit to Shetland in August 1814;[49] or the 'small Roman pot and silver ring' from Chichester, obtained for him by his eldest son in 1829.[50] While some at least of the Shetland artefacts are still in the collection at Abbotsford, the latter items are unfortunately no longer traceable.

BRONZE AGE METALWORK: 'THE BATTLE ARRAY OF THE BRITISH'[51]

Our aim in this, and the following section, is chiefly to draw attention to the range of *extant* Scottish archaeological material acquired by Scott and now in the national collections (see Appendix 1). As we know so little about their circumstances of acquisition, the artefacts will be discussed in a broadly chronological order, particular reference being made to provenanced finds.

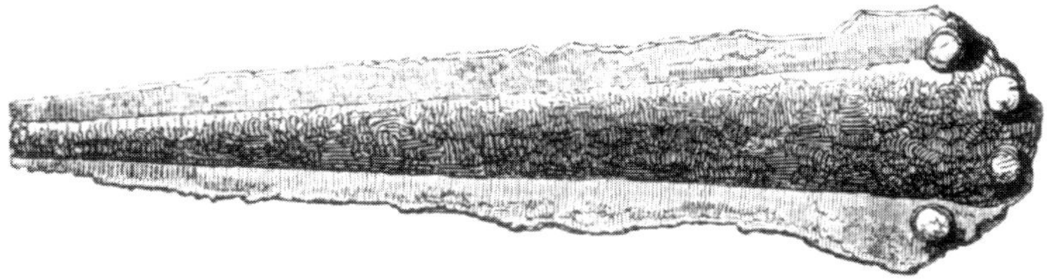

FIGURE 4a
The artefact as illustrated in the Library Edition of the Waverley *Novels (vol. ii,* The Antiquary, *1843): 'Spear-head found in the Roman Camp on Eildon Hills. Abbotsford. Drawn by Dickes, engraved by Gray'.*
(Reproduced by permission of the Trustees of the National Library of Scotland)

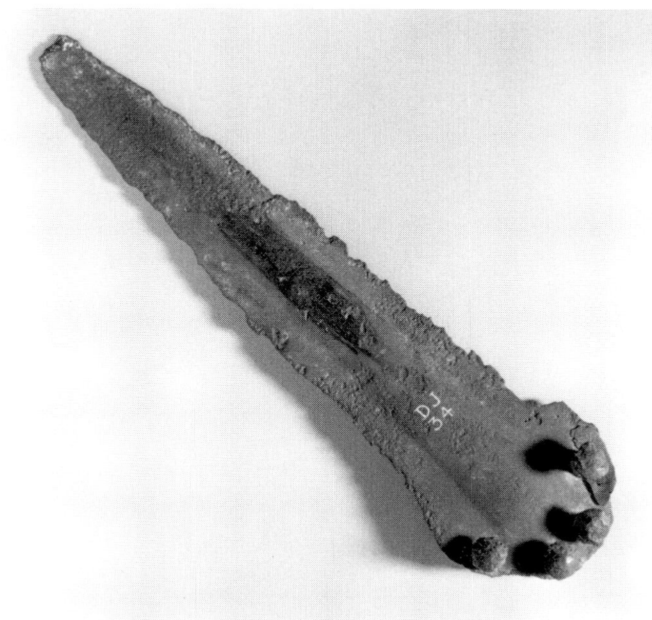

FIGURE 4b
The Early Bronze Age halberd said to have been found on the Eildon Hills but here tentatively identified as from Friarshaugh.
(Copyright Trustees of the National Museums of Scotland)

Among the objects formerly in the collection at Abbotsford the largest group comprises a number of items of Bronze Age metalwork. We are fortunate that a number of the antiquities in the collection were depicted in the illustrations to *The Antiquary* in the Library Edition of the *Waverley* novels (1843).

One of these illustrations (Fig. 4a) is said to depict a 'Spear-head found in the Roman Camp on Eildon Hills. Abbotsford'.[52] Allowance must be made for the terminology employed by the early antiquarians; the object in this illustration is actually a type of artefact which has come to be widely known as a *halberd*,[53] dating from the Early Bronze Age, c. 2300–2000 BC. Depictions on contemporary rock-art suggest that these blades were mounted at right angles on wooden shafts for use as pole-arms.

Unfortunately, no details of provenance accompanied the halberd when it was purchased for the national collections in 1935 (NMS: X.DJ 34). As noted above, the 1843 caption indicates that it was 'found in the Roman Camp on Eildon Hills', but this is not corroborated elsewhere. Taken at face value, the description of the findspot does seem to suggest that this artefact was found *on* the Eildons (as opposed to the spearhead mentioned below which is said to have been dug out from an encampment *near* the Eildon Hills). However, Scott's cataloguing was intermittent and idiosyn-cratic[54] and it is tempting to speculate whether the provenance of some items in the collection may have become confused or lost, possibly in Scott's own lifetime. It is therefore worth noting that the form of the halberd would be fully in keeping with the 'very broad-headed metal javelin or spear' said to have been found near Friarshaugh, Melrose, and given to Scott (see above). This he described as a 'curious weapon . . . about a palm's-breadth at the bottom, tapering to the length of about nine inches, or perhaps more, (for it is considerably decayed towards the point)'. Although this can be no more than a tentative suggestion, there is no other obvious object fitting this description in the Abbotsford collection.

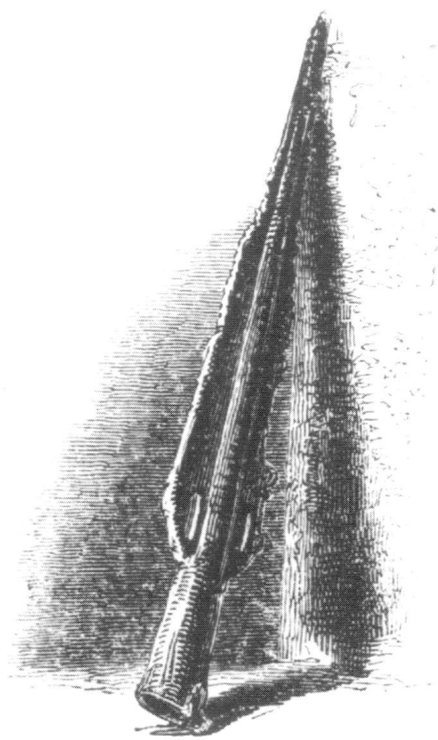

FIGURE 5
Middle Bronze Age spearhead 'dug out from encampment near the Eildon Hills', as illustrated in the Library Edition of the Waverley *Novels: 'Ancient British Spear-head, Abbotsford. Drawn by Dickes, engraved by Slater'.* (Reproduced by permission of the Trustees of the National Library of Scotland)

A second Bronze Age artefact (Fig. 5) is illustrated with the caption 'Ancient British Spear-head. Abbotsford'.[55] However, in this instance the actual object – a basal-looped spearhead from the Middle Bronze Age, c. 1400–1100 BC – was formerly labelled as a 'Spear-head dug out from encampment near the Eildon Hills' in Scott's handwriting (NMS: X.DG 95). This is echoed in Mary Monica Maxwell-Scott's catalogue of the armour at Abbotsford; one piece (no. 112) is described as

'An Old Scotch Spear-Head Dug out of an encampment near the Eildon Hills'. There seems no reason to doubt the provenance: most of the examples of what is a relatively uncommon type north of the Border come from southern Scotland.[56]

The third illustration is captioned 'Ancient British Sword (*cledyr*) of Bronze. Abbotsford'.[57] The woodcut (Fig. 6b) actually shows fragments of bronze swords generally accepted as being from the important hoard of Late Bronze Age metalwork found in Duddingston Loch, Edinburgh. This large hoard, mostly consisting of weaponry, was found in 1778 by workmen dredging for marl in Duddingston Loch, adjoining the King's Park.[58] Sir Alexander Dick of Prestonfield, the landowner, presented most of the fragmentary objects, then described as 'a quantity of Roman arms', to the fledgling Museum of the Society of Antiquaries of Scotland in January 1781: they represent, indeed, the very first donations to what was to become the national collection. It is known that some objects from the loch were presented to the King, while others were given to Sir Walter Scott. In 1935, the National Museum acquired four pieces (NMS: X.DQ 302–5) from the Abbotsford collection. These included the three items depicted in the woodcut – one complete sword (in two pieces) and the blade of a second sword – as well as the point of a spearhead.[59] Although there are no grounds for doubting their

FIGURE 6a
The collection of Late Bronze Age metalwork dredged from Duddingston Loch.
(Copyright Trustees of the National Museums of Scotland)

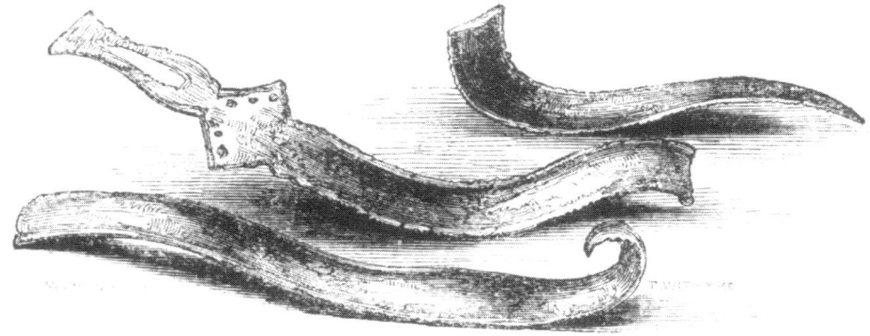

FIGURE 6b
The sword fragments which were in Scott's possession, as they appear in the Library Edition of the Waverley Novels*: 'Ancient British Sword* (cledyr) *of Bronze. Abbotsford. Drawn by Dickes, engraved by Withy.'*
(Reproduced by permission of the Trustees of the National Library of Scotland)

provenance, the condition of the Abbotsford pieces differs markedly from the items presented directly to the Society. This may simply reflect different cleaning and treatment after recovery, but it may also have a bearing on the original circumstances of deposition, possibly indicating that metalwork was placed in the loch on more than one occasion rather than as a single 'hoard'.

Other Bronze Age metalwork formerly in the collection at Abbotsford includes a number of bronze axeheads and a Late Bronze Age sword (Fig. 7: see Appendix 1). The axeheads include an Early Bronze Age decorated flat axe, flanged axes and palstaves of the Middle to Late Bronze Age and Late Bronze Age socketed axes, representative of axe-types current at various times between about 2200 and 800 BC. None of the extant specimens has a provenance, but there is an assumption that these and other examples of metalwork from the Abbotsford collection were all found probably in the south of Scotland if not the immediate Borders counties. There are hints that the estate at Abbotsford itself was reasonably 'finds-rich'. Scott himself mentions 'some bronze vessels and Roman antiquities, found by the author in improving . . . his property' (above). Two bronze rings from Abbotsford were listed in the collection of the artist Tom Scott[60] while a socketed axe was found in 1927 'beside a rabbit-hole, in the Lower Thicket' (NMS: X.DE 102).[61]

In several instances, provenances are recorded but the artefacts themselves can no longer be identified. We know that Joseph Train presented Scott with a 'Roman battle-axe' found in the Moss of Cree in Galloway (above). Unfortunately, the object in question cannot be identified with certainty, but one possible candidate may be the bronze flat axe (NMS: X.DA 100), which has been reshaped and drilled for attachment to a handle in modern times. Train also acquired and sent on to Abbotsford what were later described (in a local source of 1894) as 'several valuable Roman relics, a sword, a tripod and a brass plate' from the Kirkintilloch area.[62] Almost certainly, the attributions

FIGURE 7

A selection of Scott's collection of bronze, including specimens of axeheads, a spearhead, sword and a plain ring. The Middle Bronze Age spearhead (lower right) appears to be that 'dug out from [an] encampment near the Eildon Hills' (Fig. 5). It is suggested in the text that the sword may tentatively be identified as a weapon from Kirkintilloch.

(Copyright Trustees of the National Museums of Scotland)

of a Roman date reflect no more than the then prevailing interpretation of most finds of bronze metalwork. Train himself said that the brass plate came from Castlecary. The so-called tripod, described by Train as 'turned up by the plough in a field immediately adjoining Graeme's Dyke at Croy near Kilsyth', certainly refers to a ewer of medieval type (on display in the Armoury at Abbotsford).[63] Train's sword was said to have been found 'in the Peel at Kirkintilloch'. It may be for this reason that the sword has hitherto also been assumed to have been medieval, but it is bronze weapons that were customarily described as 'Roman' by the early antiquaries. If so, it may tentatively be suggested that this account provides a provenance for the otherwise unlocated Late Bronze Age sword in the Scott collection (NMS: X.DL 57; Fig. 7).

Scott had thus obtained a reasonably impressive group, representative of several Bronze Age metalwork types. It is particularly interesting that Scott (or at least the publisher of this posthumous edition of the *Waverley* novels) portrayed the Duddingston weaponry as Ancient British – running counter to the prevailing interpretation at the time which would have preferred to see these as Roman weapons. Scott himself offered two views of the date of the halberd mentioned earlier: ancient British (drawing on ethnographic parallels) and Roman. In his archaeological essay prefacing the *Border Antiquities*, his discussion of the weapons we now call Bronze Age swords noted that 'such weapons, by the common consent of antiquaries, have hitherto been termed Roman swords'. But Scott went on to set out clearly 'facts which certainly go far to establish that these brazen swords . . . are of British, not of Roman manufacture'.[64] Daniel Wilson (familiar with the Abbotsford collection from the illustrations in the Library Edition of *The Antiquary*) wrote of work like this as marking 'the transition from profitless dilettantism to the intelligent spirit of scientific investigation'.[65]

IRON AGE, ROMAN AND PICTISH ARTEFACTS: 'THE COLLECTION WAS, INDEED, A CURIOUS ONE'[66]

As we have said, Joseph Train was also the intermediary through whom Scott acquired the most significant prehistoric artefact associated with the Abbotsford collection: the so-called Torrs Chamfrein or pony cap (NMS: X.FA 72; Fig. 8), one of the best-known items of Iron Age metalwork from Scotland.[67] Around the time of finding and for some years after, it was considered to be medieval ('a mummer's head mask'[68]). The original discovery was made about 1820 in a moss on the farm of Torrs, Kelton, Kirkcudbrightshire.[69] A cast replica of the 'pony mask', made in 1899 for the museum of the Society of Antiquaries of Scotland, was sent to Abbotsford in place of the original in 1921.

A question mark hangs over the possible provenance of the plain bronze ring (now NMS: X.DO 42) formerly in the Abbotsford collection (see Fig. 7). A simple ring is depicted alongside the chamfrein in Train's full-size pencil drawing of the Torrs find, sent to Scott about 1829.[70] However, as Atkinson and Piggott noted, the dimensions of the ring in the drawing match closely those of another solid bronze ring (NMS: X.DO 49), said to have been discovered in the vicinity of Dungyle Camp, Kelton, Kirkcudbrightshire. Together with a cast bronze bar torc with which it is supposed to have been found, that ring was acquired by the National Museum in 1948 from a descendant of Joseph Train.[71]

One assumption is that the 'Dungyle' ring had been retained by Train, and passed on through his family, rather than being dispatched to Scott along with the chamfrein. We have, however, found no reference to objects from Dungyle in the various lists describing the objects Train had collected. While there is no reason to doubt the provenance of the ring or the torc said to have been found near Dungyle Camp, it does raise the question of whether the 'Dungyle' ring was in Train's hands as early as 1829. The apparent discrepancies in size argue against the 'Abbotsford' ring being that

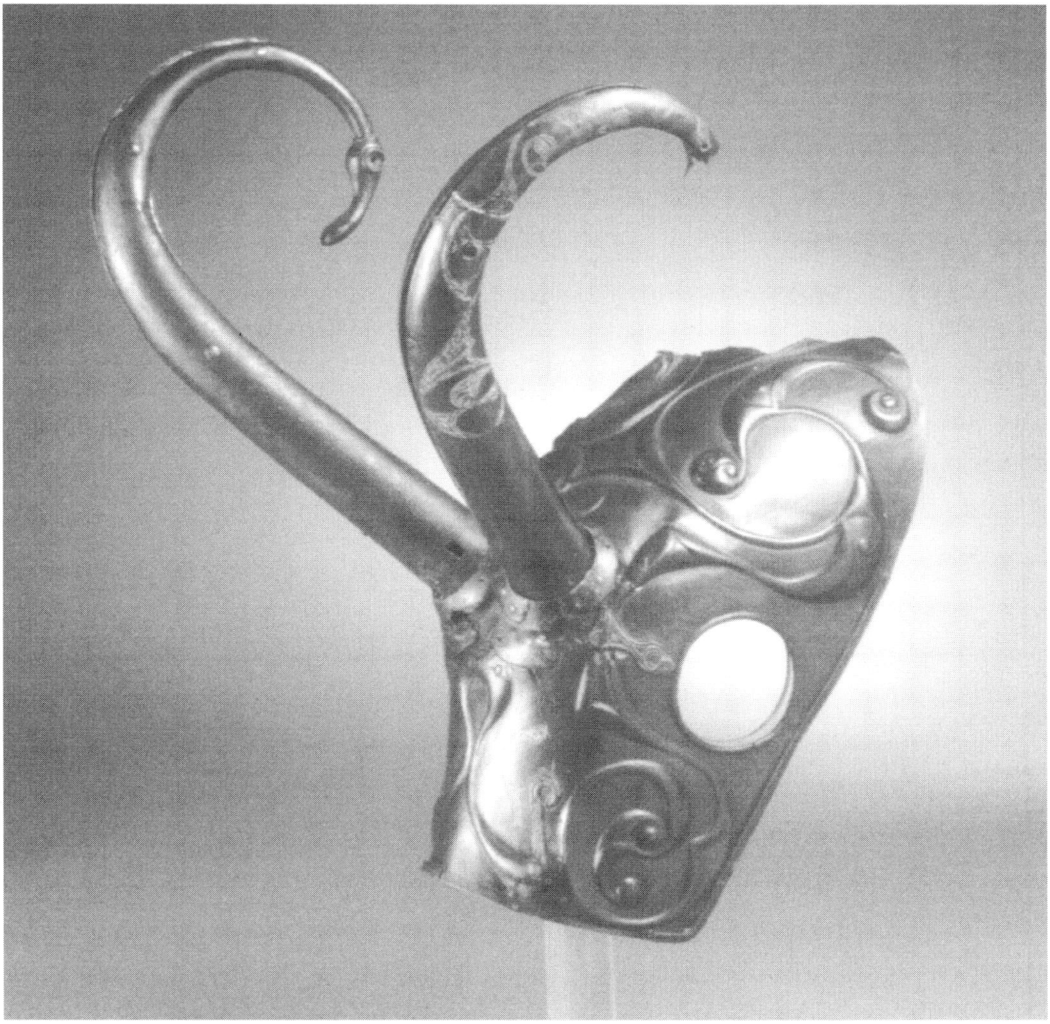

FIGURE 8
The Torrs Chamfrein. The horns were made as separate objects from the pony cap, but at some point – either during the last three centuries BC *or after its discovery – they were attached to the cap.*
(Copyright Trustees of the National Museums of Scotland)

illustrated in Train's drawing, unless depicted schematically rather than full-size. Yet having been grouped together for the purposes of the drawing it would seem strange if Scott's agent had not kept pony cap and ring together when passing on the former. In the light of all these difficulties, the 'Abbotsford' ring must remain unprovenanced. As we noted earlier, two bronze rings from Abbotsford were recorded in a private collection in the 1890s, so that the National Museum's 'Abbotsford' ring may even be a local Borders find.

The collection also includes a Roman bronze offering-pan (*patera* or *trulleus*), perhaps originally part of a libation set. The exact findspot of this Roman vessel (NMS: X.FT 94; Fig. 9) is again unknown but is likely to be from one of the Border counties. It is illustrated with the caption 'Roman urns Abbotsford', again in the Library Edition of *The Antiquary*.[72] In his sketch of regional archaeology in the Introduction to his *Border Antiquities*, Scott mentions 'some bronze vessels and Roman antiquities, found by the author' and also other Roman finds that were not necessarily in his possession at the time.[73] In Scott's published letters, one vessel is given a more specific Abbotsford-area provenance, but it may have been medieval.[74]

Train had also sent to Scott 'an antique spoon of Roman metal, found in the camp at Burnswark'. This became NMS: H.SK 46, and it is, in fact, a slip-top spoon of c. 1630–50 (*ex inf* George Dalgleish). If it really was a Burnswark find, as the nineteenth-century engraved label on it repeats, it would relate better to the mid-seventeenth-century artillery redoubt there than to the Roman fortlet and camps.[75]

FIGURE 9

The Roman patera, *probably from the south of Scotland, as depicted in the Library Edition of the* Waverley *Novels: 'Roman urns Abbotsford Drawn by Dickes, engraved by Withy'. The three-legged vessels in the background are of medieval date: the largest is probably that from Riddell, the subject of Scott's anecdote at the start of our paper, while that on the left is from Croy.*

(Reproduced by permission of the Trustees of the National Library of Scotland)

The antiquities at Abbotsford were by no means limited to readily portable objects. A number of pieces of Roman sculpture were brought to the house and built into the garden wall. They include part of a commemorative slab erected by *Legio XXII Primigenia*, with no provenance but which may have come from the eastern part of the Antonine Wall.[76] Here also are the five sculptured panels found at Old Penrith in Cumbria in 1813, where they may originally have been associated with a shrine (Fig. 10).[77] The Royal Commission has listed the large amount of medieval and later architectural details built into the house and garden walls at Abbotsford.[78]

When the remains of Woodwray (now Woodrae) Castle near Aberlemno in Angus were cleared in 1819, two Pictish sculptured cross-slabs were recovered from the foundations, apparently having been reused as floor slabs. One of them was lost by

FIGURE 10
One of the five sculptured panels found re-used in the defences of the Late Roman fort at Old Penrith and now set into the wall of the formal garden at Abbotsford. The subject of this panel is interpreted as Venus, the others being Jupiter, Apollo, Mercury and Mars.
(Reproduced by permission of the Royal Commission on the Ancient and Historical Monuments of Scotland)

1854, but the other was presented to Sir Walter Scott and erected at Abbotsford[79] (Fig. 11). It was first recorded in about 1832 by Scott's friend, James Skene of Rubislaw (1775–1864). Both Skene and the later publication by Jervise[80] mention a Mr Somerville as sending the stone to Scott. This was Samuel Somerville WS (1776–1823), son of the Rev. J. Somerville of Kelso and the factor to the landowner concerned (Lord Minto). A Borders connection is apparent, for Somerville lived at Lowood in Roxburghshire and Minto House, the home of the 2nd Earl of Minto, was near Ancrum. We presume that the proximity of Scott at Abbotsford to the Woodwray stone's guardians led to his acquisition of it.

The imposing red sandstone slab bears a cross, decorated with interlace and surrounded by fantastic beasts. The other face is divided into panels, bearing Pictish double-disc and step symbols, horsemen and beasts (NMS: X.IB 202).[81] The Woodwray cross-slab remained at Abbotsford until it was presented to the National Museum of Antiquities of Scotland by his descendant Colonel [later Major-General, Sir] Walter J. C. Maxwell-Scott in 1923.[82]

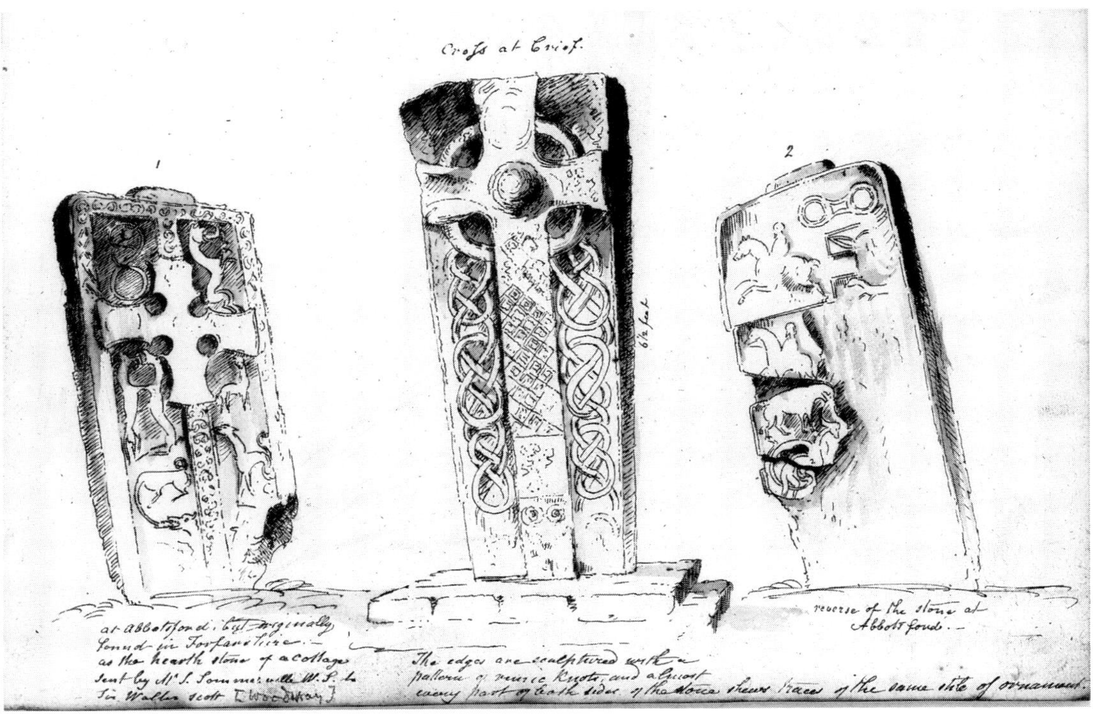

FIGURE 11

Drawing of 1832 by J. Skene, depicting the cross-slab from Woodwray Castle, Angus (to either side of the Crieff Burgh cross). The main annotation reads: 'at Abbotsford but originally found in Forfarshire – as the hearth stone of a cottage. Sent by Mr J. Sommerville, W.S., to Sir Walter Scott'. The artist, James Skene, was a friend of Scott.

(Society of Antiquaries of Scotland MS collection: reproduced by permission of the Royal Commission on the Ancient and Historical Monuments of Scotland)

OBJECTS INTRODUCED BY SCOTT INTO HIS NOVELS

As we have seen, some of the archaeological finds in Scott's collection appeared in his publications, but the illustrations in the Library Edition of *The Antiquary* are marginal, both figuratively and literally. We now turn to objects which were actually woven into the body of his work. References are to the new Edinburgh Edition of the *Waverley* novels, where possible.

In *The Antiquary* (1816), the description of Jonathan Oldbuck's 'Sanctum Sanctorum' includes 'antique spurs and buckles, . . . [and] three ancient calthrops, or craw-taes, lately dug up in the bog near Bannockburn'.[83] Some rare and highly prized items of thirteenth-century date entered the national collections in the nineteenth century, for example spurs from Urquhart Castle (occupied by the English during the War of Independence), from Skye and from Linlithgow (with a possible link to the Battle of Falkirk in July 1298), NMS: H.HY 72–3, ML 94 and ML 1, and an iron caltrop from Bannockburn, NMS: H.LM 19.

One of the 'gabions' described in the *Reliquiae Trottcosienses* was the Border war-horn which had been a 'trophy' from a raid into the Armstrong country of Liddesdale. Such items are mentioned in the Border ballads which Scott edited into his *Minstrelsy of the Scottish Border* (1802) and wove into his poetic creation *The Lay of the Last Minstrel* (1805). The *Minstrelsy*, which brought him such fame, was an intense and personal production, dedicated to his 'chief', Henry, Duke of Buccleuch – probably one of the greatest 'reivers' of them all – and sang of the exploits of the folk who were his own ancestors. One of these in particular was the hero of ballad and story, Walter Scott of Harden, whose spurs and horn were given to the then National Museum of Antiquities in 1931.[84] These items had inspired the tale of the spurs served up on a plate as the sardonic prompt to go reiving, which story was duly noted in the *Minstrelsy*[85] and introduced by Scott into *The Reiver's Wedding*.

Scott was present when the Maiden, used between 1564 and 1710 for beheading criminals (NMS: H.MR 1; Fig. 12), was handed over to the Society of Antiquaries of Scotland by the Lord Provost and Magistrates of the City of Edinburgh.[86] He owned a box alleged to have been made from the wood of its pulley.[87] In *Rob Roy* (1818), the Maiden is invoked as a means of bringing Highland feuding to an end: 'it will be time to sharp the Maiden for shearing o' craigs and thrapples. I hope to see the auld rusty lass linting at a bluidy hairst again'.[88] The beheading machine was acquired for the museum of the Society of Antiquaries of Scotland in 1797 coincidentally but no doubt significantly when the French 'Terror' was at its height. The Earl of Buchan had written to the Edinburgh city fathers in 1781, requesting the Maiden for the Museum on its foundation, as the machine then languished in the Laigh Parliament House.

It is in *Rob Roy*, too, that we find a sporran clasp, of brass and steel with four concealed pistols which are fired by any incautious attempt to open the purse (NMS: H.NE 12; Fig. 13). Given by Francis MacNab of MacNab in 1783, this was among the earliest donations to the collections of the Society's museum. Its unusual nature seems to have inspired Scott to give such an extraordinary item to Rob Roy:

'I advise no man to attempt opening this sporran till he has my secret,' said Rob Roy; and then twisting one button in one direction, and another in another, pulling one stud upward, and pressing another downward, the mouth of the purse, which was bound with massive silver-plate, opened and gave admittance to his hand. He made me remark, as if to break short the subject on which Bailie Jarvie had spoken, that a small steel pistol was concealed within the purse, the trigger of which was connected with the mounting, and made part of the machinery, so that the weapon would certainly be discharged, and in all probability its contents lodged in the person of any one, who, being unacquainted with the secret, should tamper with the lock which secured his treasure. 'This,' said he, touching the pistol – 'this is the keeper of my privy purse.'[89]

The object had no known connection with Rob Roy himself, but, inspired by Scott's fictional treatment, the Museum of Scotland has chosen to display the sporran top in the section on the eighteenth-century cattle trade. A gun in Scott's own collection of arms and armour at Abbotsford is said to have belonged to Rob Roy, attributed by Scott with undisguised frisson: 'This is the same gun with which his son, Robin Oig, shot McLaren of Invernenty.'[90] Scott read a paper to the Society of Antiquaries of Scotland in 1831 on a contemporary account of the escape of Rob Roy in 1717.[91] This incident, which must have been the stuff of ceilidh-house storytelling, helped to raise the life and career of Rob Roy (1671–1734) to legendary proportions. Symbolising, as the character did, the old order of Gaelic Scotland, Rob Roy was used by Scott to represent older and nobler traits such as the man of gentle birth (Rob was a nephew of the clan chief, MacGregor of Glengyle) forced into banditry by the *force majeure* of his feudal overlords.

FIGURE 12
The beheading machine called The Maiden: 'it will be time to sharp the Maiden for shearing o' craigs and thrapples. I hope to see the auld rusty lass linting at a bluidy hairst again'. (Copyright Trustees of the National Museums of Scotland)

FIGURE 13
Sporran clasp with four concealed pistols: '"I advise no man to attempt opening this sporran till he has my secret," said Rob Roy.'
(Copyright Trustees of the National Museums of Scotland)

In *The Antiquary*, the collections of Jonathan Oldbuck include 'a collar with the name of a fellow convicted of theft, whose services, as the inscription bore, had been adjudged to a neighbouring baron in lieu of the modern Scottish punishment'.[92] This refers to NMS: H.MR 3, a brass serf's collar, found in the Forth at Logie, Stirlingshire, inscribed: 'Alexr Steuart found guilty of death for theft at Perth the 5th December 1701 and gifted by the Justiciars as a perpetual servant to Sir Jo. Areskin of Alva' (Fig. 14). It was given to the Society of Antiquaries of Scotland by William McKillope in 1784. Sir John Erskine owned coal mines in the Alva area and it is believed that the convicted Alexander Steuart worked in these mines as a collier 'serf', duly bound to the mine owner and deprived of the right to move or change employer. Two Acts of Parliament, in 1775 and 1799, completed the emancipation of Scottish colliers, coalbearers and salters (also in a state of serfdom since the seventeenth century)[93] and it is noteworthy that the brass collar came into the Museums' collections while this form of serfdom still existed in law.

Lastly, there is a calf's heart stuck full of pins, which had been used as a charm in witchcraft, found in an old house in Dalkeith (NMS: H.NO 22; Fig. 15). Although the donation of this 'counter-charm' is otherwise attributed ('given by James Bowd, 1827'), Scott's *Journal* makes it clear that it was he who brought it into the Museum that year.[94]

It was one of the earliest donations that laid the foundations of the National Museums' very important collection of Scottish charms and amulets.[95] The circumstances of the discovery of the calf's heart are described by Scott in *Letters on Demonology and Witchcraft* (1830):

> About two years since, as they were taking down the walls of a building formerly used as a feeding-house for cattle, in the town of Dalkeith, there was found below the threshold-stone the withered heart of some animal stuck full of many scores of pins; a counter-charm, according to tradition, against the operations of witchcraft on the cattle which are kept within.[96]

Curiously, a copy of this book was buried (some time after 1831) in a shallow pit at the centre of the round barrow on White Horse Hill in Oxfordshire, near the famous Bronze Age hill figure. Inside it had been daubed a pentangle and the inscription 'Demon de Uffing'.[97]

SCOTT AND SCOTTISH MATERIAL CULTURE

Just as history was equated in Scott's time and after with personalities and events, so was it natural for the predecessor institution of the National Museums to collect material connected with personalities and events – such as the Scott memorabilia mentioned at

FIGURE 14
Serf's collar: 'with the name of a fellow convicted of theft, whose services, as the inscription bore, had been adjudged to a neighbouring baron'.
(Copyright Trustees of the National Museums of Scotland)

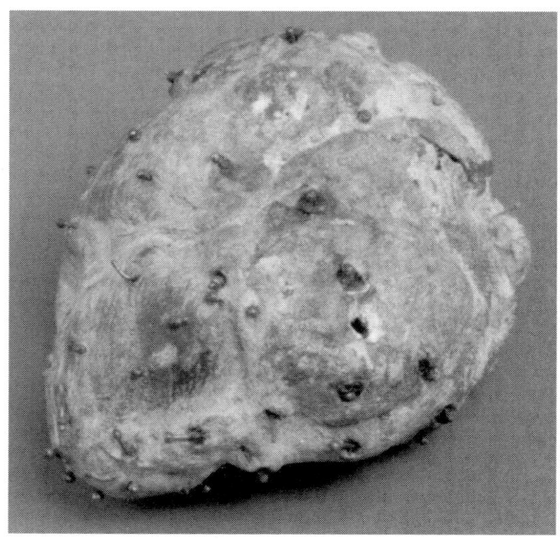

FIGURE 15
Calf's heart: 'a counter-charm, according to tradition, against the operations of witchcraft on the cattle which are kept within'.
(Copyright Trustees of the National Museums of Scotland)

the start of this paper. It can even be argued that the dynamic of object-survival generally, in the medieval and later periods, is associated with personalities and events. Broadly narrative and analytical or taxonomic collections are a more recent phenomenon. Scott, according to the Abbotsford *Catalogue* published by his descendants, himself owned several relics of William Wallace, Mary Queen of Scots, Rob Roy, Bonnie Prince Charlie, Flora Macdonald, Burns, Napoleon and others. Interesting vignettes of tradition and storytelling, as we saw at the start of this paper, can still be supplied by such items of personalia.

The late Marinell Ash discussed the historical worlds of Walter Scott and his influence on the development of archaeology, as distinct from his involvement with Romanticism.[98] In the present brief review, we have seen how his archaeological contacts and energies, diverted away from excavation and research on his own account by his literary concerns that began with his gathering of material for *The Minstrelsy of the Scottish Border* (1802), still gave him the view of the Scottish antiquarian tradition expressed in the pages of *The Antiquary* (1816).

The building and furnishing of Abbotsford in the period 1813–25 is acknowledged to have been an important impulse for Scott's collecting.[99] It is not known how many of the objects were acquired before then, nor do we have the full details of how Scott obtained most of the various portable antiquities from southern Scotland listed above.[100] It would be useful to know more of the background to the acquisition and display of the Roman and the carved stones that are still a physical part of the romantic exterior at Abbotsford.[101] We have been able to sketch out a network of archaeological and antiquarian contacts – some of whom, like Joseph Train, deserve more detailed study – and to show that Scott certainly continued to take an interest in archaeological discoveries and was obviously considered as someone to whose attention finds should be brought or the finds themselves given. Our view of Scott as this sort of an archaeologist has been submerged by that of Scott the medievalist.[102]

His description of the timber-laced rampart at Greencairn, though concise, was clear. His opinion of Bronze Age artefacts was, we have seen, advanced for its time. Even though it was not published or documented by Scott in his lifetime, we suggest that the Bronze Age metalwork in his collection was special enough to him to impress on his successors the idea that some items be shown off in the pages of the posthumous Library Edition of the *Waverley* novels.[103] The Torrs Chamfrein was prominent enough from the time of its arrival at Abbotsford to become the chief archaeological object personally associated with him in the rest of the Scott literature. Scott was familiar with a number of important and interesting Scottish pieces in the collection of the Society of Antiquaries of Scotland and incorporated them into his novels. This was, perhaps, an indication of Scott the antiquary's relish of the past for its own sake. It may also imply that he, in the manner of Jonathan Oldbuck, would have loved to have owned them himself. It may simply have been as a nod to fellow Fellows among his readers. One of Scott's last acts for archaeology was his involvement in bringing to the attention of the British Museum authorities the discovery of the renowned hoard of twelfth-century walrus ivory chessmen at Uig, Lewis, about 1831.[104] These activities of observation and collection, a *leitmotiv* of

Scott's whole life from boyhood, tend to be ignored in the predominantly literary assessment of the 'Wizard of the North'. Such omission and neglect has, arguably, been more critical when we come to look at Scott's attention to detail of place and landscape. It therefore leaves the extent of his achievements undervalued or too narrowly perceived in any representations of Scott's influence on the taste for the picturesque and romantic or his satisfying of a contemporary appetite for the Gothic.[105]

ACKNOWLEDGEMENTS

We are indebted to Dr Iain Gordon Brown of the National Library of Scotland, Iain Fraser and Bob Mowat of the National Monuments Record of Scotland, George Dalgleish (History and Applied Art, National Museums of Scotland), Andrew Martin (Library, NMS), Lyn Wall (Documentation, NMS), Duncan Anderson (Photography, NMS), Ian Davies, Brendan O'Connor, Ronan O'Flaherty and the Special Collections Department Edinburgh University Library for information and assistance. Trevor Cowie wishes to thank Dame Jean Maxwell-Scott and her staff at Abbotsford for all their help and kind hospitality in the course of a most productive search for 'lost' archaeological finds. The RCAHMS CANMORE database was the catalyst for several fruitful lines of enquiry, while Frances Coakley's *Manx Notebook* website drew our attention to Charles Dickens' account of Train. Fraser Hunter (Archaeology, NMS), Gordon Maxwell, Dr Stephen Briggs and the editor have read and commented on the paper to its advantage. Colin Wallace wishes to acknowledge the assistance he received from Craig Angus (Department of Archaeology, NMS) and Fionna Ashmore (Society of Antiquaries of Scotland) during the preparation of the original 'trail' which was created to highlight Scott-related artefacts on display in the Museum of Scotland on the occasion of the Conference.

The costs of the illustrations were kindly met by the Society of Antiquaries of Scotland and the National Museums of Scotland. The illustrations are reproduced by courtesy of the Trustees of the National Museums of Scotland (1, 2, 4, 6, 7, 8 and 12–15) and the National Library of Scotland (4, 5, 6 and 9); illustrations 3, 10 and 11 are Crown Copyright, The Royal Commission on the Ancient and Historical Monuments of Scotland.

APPENDIX 1

An interim handlist of the Prehistoric, Roman and Pictish material formerly in the Abbotsford collection:

Extant

Unless otherwise stated, all the following are of copper alloy and are unprovenanced.

1. Halberd, 'found in the Roman Camp on Eildon Hills', but here tentatively reprovenanced to Friarshaugh, near Melrose, Roxburghshire (NMS: X.DJ 34) [see notes to main text, above, for references].

2. Flat axe (NMS: X.DA 100): Migdale type (Schmidt and Burgess, Axes, no. 207).
3. Flanged axe (NMS: X.DC 117): Ulrome type (Schmidt and Burgess, Axes, no. 555).
4. Palstave (NMS: X.DC 118): Unclassified Low-flanged (Broad-bladed), Early Palstave Group III (Schmidt and Burgess, Axes, no. 839).
5. Palstave (NMS: X.DC 119): South-Western type (Schmidt and Burgess, Axes, no. 840).
6. Socketed axe (NMS: X.DE 103): Fulford type (Schmidt and Burgess, Axes, no. 994).
7. Socketed axe (NMS: X.DE 104): South-Eastern type (Schmidt and Burgess, Axes, no. 1292).
8. Socketed axe (NMS: X.DE 105): South-Eastern type (Schmidt and Burgess, Axes, no. 1294).
9. Socketed axe (NMS: X.DE 106): Everthorpe type (Schmidt and Burgess, Axes, no. 1309).
10. Socketed axe (NMS: X.DE 107): Yorkshire type (Schmidt and Burgess, Axes, no. 1374).
11. Basal-looped spearhead, 'from encampment near the Eildon Hills' (NMS: X.DG 95) [see notes to main text, above, for references].
12–15. Parts of two swords and a spearhead fragment, Duddingston Loch, Edinburgh (NMS: X.DQ 302–305) [see notes to main text, above, for references].
16. Sword (NMS: X.DL 57): Ewart Park type [see notes to main text, above, for references].
17–19. Three Late Bronze Age gold ornaments from the south of Ireland (the so-called Mull Hoard, NMS: X.FE 80–82) [see notes to main text, above, for references].
20. Ring, unprovenanced (NMS: X.DO 42) [see notes to main text, above, for references].
21. Pony-cap and horns, Torrs, Kelton, Kirkcudbrightshire (NMS: X.FA 72) [see notes to main text, above, for references].
22. Roman *patera* or *trulleus*, here tentatively provenanced to the Abbotsford area (NMS: X.FT 94) [see notes to main text, above, for references].
23. Pictish cross-slab of sandstone, Woodwray, Angus (NMS: X.IB 202) [see notes to main text, above, for references].

Probably extant

24. Moss of Cree, bronze axe (NLS MS. 3277, pp. 58 and 278 [no. 3]; *New Statistical Account* IV (Wigtownshire), p. 177 [dated 1838] and Mackenzie, *Galloway*, p. 63 (no. 2); this may possibly be no. 2 [NMS: X.DA 100], above.
25. The Peel, Kirkintilloch, Dunbartonshire, sword (NLS MS. 3277, pp. 132 and 280 [no. 15]; W. Train, *Biographical Memoir*, p. 15). This may be no. 16 [NMS: X.DL 57], above.
26. Bronze vessels and Roman antiquities, Roxburghshire, 'found by the author in improving that part of his property through which these lines run'. From his description of the location in *Border Antiquities*, Scott is referring to a late prehistoric boundary work called 'The Military Way' and the Bowden Moor group of late medieval woodbanks (see also *Letters*, IV, p. 539).[106] No. 22 [NMS: X.FT 94], above may possibly have been among this material, though it is a little hard to imagine it as the 'ill made coffee pot' mentioned in a letter by Scott (below).
27. Kilgow-bridge, Minnigaff, Kirkcudbrightshire, 'an earthen urn . . . about half full of a black substance' (G. Chalmers, *Caledonia: or, An Account Historical and Topographic, of North Britain . . .* [vol. III] (London 1824), pp. 232–3 [hereafter Chalmers, *Caledonia*]; NLS MS. 3277, pp. 58–9 and 278 [no. 4]). Among the archaeological collection still at Abbotsford there is a complete Bronze Age food vessel containing burnt human bones: in the absence of any record of other pottery having been sent to Scott, this may be identified with some confidence as the pot from Kilgow-bridge (presumably in the vicinity of present day Calgow, NX 431 652). Although the pot has not previously been recorded in the archaeological literature, it has long stood on the mantelpiece in the Entrance Hall.[107]

28. Repentance Tower, near Hoddom, Dumfriesshire, flint arrowhead (NLS MS. 3277, pp. 177–8 and 282 [no. 28]; Patterson, *Memoir*, p. 121). Among the artefacts still at Abbotsford are two Neolithic arrowheads[108] but neither can now be provenanced.
29. Shetland, stone axes (*Border Antiquities*, p. vii). Among the artefacts still at Abbotsford are four ground and polished stone axes, a utilised pebble and a polished stone knife of the type known as 'Shetland knives'. At least three of the axes are of a distinctive rock type found in Shetland.
30. Castlewigg, Glasserton, auroch's head and horns (NLS MS. 3277, pp. 177 and 282 [no. 26]; Mackenzie, *Galloway*, pp. 64–5 [no. 10]; *New Statistical Account* IV (Wigtownshire), p. 41 [dated 1838]). This may well be the set on display in the Entrance Hall at Abbotsford.
31–2. Water of Cree (near Machermore), human remains and antlers (MS. 3277, pp. 118–20 and 279 [no. 9]; Mackenzie, *Galloway*, pp. 65–6 (no. 12); *New Statistical Account* IV (Kirkcudbrightshire), p. 131 [dated 1842]). The NMS has several later finds of antlers from here (NMS: X.IR 10, 29, 30 and 66). Scott showed his to 'our professor of Natural History, Mr Barklay' [?John Barclay, 1758–1826] and – as quoted by Train (Mackenzie, *Galloway*, pp. 65–6) – they were 'now deposited in the college museum'.

Unclear as to whether still extant or not

33. Knockbrex Moor, stone axe (NLS MS. 3277, pp. 105–6 and 279 [no. 7]; *New Statistical Account* IV (Wigtownshire), pp. 177–8 [dated 1838]; Mackenzie, *Galloway*, p. 64 [no. 8]).
34. Auchengibbert, Urr, 'Roman javelin' (NLS MS. 3277, pp. 202–3 and 282 [no. 32]; Mackenzie, *Galloway*, pp. 63–4 (no. 5); *New Statistical Account* IV (Kirkcud-brightshire), p. 351 [dated 1843]).
35. Milton, near Kirkcudbright, 'Stone Chisel' (NLS MS. 3277, pp. 126–7 and 279 [no. 11]).
36. Repentance Tower, near Hoddom, Dumfriesshire, Roman coin (NLS MS. 3277, pp. 177–8 and 282 [no. 29]; Patterson, *Memoir*, p. 121).
37. Castlestead, Kaeside, Roxburghshire, 'pair of Roman [iron] forceps' (*Letters*, IV, p. 540 and XII, p. 153).

APPENDIX 2

An interim handlist of the archaeological material collected by Joseph Train (1779–1852), in alphabetical order by place of origin. Please note: unless stated otherwise, the items are from localities in Kirkcudbrightshire. Original spellings are used for place names.

No single source lists all of Train's collected objects;[109] we have used five to compile this list. We hope that there are no duplicated entries, through different names being given to the same place. Alexander Trotter's brief biography of Train notes the dispersal of some of the collections after Train's death in 1852.[110] In the references below, 'Mackenzie, *Galloway*' refers to the appendix by Train, in W. Mackenzie, *The History of Galloway from the Earliest Period to the Present Time* (Kirkcudbright 1841), 'NSA' refers to the parish reviews in the *New Statistical Account*, volume IV, 'MS 3277' refers to the 'List of Relics presented to Sir Walter Scott', pages 277–83 of Joseph Train's 'Brief Sketch of a Correspondence with Sir Walter Scott commencing in the year 1814' (National Library of Scotland, MS 3277), 'W. Train, *Biographical Memoir*' refers to the son's 'Biographical Memoir of the Author', in J. Train, *An Historical and Statistical Account of the Isle of Man, from the earliest times to the present date . . .* (Douglas, IoM 1845), pp. 1–29 and 'Patterson, *Memoir*' to J. Patterson's *Memoir of Joseph Train F.S.A. Scot. the antiquarian correspondent of Sir Walter Scott* (Glasgow 1857). Train's 1841 publication included material that had never belonged to him (these others have been omitted from the list below). Several of Scott's collection of charms (cf. C. O. Parsons, *Witchcraft and Demonology in Scott's Fiction* ([Edinburgh 1964], pp. 134–8) were also obtained for him by Train (e.g. Patterson, *Memoir*, p. 43); there were yet other charms still in Train's possession (Mackenzie, *Galloway*, p. 72).

The following abbreviations are used for archaeological journals: *PSAS* for the *Proceedings of the Society of Antiquaries of Scotland* and *TDGNHAS* for the *Transactions of the Dumfriesshire & Galloway Natural History and Antiquarian Society*.

PLACE OF ORIGIN	ITEM	LOCATION	REFERENCE
Auchengibbert, Urr	'Roman javelin'	to Walter Scott	(see Appendix 1, above)
Barlochan, Buittle	Roman coin	with Train by 1844	*NSA* IV, p. 209
Barskeoch Moss	palstave	with Train after 1850; in private hands 1948; now Dundee Museum	*TDGNHAS* 26, p. 124 and 42, p. 93
(near) Bladenoch	stone axe	to Dr Symons of Dumfries	Mackenzie, *Galloway*, p. 64 (no. 9)
Breoch, Buittle	prehistoric pottery	with Train by 1841	Mackenzie, *Galloway*, p. 67 (no. 15); *NSA* IV, p. 209
Burnswark, Dumfriesshire	'Antic Spoon of Roman Metal'	to Walter Scott (now NMS H.SK 46)	MS 3277, pp. 178 and 282 [no. 30]; Patterson, *Memoir*, p. 121; *PSAS* 69, p. 441
Carlingwark Loch	horseshoe	with Train by 1844	*NSA* IV, p. 155
Castlecary, Stirlingshire	'curious Brass Plate found in the Ruins'	to Walter Scott, 1820s	MS 3277, pp. 132 and 280 [no. 17]
Castlewigg, Glasserton Wigtownshire	aurochs' head and horns	to Walter Scott, 1820s	(see Appendix 1, above)
Croy, near Kilsyth, Stirlingshire ('Graeme's Dyke')	'a Roman tripod'	to Walter Scott, 1820s	MS 3277, pp. 132 and 280 [no. 16]
(near) Dungyle, Kelton	bronze chisel	Dumfries Museum	*TDGNHAS* 27, p. 206 and 42, p. 91
(near) Dungyle Camp, Kelton	bronze ring	NMS (X.DO 49)	*PSAS* 82, p. 321; NMAS Register 1948 (and see also main text, above)
(near) Dungyle Camp, Kelton	torc	NMS (X.FA 96)	*PSAS* 82, pp. 293–4 and 321; NMAS Register 1948

PLACE OF ORIGIN	ITEM	LOCATION	REFERENCE
Edingham, Urr	3-legged vessel ('a tripod of Roman construction')	with Train from 1832	Mackenzie, *Galloway*, p. 63 (no. 3); *NSA* IV, p. 351; *TDGNHAS* 27, p. 205
Falkirk (battle of, 1298), Stirlingshire	'the Steel Bow of Sir John the Graeme'	from Joseph Stainton of Falkirk, 1824 and on to Walter Scott	MS 3277, pp. 161 and 281 [no. 20]; W. Train, *Biographical Memoir*, p. 16
Hallferne, Crossmichael	bead	with Train by 1841	Mackenzie, *Galloway*, pp. 71–2; *NSA* IV, p. 196
Hallferne, Crossmichael	perforated stone charm	with Train by 1844	*NSA* IV, p. 196
Repentance Tower, Hoddom, Dumfriesshire	'an Elfin arrow'	to Walter Scott, 1820s	(see Appendix 1, above)
(near) Repentance Tower, Hoddom, Dumfriesshire	'a Roman denarius'	to Walter Scott, 1820s	(see Appendix 1, above)
Ironmacannie Moss, Balmaclellan	8 wooden objects	with Train by 1841	Mackenzie, *Galloway*, pp. 66–7 (no. 14); *NSA* IV, 103–4
Kelton area (Arieland Moss?)	dagger (or atypical halberd)	NMS (X.DJ 41)	*TDGNHAS* 27, 206–7; *PSAS* 82, p. 321; NMAS Register 1948; *PSAS* 125, p. 365
Kilgow-bridge, Minnigaff	food vessel	to Walter Scott	(see Appendix 1, above)
Kingscase, Ayrshire[111]	'one of the mazers used by the lepers'	to Walter Scott, 1810s	MS 3277, pp. 10 and 277 [no. 1]; W. Train, *Biographical Memoir*, p. 5
Kirkcudbright Castle	metal cup	with Train by 1841	Mackenzie, *Galloway*, p. 64 (no. 7); *NSA* IV, p. 24
Kirkintilloch, Dunbartonshire	sword	to Walter Scott, 1820s	(see Appendix 1, above)

PLACE OF ORIGIN	ITEM	LOCATION	REFERENCE
Knockbrex Moor, Penninghame, Wigtownshire	stone axe	to Walter Scott	(see Appendix 1, above)
(near) Loudon Hill, Ayrshire	'a Roman tripod'	from Joseph Stainton of Falkirk, 1824 and on to Walter Scott	MS 3277, pp. 162 and 281 [no. 22]; Patterson, *Memoir*, p. 112
Maclellan's Castle, Kirkcudbright	bag of oats	with Train by 1841	Mackenzie, *Galloway*, p. 66 (no. 13)
Merton-Hall, Penninghame, Wigtownshire	'head of a Roman spear'	to Dr Black of Manchester (not to Scott, as in *Memoir*; Patterson, p. 55)	Mackenzie, *Galloway*, p. 63 (no. 1); W. Train, *Biographical Memoir*, p. 8
Mid Kelton	3-legged vessel ('Roman tripod')	with Train by 1841	Mackenzie, *Galloway*, p. 64 (no. 6); *NSA* IV, p. 153
Milton, near Kirkcudbright	flint implement	to Walter Scott	(see Appendix 1, above)
Moss of Cree, Wigtownshire	bronze axe	to Walter Scott, 1818; now NMS?	(see Appendix 1, above)
Munshes, Buittle	aurochs' horns	with Train by 1841	Mackenzie, *Galloway*, p. 65 (no. 11); *NSA* IV, p. 209
Threave Castle	8 stone balls and a gold ring	with Train from 1843	*NSA* IV, p. 182
Torrs, Kelton,	pony cap	to Walter Scott, c. 1829; now NMS (X.FA 72)	(see main text, above)
Water of Cree	deer antlers	to Walter Scott, c. 1819	(see Appendix 1, above)
Water of Cree	human bone	to Walter Scott, c. 1819	(see Appendix 1, above)

NOTES

1 D. Wilson, *The Archaeology and Prehistoric Annals of Scotland* (Edinburgh 1851), preface, p. xi [hereafter Wilson, *Prehistoric Annals*]; cf. B. G. Trigger, 'Daniel Wilson and the Scottish Enlightenment', *Proceedings of the Society of Antiquaries of Scotland* [hereafter *PSAS*], 122 (1992), pp. 55–75 and other references in notes 12 and 98 below.

2 *Waverley, Or 'Tis Sixty Years Since* (Magnum Edition, 1829), vol. 1, p. 80/chapter 8.

3 *Waverley* (Magnum Edition, 1829), vol. 1, p. 106/chapter 11.

4 *Waverley* (Magnum Edition, 1829), vol. 1, Note V on p. 114. Scott adds: 'The Author ought perhaps to be ashamed of recording that he has had the honour of swallowing the contents of the Lion; and the recollection of the feat served to suggest the story of the Bear of Bradwardine.'

5 M. M. Maxwell-Scott, 'Gabions of Abbotsford: A Hitherto Unpublished Fragment by Sir Walter Scott', *Harper's Monthly Magazine* (European edition), 17 (1888–9), pp. 778–88 [hereafter *Gabions*], at p. 780 (= pp. xiv–xv of M. M. Maxwell-Scott, *Abbotsford: The Personal Relics and Antiquarian Treasures of Sir Walter Scott* (London 1893) [hereafter *Personal Relics*]). This 'Roman' object is illustrated on p. vii of the 1893 volume, from which it is clear that it is a medieval tripod cauldron with angular handles. Scott writes in August 1819 about the sale at Riddell: 'I attend myself to look out for wine & any odd matters' (*Letters*, V, p. 467).

6 *Oxford English Dictionary* (2nd edn), vol. VI, p. 302 (cf. *Letters*, VIII, p. 457, of 1824).

7 *Gabions*, p. 779.

8 *Romantic Interior*, p. 151.

9 *Life*, vol. 1, pp. 219 and 224–5; cf. *Gabions*, p. 781 and *Personal Relics*, pp. 57–8.

10 *Life*, vol. 5, p. 160.

11 *Tales of a Grandfather* I (1836), p. 55/chapter VII.

12 M. Ash, 'Scott and historical publishing: the Bannatyne and Maitland Clubs', in R. P. Doig (ed.), *Scots Antiquaries and Historians*, Abertay Historical Society Publication 16 (Dundee 1972), pp. 26–42; M. Ash, '"A fine, genial, hearty band": David Laing, Daniel Wilson and Scottish Archaeology', in A. S. Bell (ed.), *The Scottish Antiquarian Tradition* (Edinburgh 1981), pp. 86–113.

13 J. C. Hodgson, 'A Visit to Tweedside in 1833, being the Journal of John Trotter Brockett, the younger, of Newcastle', *History of the Berwickshire Naturalists' Club*, 20 (1906), pp. 55–81 (at pp. 76–7).

14 For the more significant events: D. A. Low, 'Walter Scott and Williamina Belsches', *Times Literary Supplement*, 23 July 1971, pp. 865–6.

15 *Letters*, I, pp. 48–51.

16 L. M. MacL. Wedderburn, *Excavations at Greencairn Cairnton of Balbegno Fettercairn, Angus A Preliminary Report* (Dundee 1973); *Discovery and Excavation in Scotland* 1974, p. 41. Radiocarbon dates of 2490 ± 95 BP (N–1376), 2340 ± 95 BP (N–1375) and 2130 ± 100 BP (N–1318) were obtained (*Radiocarbon*, 16 [1974], pp. 348–9). Some vitrified rock from here was added to the national collections in the 1950s (NMS: X.HH 644). On vitrified forts generally, see H. Nisbet, 'Excavation of a Vitrified Dun at Langwell, Strath Oykell, Sutherland', *Glasgow Archaeological Journal*, 19 (1994–5), pp. 51–73 (esp. pp. 70–3) and D. Gentles, 'Vitrified forts', *Current Archaeology*, 133 (1993), pp. 18–20.

17 Scott may have retained an interest in vitrified forts; see G. S. Mackenzie, *A Letter to Sir Walter Scott, Baronet containing observations on the vitrified forts . . .* (Edinburgh 1824), a response to J. MacCulloch, *The Highlands and Western Isles of Scotland, containing descriptions of their scenery and antiquities . . . founded on a series of annual journeys between the years 1811 and 1821 . . . in letters to Sir Walter Scott, Bart.* (London 1824), at Volume I, pp. 287–301. Stephen Briggs tells us that

there are two letters in the Royal Archive, Copenhagen (*Riksarkivet*) that shed some light on Scott and his connection with Scandinavian antiquaries. Written by the Royal Society of Antiquaries of the North, they are a draft of 15 August 1827 from C. C. Rafn (1795–1864), possibly including a present of a book to Scott, and another of 4 March 1828. These letters invite Scott to become a member of the Society but as no replies are included, Scott's reaction is unknown. It is of interest that this was only two years after the establishment of the Society, and his membership was obviously considered of some importance to them. Rafn's main aim was to bring out editions of Old Icelandic texts. From early on in his career, Scott was interested in old northern literature, his enthusiasm coming to fruition in his novel *The Pirate* of 1822: see A. Wawn, *The Vikings and the Victorians: Inventing the Old North in Nineteenth-century Britain* (Cambridge 2000), at pp. 60–83.

An edition of Sir Walter's archaeological correspondence would no doubt help provide a fuller context for his contacts and collecting activities than we have been able to give in this paper. It would also be useful, in the context of any larger study, to discuss at greater length possible influences on Scott of a collection such as that of Sir John Clerk of Penicuik (1676–1755).

18 *New Statistical Account of Scotland* III (Selkirkshire) 1845, p. 47; a drawing of it made for Scott was later presented by him to the Society of Antiquaries of Scotland (below).

19 Scott had asked for an account of the find: see the 'Letter from John Lawson of Cairnmuir, Esq., to Sir Walter Scott, Baronet, describing some Golden Ornaments found in March, 1806, near the house of New Cairnmuir, Peeblesshire', *Archaeologia Scotica*, 4 (1857), pp. 217–19. See W. Scott, *Border Antiquities* (London 1814) [hereafter *Border Antiquities*], at p. xv. NMS: X.FE 46–8 and 90–2 are the surviving pieces and replicas in the National Collections: F. Hunter, 'Iron Age coins in Scotland', *PSAS* 127 (1997), pp. 513–25 (at pp. 515–16) summarises the earlier literature on the hoard.

20 *Letters*, VI, p. 139. It passed into the possession of the Dukes of Buccleuch, who have loaned it for public exhibition (NMS: Q.L. 1920.1). G. Macdonald, 'Note on some fragments of Imperial statues and of a statuette of Victory', *Journal of Roman Studies*, 16 (1926), pp. 1–16 and J. Curle, 'The Leg from a Roman Bronze Statue found at Milsington', *History of the Berwickshire Naturalists' Club*, 29 (1936), pp. 193–5 describe it and its history.

21 See pp. 88 and 142–43 and fig 16 of I. A. Richmond, 'The Romans in Redesdale', in M. H. Dodds (ed.), *A History of Northumberland* Volume XV (Newcastle 1940), pp. 63–154.

22 *Letters*, III, 1811–14, p. 525. Scott replied in December: 'I cannot yet digest the fate of Robin of Redesdale poor old fellow. I little thought our adventure in quest of him would have brought him to untimely destruction after having occupied his secluded situation for many centuries. I wish you would keep an eye on the perpetrator – he certainly cannot come to a good end – a halter is greatly too good for him.' *Letters*, III, 1811–14, p. 526. The 'maledictions' that Scott goes on to heap on this man bring to mind the attacks mounted by Stukeley and others on the demolisher of Arthur's O'on some seventy years earlier (p. 32 of Brown, *Hobby-Horsical*).

23 *Letters*, IV, 1815–17, p. 271 (of 1816). The figure that was called 'an outlaw's image on the stone' in *Rokeby* (canto I.xx), see note IX to Scott's 1830 edition. The story of the destruction is repeated in Scott's 'Dedicatory Epistle' to *Ivanhoe* of 1819.

24 I. G. Brown, '"This Old Magazine of Antiquities" The Advocates' Library as National Museum', in P. Cadell and A. Matheson (eds), *For the Encouragement of Learning: Scotland's National Library 1689–1989* (Edinburgh 1989), pp. 149–85 [hereafter Brown, 'Old Magazine of Antiquities']. For example, Scott mentions in his synthesis of Borders archaeology (p. xiii of *Border Antiquities*) the altar to the Goddesses of the Parade-ground from Newstead then in the Advocates' collections

(now NMS: X.FV 26/Roman Inscriptions of Britain 2121). As one of the Curators of the Advocates' Library in 1796, Scott was involved in cataloguing the coin collection (Brown, 'Old Magazine of Antiquities', p. 172).

25 See J. Anderson, *Sir Walter Scott and History, with other papers* (Edinburgh 1981), at pp. 2–4.

26 This is the most developed aspect of Scott literature in the field of his archaeological interests: see S. Piggott, *Ruins in a Landscape Essays in Antiquarianism* (Edinburgh 1976) [hereafter *Ruins*], at pp. 133–70 and I. G. Brown, *The Hobby-Horsical Antiquary: A Scottish Character 1640–1830* (Edinburgh 1980) [hereafter Brown, *Hobby-Horsical*].

27 *Journal*, p. 550; cf. Brown, *Hobby-Horsical*, pp. 9–10 and 45–6, and R. G. Cant, 'David Steuart Erskine, 11th Earl of Buchan: Founder of the Society of Antiquaries of Scotland', in A. S. Bell (ed.), *The Scottish Antiquarian Tradition* (Edinburgh 1981), pp. 1–30 (at pp. 25–6).

28 *Journal*, p. 257: entry for 26 December 1826.

29 As Vice-President: S. Hibbert and D. Laing, 'Account of the Institution and Progress of the Society of Antiquaries of Scotland Part III 1784–1830', appendix to *Archaeologia Scotica*, 3 (1831) [hereafter Laing, *Account*], at p. 201. In the Scott literature, he appears as President (e.g. *Journal* (1827), p. 386), but this is not so as the Society's published records confirm.

30 Papers read: Laing, *Account*, pp. 179 and 188 (1824, letter by Lord Lovat about the '45 and 1828, about the 'Laird Jock's Stone' in Liddesdale) and appendix to *Archaeologia Scotica*, 4 (1857), p. 14 (1831, contemporary account of the escape of Rob Roy in 1717). D. R. Dean, 'Four Notes on Scott', *Studies in Scottish Literature*, 10 (1972), pp. 51–3 draws attention to an instance of Scott's 'graceful social wit', responding to a toast at a meeting of the Society in 1824 when the mystery of the authorship of the *Waverley* novels was mentioned.

31 Donations: Laing, *Account*, pp. 101 and 187 (coins from Jedburgh, 1822 and a drawing of the sixth-century AD Yarrow Stone, 1828).

32 *PSAS* 56 (1921–2), p. 21 (Torrs); 58 (1923–4), p. 100 (Woodwray); 68 (1933–4), pp. 191–2 (gold hoard) and 69 (1934–5), pp. 439–41 (Bronze Age metalwork, etc.).

33 Brown, *Hobby-Horsical*, p. 20.

34 We have left out of this account the objects of medieval and later date. At least five medieval three-legged metal vessels were in Scott's possession at various times, for example (from Riddell, Edgerston, Galashiels, Croy and Loudon Hill). Three were illustrated in the Library Edition of *The Antiquary* (1843).

35 See pages 514–15 of I. G. Brown, 'Collecting Scott for Scotland: 1855–2000', *The Book Collector*, 49, no. 4 (2000), pp. 502–34.

36 *Gabions* (above) and M. M. Maxwell-Scott, 'Sir Walter Scott on his "Gabions"', *The Nineteenth Century and After*, 58 (1905), pp. 621–33. A new edition is in preparation by Alison Lumsden.

37 *Personal Relics*, p. 38 and pl. XVI.

38 *PSAS* 69 (1934–5), p. 440.

39 This is the group NMS: X.FE 80–2, purchased 1934 (*PSAS* 68 [1933–4], pp. 191–2). Bought in Cork in 1825 and given to Scott in 1826 (*Journal* [1826], p. 221): see G. Eogan, 'The Mull ('South of Ireland') Hoard', *Antiquity*, 41 (1967), pp. 56–8 [hereafter Eogan, *Mull Hoard*].

40 Cf. *Letters*, III, p. 70 and W. A. J. Prevost, 'Joseph Train's Letter to Sir Walter Scott Concerning Wandering Willie', *Scottish Studies*, 20 (1976), pp 117–23. There is a useful entry on Joseph Train in the *Dictionary of National Biography* and at least three brief biographies (A. Trotter, *East Galloway Sketches: Biographical, Historical and Descriptive Notices of Kirkcudbrightshire*, (Castle Douglas 1901), pp. 140–6 [hereafter Trotter, *East Galloway Sketches*], W. Train's 'Biographical Memoir of the Author', in J. Train, *An Historical and Statistical Account of the Isle of Man, from the earliest times to the present date . . .* (Douglas, IoM 1845), pp. 1–29 [hereafter W. Train, *Biographical Memoir*] and J. Patterson, *Memoir of Joseph Train F.S.A. Scot.: the antiquarian correspondent of Sir*

Walter Scott (Glasgow 1857) [hereafter Patterson, *Memoir*]). He deserves a fuller study, however, one that would set his collecting activities in context. As well as researching for Scott, he carried out fieldwork for George Chalmers (1742–1825), the author of *Caledonia* (1807–24), especially on the Deil's Dyke, a medieval linear earthwork incorporating earlier separate elements (W. Train, *Biographical Memoir*, pp. 11–12). We have not been able to consult a copy of W. C. van Antwerp's publication on Train, *A Forgotten Antiquary* (San Francisco 1933).

41 We publish here, in Appendix 2, an outline of his archaeological collections compiled from Train's publications (e.g. the notes on antiquities which he contributed to the *New Statistical Account* in the 1830s–40s: IV (Kirkcudbrightshire), 1842, pp. 130–2 and 195–7; IV (Wigtownshire), 1838, p. 177–8, originally collected for a History of Galloway?) and other sources. Train, as a collector of personal relics of Scott and others, is discussed by one of his descendants: M. Train Dunn, 'A Bookcase and Its Contents Mementos of Scott, Burns and the Black Douglas', *The Scots Magazine*, 29 (1938), pp. 255–62.

42 R. De Bruce Trotter, *Galloway Gossip or the Southern Albanich 80 Years Ago* (Dumfries 1901), at pp. 114–18. The item itself is described as 'a tolerable sized smooth bluish natural stone, most probably brought from the bed of the Water of Ken. Its shape is similar to a chair and it is traditionally said that it was used by St John, or more likely one of his followers. It formerly belonged to the old church, but has been moved from there to its present position' (Ordnance Survey Name Book 1849, quoted in CANMORE entry NMRS NX68SW 2).

43 For Charles Dickens' *Household Words*, 173 (16 July 1853), pp. 475–6.

44 See Appendix 1 for references to the Water of Cree, Moss of Cree, Knockbrex Moor, Milton, Auchengibbert, Kilgow-bridge (Minnigaff), Kirkintilloch, Repentance Tower and Castlewigg finds. Scott may have referred to the last-named in his account of the Abbotsford interiors: *Gabions*, p. 782. As regards the finds from around 'The Tower of Repentance' in Dumfriesshire, it is presumed that the sixteenth-century Repentance Tower on Trailtrow Hill near Hoddom is meant. The sources for this location (*NSA* IV (Dumfriesshire) [1834], pp. 248–50; *TDGNHAS* 13 [1897], pp. 82–94) do not mention the arrowhead or the coin. Most of the flint implements from the Milton inhumation burial were sent to the Earl of Selkirk (NLS MS 3277, p. 127; cf. also *New Statistical Account* IV (Kirkcudbrightshire), pp. 23–4 [dated 1843] and *Caledonia*; Chalmers, p. 230). J. M. Corrie sought them in vain in 1926 (*TDGNHAS*, 3rd series, 14 [1930], p. 296).

45 Friarshaugh: *Border Antiquities*, pp. viii–ix.

46 Bronze vessels: *Border Antiquities*, p. xx.

47 Tongs: *Letters*, IV, p. 540 and *Border Antiquities*, p. xxi (the same as the 'pair of tongs unquestionably Roman' from the 'fine old Roman station' at Keaside [*sic*] found before 1815 [*Letters*, XII, p. 153] and acquired as a consequence of extending his landholdings). This site was presumably the now-destroyed enclosure at Castlestead, Kaeside (National Monuments Record of Scotland NT 53SW 8).

48 *New Statistical Account* III (Roxburghshire) 1845, p. 13 [dated 1834]; perhaps one of the tripod spouted jugs illustrated on p. 12 of the Library Edition of the *Waverley* novels (vol. ii, *The Antiquary*, 1843; Fig. 8 here). It was yet another example (Scott's first, from the Galashiels area) that led him to coin the phrase 'a hobby-horsical Antiquary' in 1811 (*Letters*, XII, pp. 409–10; Brown, *Hobby-Horsical*, p. 6). We have already quoted Scott, at the start of our paper, referring to an example of a related type that had been purchased and came from 'the domain of Riddle'.

49 Scott visited Shetland on the yacht belonging to the Commissioners for Northern Lights; the journal he kept was later published in Lockhart's *Life of Sir Walter Scott* (1837–8). The particular entry of interest here runs: 'Visit Mr Ross, collector of the customs, who presents me with the

most superb collection of the stone axes (or adzes, or whatever they are), called *celts*. The Zetlanders call them *thunderbolts*, and keep them in their houses as a receipt against thunder, but the Collector has succeeded in obtaining several' (quoted from the 1902 edn, vol. iv, p. 193). *Border Antiquities*, p. vii says that there were six 'stone axes': at Abbotsford today there are four stone axes, a utilised pebble and a polished stone knife.

50 Roman pot and ring: *Letters*, XII, note on p. 466.

51 *Border Antiquities*, p. xi.

52 Library Edition of the *Waverley* novels (vol. ii, *The Antiquary*, 1843), p. 17. For the piece itself, see J. M. Coles, 'Scottish Early Bronze Age Metalwork', *PSAS* 101 (1968–9), pp. 1–110, at fig. 30.3 and p. 88.

53 The term halberd was coined by John Evans much later in the nineteenth century (*The Ancient Bronze Implements, Weapons and Ornaments of Great Britain and Ireland* [London 1881], pp. 261–72). For halberd depictions on contemporary rock-art, see R. Chenorkian, *Les Armes Metalliques dans l'art protohistorique de l'Occident Mediterranean* (Paris 1988).

54 Apart from the suspicious Eildon Hills origin accorded to the halberd NMS: X.DJ 34, we would cite the attachment of an wholly erroneous Scottish island provenance to Scott's group of three Late Bronze Age gold ornaments from Ireland: see Eogan, *Mull Hoard*.

55 Library Edition of the *Waverley* novels (vol. ii, *The Antiquary*, 1843), p. 30. For the piece itself, see J. M. Coles, 'Scottish Late Bronze Age Metalwork: Typology, Distributions and Chronology', *PSAS* 93 (1959–60), pp. 16–134 [hereafter Coles, *LBA*], at p. 80.

56 M. M. Maxwell-Scott, *Catalogue of the Armour and Antiquities at Abbotsford* (Edinburgh 1915, originally 1888) [hereafter *Catalogue*], at p. 26. Distribution: e.g. J. M. Coles, 'Scottish Middle Bronze Age Metalwork', *PSAS* 97 (1963–4), pp. 82–156, at p. 108 and fig. 11.

57 Library Edition of the *Waverley* novels (vol. ii, *The Antiquary*, 1843), p. 103.

58 Coles, *LBA*, p. 117 summarises the earlier literature on the hoard (X.DQ 1–44 and 302–5).

59 *PSAS* 69 (1934–5), pp. 439–40.

60 Two bronze rings: T. Scott, 'Collection of Flint Arrow-heads, Spear-Heads, Knives, Scrapers, Borers, Flakes . . .', *History of the Berwickshire Naturalists' Club*, 15 (1894), pp. 166–9, at p. 166.

61 Axe: *PSAS* 69 (1934–5), p. 439 and P. K. Schmidt and C. B. Burgess, *The Axes of Scotland and Northern England*, Prähistorische Bronzefunde Ab. IX Band 7 (Munich 1981) [hereafter Schmidt and Burgess, *Axes*], no. 1055.

62 G. Macdonald, *The Roman Wall in Scotland* (Glasgow 1911), p. 179 (p. 294 of the 1934 edn), quoting T. Watson, *Kirkintilloch Town and Parish* (Glasgow 1894), p. 77. For the sword, see now I. Colquhoun and C. B. Burgess, *The Swords of Britain*, Prähistorische Bronzefunde Ab. IV Band 5 (Munich, 1988), no. 552. For Train's own account: J. Train, 'Brief Sketch of a Correspondence with Sir Walter Scott commencing in the year 1814' (NLS, MS 3277), pp. 132 and 280. He noted that 'a detailed and learned account was given of these Relics by Mr Thomson of the Ayr Academy in one of the periodical publications of the day'. This was presumably Ebenezer Thomson (1783–1861), sometime classical master at Ayr Academy; we have not yet been able to trace the publication.

63 Curiously, James Curle, when researching the 'Kirkintilloch' pieces at Abbotsford for Macdonald, came up with a quotation different from a Train manuscript from that which we have found ('a Roman flagon found . . . amid the ruins of Graham's Dyke about a mile from [Kirkintilloch]'). This ought to mean that at Abbotsford before the First World War were preserved either Train's original letters or the account he supplied Robert Cadell in 1841. The source we have used – National Library of Scotland, MS 3277, acquired in 1944 from a London bookseller – was retained by the Train family and is referred to by M. Train Dunn in her 1938 *Scots Magazine* article noted above.

64 *Border Antiquities*, pp. ix–xi. See further on the developing knowledge of prehistoric bronze implements S. Piggott, 'Bronze, Britons and Romans: An Early Antiquarian Problem', in R. Miket and C. Burgess (eds), *Between and Beyond the Walls* (Edinburgh 1984), pp. 117–25. A recognition of the distinction between medieval and Roman metal vessels came yet later (Wilson, *Prehistoric Annals*, pp. 276–9): Scott continued to regard three-legged cooking vessels like the ones he had collected (above) as Roman (e.g. *Border Antiquities*, p. xxi).

65 Wilson, *Prehistoric Annals*, p. xi. Wilson's *Synopsis of the Museum of the Society of Antiquaries of Scotland* (Edinburgh 1849) partly depends on illustrations of museum objects that were made for the Library Edition, e.g. a 'Skein Dhu, found on Culloden Moor' (NMS: H.LC 9) that figured in *Waverley* (1842), p. 330.

66 *The Antiquary* (Edinburgh Edition, 1995), p. 23/chapter 3.

67 E. M. Jope, *Early Celtic Art in the British Isles* (Oxford 2000), especially pp. 72–4, 246 and 251 and pls 100–1 and 58–59, which describe the pony cap and summarise the earlier literature.

68 For example, J. Train, appendix to volume II of W. Mackenzie, *The History of Galloway from the Earliest Period to the Present Time* (Kirkcudbright 1841) [hereafter Mackenzie, *Galloway*], pp. 63–72 (at pp. 70–1), W. Train, *Biographical Memoir*, p. 21 or NLS MS 3277, pp. 202 and 282 [no. 31].

69 J. A. Smith, 'Notice of a Remarkable Bronze Ornament with Horns found in Galloway, now at Abbotsford . . .', *PSAS* 7 (1867–8), pp. 334–57 (pages 334–5 summarise earlier accounts of its discovery).

70 NLS, MS 912 (fo. 80). Illustrated as plate LXXI of R. J. C. Atkinson and S. Piggott, 'The Torrs Chamfrein', *Archaeologia*, 96 (1955), pp. 197–235.

71 Acquisition: *PSAS* 82 (1947–8), p. 321. For Train's descendants, see p. 146 of Trotter, *East Galloway Sketches*. The torc: M. Macgregor, *Early Celtic Art in North Britain*, 2 vols (Leicester 1976), 2, no. 195, there erroneously attributed to Joseph Tait [*sic*].

72 Library Edition of the *Waverley* novels (vol. ii, *The Antiquary*, 1843), p. 12. See A. Robertson, 'Roman Finds from non-Roman Sites in Scotland', *Britannia*, 1 (1970), pp. 198–226, at fig. 6 and p. 221 (also mentioned in passing in *PSAS* 62 [1927–8], p. 246).

73 *Border Antiquities*, p. xx.

74 In 1811 Scott writes that 'the people who are planting Abbotsford have rejoiced my heart by digging up a brazen utensil much resembling an ill made coffee pot but termed by the learned a sacrificial vessel for pouring the wine on the brows of the victim. Was this not having great Luck?' (*Letters*, III, p. 46). This could be X.FT 94, but Scott also describes a medieval three-legged vessel from the Galashiels area (above) using the same sort of 'sacrificing vessel' terms (*Letters*, XII, p. 409). Despite both appearing in the same year, we think that two different pieces are referred to in the two different letters of December 1811, as the locations given are different enough.

75 NLS, MS 3277, pp. 178 and 282 [no. 30]; Patterson, *Memoir*, p. 121; *PSAS* 69 [1934–5], p. 441. Artillery redoubt: G. Jobey, 'A Military Redoubt on Burnswark Hill, Dumfriesshire', *TDGNHAS* 50 (1973), pp. 72–81.

76 *Roman Inscriptions of Britain*, no. 2216; L. J. F. Keppie and B. J. Arnold, *Corpus Signorum Imperii Romani Great Britain*, Vol. 1, fascicule 4 (Oxford 1984), no. 72 (p. 29 and pl. 22).

77 F. Haverfield, 'Voreda, the Roman fort at Plumpton Wall', *Transactions Cumberland Westmorland Antiq Archaeol Society*, *new series*, 13 (1913), pp. 176–98 (pp. 194–7 summarise the earlier literature on the sculptured panels).

78 RCAHMS, *An Inventory of the Ancient and Historical Monuments of Roxburghshire* (Edinburgh 1956), vol. II, pp. 299–301.

79 Scott, an opponent of John Pinkerton's arguments about 'Gothic' Picts, published both a scholarly essay on the matter (in a review article in the *Quarterly Review*, vol. 41 no. 81 of 1829) and a satire of the excesses of this important debate on Celtic vs Germanic national origins, in Chapter VI of *The Antiquary*. In the former, he reflected on 'a controversy in which the most violent opinions have been maintained on the slightest authorities, and which may be termed to Scottish antiquaries the very slough of despond, whereon much learning has been thrown without mending the path' (quoted from p. 319 of *The Miscellaneous Prose Works of Sir Walter Scott*, vol. 20 [Magnum Edition of 1835]. See especially W. Ferguson, *The Identity of the Scottish Nation: An Historic Quest* (Edinburgh 1998), at pp. 312–14 and C. Kidd, 'The Ideological Uses of the Picts, 1707 – c 1990', in E. J. Cowan and R. J. Finlay (eds), *Scottish History: The Power of the Past* (Edinburgh 2002), 169–90, at p. 176.

80 The story of the discovery is given only in 1856 by Andrew Jervise (1820–78) from a local source (see his 'Notices descriptive of the localities of certain sculptured stone monuments in Forfarshire . . . (Part I)', *PSAS* 2 (1859), pp. 187–99, at p. 194). Skene wrote on his sketch that it was 'originally found . . . as the hearth stone of a cottage' [Society of Antiquaries MS 464, f11; housed at the NMRS]. For Samuel Somerville WS, see *Letters*, V, p. 509.

81 RCAHMS, *Pictish Symbol Stones An Illustrated Gazetteer* (Edinburgh 1999), p. 23 no. 69.

82 *PSAS* 58 (1923–4), p. 100.

83 *The Antiquary* (Edinburgh Edition, 1995), p. 22/chapter 3. In 1833, it was recorded that 'an old spur, with a rowel nine inches in circumference, was found by Sir W. Scott in Huntly Meadow [Yarrow parish]' (*New Statistical Account* III (Roxburghshire) 1845, p. 38 [account dated 1833]). This was illustrated on p. 183 of the Library Edition of *The Antiquary* (1843).

84 Spurs, NMS: H.ML 85 and horn NMS: H.LT 45; see *PSAS* 65 (1930–1), pp. 408–10.

85 W. Scott, *Minstrelsy of the Scottish Border: consisting of Historical and Romantic Ballads collected in the Southern Counties of Scotland* [3 vols] (2nd edn, Edinburgh 1803).

86 R. B. K. Stevenson, 'The Museum, its Beginnings and its Development part I: to 1858: the Society's Own Museum', in A. S. Bell (ed.), *The Scottish Antiquarian Tradition* (Edinburgh 1981), pp. 31–85 [hereafter Stevenson, *Museum*], at p. 56.

87 *Catalogue*, p. 5.

88 *Rob Roy* (Magnum Edition, 1831), vol. II, p. 186/chapter 12.

89 *Rob Roy* (Magnum Edition, 1831), vol. II, p. 292/chapter 17. Robert Cadell had it drawn and engraved as a 'Purse Clasp, with concealed Pistols', for the Library Edition of *Rob Roy* (Edinburgh 1843), p. 265.

90 *Personal Relics*, p. 47. Gun: A. V. B. Norman, 'Arms and Armour at Abbotsford', *Apollo*, 77 (1962), pp. 525–9 [hereafter Norman, *Arms & Armour*], at p. 528 and fig. 6.

91 Escape paper: appendix to *Archaeologia Scotica*, 4 (1857), p. 14.

92 *The Antiquary* (Edinburgh Edition, 1995), p. 23/chapter 3.

93 T. C. Smout, *A History of the Scottish People 1560–1830* (London 1970), at pp. 180–3 and 430–4, charts the enserfment of colliers in the early seventeenth century and their emancipation by the end of the eighteenth century.

94 *Journal*, p. 272: Bowd wrote to Scott and his letter was read to the Society in 1827 by James Skene (Laing, *Account*, p. 185). See also Stevenson, *Museum*, p. 69 and C. O. Parsons, *Witchcraft and Demonology in Scott's Fiction* (Edinburgh 1964), pp. 136–7.

95 A publication on this is in preparation by Hugh Cheape.

96 *Letters on Demonology and Witchcraft* (1968, orig. 1830), p. 273/letter IX.

97 D. Miles and S. Palmer, 'White Horse Hill', *Current Archaeology*, 142 (1995), pp. 372–8, at p. 376.

98 M. Ash, *The Strange Death of Scottish History* (Edinburgh 1980), at pp. 13–40; M. Ash, 'A past 'Filled with Living Men': Scott, Daniel Wilson, and Scottish and American Archaeology' in J. H. Alexander and D. Hewitt (eds), *Scott and His Influence: The Papers of the Aberdeen Scott Conference, 1982* (Aberdeen 1983), pp. 432–42; M. Ash, 'Old Books, Old Castles, and Old Friends: The Making of Daniel Wilson's *Archaeology and Prehistoric Annals of Scotland*', in E. Hulse (ed.), *Thinking with Both Hands: Sir Daniel Wilson in the Old World and the New* (Toronto 1999), pp. 60–80 (especially pp. 66–9). Ash's Scott is a different one from Stuart Piggott's: S. Piggott, 'The Ancestors of Jonathan Oldbuck', in *Ruins*, pp. 133–59. See, in this context, the two views of the date of the halberd NMS: X.DJ 34 set out by Scott (*Border Antiquities*, p. ix); one forward-looking, the other harking back to earlier beliefs.

99 Clive Wainwright's pioneering account of the creation of the interior is not of course concerned with such small-scale pieces (C. Wainwright, 'Walter Scott and the furnishing of Abbotsford: or the gabions of Jonathan Oldbuck Esq.', *Connoisseur*, 194 no. 779 [1977], pp. 3–15). In his later study, Wainwright made a case for Scott's collecting interests moving away from Scottish antiquities; he does not consider the evidence of the collection of Bronze Age weaponry or of Scott's interest in Borders finds at all (*Romantic Interior*, p. 151). Beyond the architectural details and furnishings, most attention has been paid to the arms and armour at Abbotsford (e.g. Norman, *Arms & Armour*, *Romantic Interior*, pp. 201–5).

100 Stuart, in the 1850s, was told that the Woodwray stone (above) had come from St Andrews (J. Stuart, *Sculptured Stones of Scotland* [Aberdeen 1856], p. 31)! As an indication of the lack of documentation, Scott's descendant alluded to 'some curiosities, such as ancient Roman pots, to which it has been impossible to give a history' (*Catalogue*, p. 12) and drew attention only to the large tripod cauldron, the Torrs pony-cap and what must be the basal-looped spearhead. We have been able to improve the situation somewhat, but it is still uncertain what happened to some of the Galloway finds sent by Train, for example, or the Kaeside 'forceps'. Were they passed on by Scott, or did they end up in other places? A much later source claims that there was a 'Walter Scott collection which passed to the Faculty of Advocates of Scotland' (R. M. Spearman, in L. Webster and J. Backhouse (eds), *The Making of England: Anglo-Saxon art and culture AD 600–900* [London 1991], p. 237) but neither we ourselves nor Dr Iain Gordon Brown have been able to substantiate this. The antiquities in the collection of the Faculty of Advocates were deposited on permanent loan with one of the predecessors of the National Museums in 1851 (Brown, 'Old Magazine of Antiquities', p. 178). Curiously, the story that Train tells of the finding of the Auchengibbert 'javelin' by an old woman breaking a peat block (NLS, MS 3277, pp. 202–3) was repeated by his descendant in relation to another item, the halberd NMS: X.DJ 41 said to have come from Arieland Moss (quoted in the NMAS Register, entry 1948–64). Were these two in fact one single find that Train did not actually send to Scott?

101 In the published edition of Scott's letters, the Old Penrith panels are recorded at Abbotsford by June 1823: 'Roman deities dug up at Old Penrith the ancient Petreia' (*Letters*, VIII, p. 14; see also one of October 1823, reporting on the progress of the building work: *Letters*, VIII, p. 112). They may have arrived through Scott's connections with the landowner, William 1st Earl of Lonsdale by the second creation (1757–1844). The familiar published sources deal with pieces of later date, e.g. 'They are pulling down so many of the old places here that carved stones are to be had for the asking' (*Letters*, IV, p. 337) and Scott to Daniel Terry in 1816: 'I expect to get some decorations from the old Tolbooth of Edinburgh, particularly the cope stones of the doorway, or lintels, as we call them, and a niche or two, one very handsome indeed! Better get a niche *from* the Tolbooth than a niche *in* it, to which such building-operations are apt to bring the projectors' (*Letters*, IV, p. 289 = *Personal Relics*, p. 63).

Scott liked the joke so much that he reused it several times (*Letters*, IV, pp. 286, 302 and 483).

102 In this connection, note too a neglected aspect of Scott's contemporary Johann Wolfgang von Goethe (1749–1832), who has been shown to have been an active prehistorian in the early nineteenth century (and even interested in Scottish vitrified forts): M. Todd, 'Goethe and prehistory', *Antiquity*, 59 (1985), pp. 197–201.

103 Joseph Train, in an addition to his manuscript 'Brief Sketch', records that at the request of Robert Cadell in August 1841 he had provided a detailed account of the thirty-three objects sent to Scott over the years. This was 'to accompany, as Notes, engravings of them in the illustrated Edition of Sir Walter Scott's works then "in busy preparation for publication"' (NLS, MS 3277, p. 283). In the end, even objects in the collections of the Society of Antiquaries of Scotland were used to illustrate the Library Edition, e.g. the sporran clasp NMS: H.NE 12 appears in *Rob Roy* and Scott's volunteer helmet NMS: H.NC 2 appears in *Waverley* (see also A. MacGregor, 'Antiquity Inventoried: Museums and 'National Antiquities' in the Mid Nineteenth Century', in V. Brand (ed.), *The Study of the Past in the Victorian Age*, Oxbow Monograph 73 (Oxford 1998), pp. 125–37 [at pp. 126–7]).

104 This was after the failure of an attempt to acquire them by the Society of Antiquaries of Scotland: *Journal*, p. 667 and N. Stratford, *The Lewis Chessmen and the enigma of the hoard* (London 1997), at pp. 4–11. Scott continues to have an effect on Scottish archaeology even long after his death. The need to consider the landscape effects on Scott's View was cited by Historic Scotland as an important factor in deciding their preferred line for the Melrose by-pass across the Newstead site in the 1990s (D. J. Breeze, 'Road Threat to Trimontium', *Current Archaeology*, 133 (1993), pp. 38–9).

105 For example, M. Ash, '"So Much that was New To Us": Scott and Shetland', in B. E. Crawford (ed.), *Essays in Shetland History: Heiðursrit to T. M. Y. Manson* (Lerwick 1984), pp. 193–207 and C. Lamont, 'Sir Walter Scott and the Discovery of the Borders' in P. Clack and J. Ivy (eds), *The Borders* (Durham 1983), pp. 125–40 (= pp. 147–59 of D. Omand (ed.), *The Borders Book* [Edinburgh 1995]), or E. Batho, 'Scott as a Mediaevalist', in H. J. C. Grierson (ed.), *Sir Walter Scott To-day: Some retrospective essays and studies* (London 1932), pp. 133–57.

106 J. Barber, 'The Linear Earthworks of Southern Scotland; survey and classification', *TDGNHAS* 73 (1999), pp. 63–164, at pp. 75 and 83–5 and fig. 5.

107 The pot is visible in plate 171 of *Romantic Interior.*

108 *Border Antiquities*, p. vii: 'the arrow-heads, made of flint, are frequently found, and are called, by the vulgar, elf-arrow-heads, from being, as they supposed, formed by the fairies or elves'.

109 Several of the items listed were purchased in 1948 by the then National Museum of Antiquities of Scotland, mostly from Miss M. T. Dunn, a descendant of Train's (NMS: X. DO 49 and X.FA 96; the NMAS Register states that NMS: X.DJ 41 was acquired through Dr James Davidson). The National Museums also acquired a bookcase of Train's, said to have been made from a bedstead at Threave Castle (Mackenzie, *Galloway*, pp. 68–70; Patterson, *Memoir*, p. 141; NMS: H.KL 131 – *PSAS* 82 [1947–8], pp. 290–2) and two other more recent items (NMS: H.ME 830 and 831 – *PSAS* 82 [1947–8], p 321). A shortened flintlock pistol, said to have been used by a Solway smuggler, may be another Train item; it came to the then NMAS through his granddaughter (object NMS: Q.L. 1948.98).

110 Trotter, *East Galloway Sketches*, at p. 141.

111 The 'King's Case' of the Train sources must be the medieval hospital at Kingscase, north of Ayr (I. B. Cowan and D. E. Easson, *Medieval Religious Houses: Scotland*, 2nd edn [London 1976], at p. 183).

SCOTTISH FURNITURE AT ABBOTSFORD

David Jones

THIS paper is a footnote to Clive Wainwright's rich scholarship on the furniture in Sir Walter Scott's collection at Abbotsford. It is about local furniture commissioned for the house and discusses the ways in which this both reflected and influenced Edinburgh fashion of the time.

The complete repertoire of furnishings at Abbotsford must be seen as a diverse collection rather than as a unified decorative scheme. The style of the furniture was not consistently Gothic, nor was it identifiably Grecian, but it was a largely deliberate mixture of these vocabularies and other, more obscure, decorative dialects. Wainwright identified two phases of supply: the first being 1816–22,[1] during which newly made furniture was supplied by George Bullock, William Atkinson, Edward Blore and Daniel Terry, and the second, 1822–32,[2] when 'Antiquarian' furniture was procured mainly by Terry in London. A good representative example of new furniture from the first phase is the dwarf cabinet of yew and gilt brass made for a plaster bust of William Shakespeare that was placed in the Library. This displayed all the idiosyncratically decorative qualities of Bullock's new 'British' style that involved the use of native woods such as yew and liberal application of brass inlay in classically inspired patterns. The antiquarian period is represented by pieces such as the intricately carved ebony chair acquired via Terry, intended for use in the Drawing Room,[3] and the Venetian baroque chair, in the style of Andrea Brustolon, that is now in the Library.[4]

But these items must be seen as highlights that add lustre to a much larger repertoire. There is a third category of furniture that provided a foundation upon which the collection was built and which is, in most cases, the work of local craftsmen.

This category is most prominently represented by a library table made by Joseph Shillinglaw of Darnick, Roxburghshire, c. 1823 (Fig. 1). The table, just under 8ft long and designed for laying out, viewing and storing outsize folios, is of rectangular design with open-fronted, lancet-arched cavities at each corner. The longer sides are fitted with three shallow frieze drawers above a central cupboard containing bookshelves and enclosed by two double-panelled doors decorated with blind arches. The arched openings at either end are ornamented with engaged clustered quarter-columns with foliate capitals in the Gothic taste (Fig. 2). The frieze is decorated with sunk field and bead panels with pointed leaf-shaped terminations, repeated on the two sham drawers on each of the shorter ends, above double-panelled sham cupboard doors decorated with blind lancets.

FIGURE 1
Library table by Joseph Shillinglaw, Darnick, Roxburghshire.
(Photograph: David Jones)

The crossbanded top of burr elm veneer is outlined twice with lines of dark stained stringing and decorated at the corners with crescents and lozenge shapes described in lines of inlaid hardwood, possibly in allusion to certain charges of Scott's arms. The whole is raised from the ground on six massive turned oak stump feet; the eight large castors screwed to pine battens are a recent addition made to enable ease of movement.

The table conforms to a late eighteenth-century type,[5] but unlike most eighteenth-century examples it was raised originally not on castors but on fixed stump feet. Its design is an ingenious reversal of the usual pedestal form in that the 'kneeholes', or in this case openings for keeping folios, have been moved to the four corners and the pedestal cupboards occupy the centre space. Because it is made in one piece and is too large to be fitted through either doors or windows in the room it must be concluded that the library table was constructed *in situ*. This is usefully corroborated by Lockhart who states in his *Life of Scott* that: 'The great table in the library (a most complex and beautiful one) was done entirely in the room where it now stands, by Joseph Shillinglaw.'[6]

The use of fine oak and elm in the making of the table is significant. This timber was almost certainly procured locally and its prestige value lay in the fact that it was home grown. The desirability of these particular cabinet woods is reflected in the Edinburgh

FIGURE 2
Library table by Joseph Shillinglaw, Darnick, Roxburghshire: detail of arched opening for folios.
(Photograph: David Jones)

cabinet-makers' *Book of Prices* for the period. To be precise, the *Supplement to the Edinburgh Book of Prices for Manufacturing Cabinet Work, 1825* specified that oak and elm were the most costly timbers available in the city at that time; their use was priced at four shillings extra in the pound than mahogany and one shilling and ninepence in the pound more than black rosewood.[7] An important distinction is made here between 'fine' oak or elm that was priced at four shillings more and plain oak (wainscot) or elm, that was priced at one shilling and sixpence less than mahogany. The popularity of oak is demonstrated by its use in interiors of this period. In addition to the use of expensive oak furniture, particularly in display apartments such as the lobby, woodwork and ceilings were grained to simulate the timber. This original decorative technique can be seen on the ceiling of the Library at Abbotsford. But elm, notably the species Wych Elm (*Ulmus Glabra*), enjoyed particular popularity in early nineteenth-century Scotland, possibly because it was underpinned by a long tradition of use in the manufacture of fashionable furniture.[8] It is worthy of remark that the timber was used by the country's more progressive designers including Andrew Fleming of Kirkcaldy[9] and William Trotter of Edinburgh. The English traveller and author T. F. Dibdin noted choice items made from this native cabinet wood in Trotter's Princes Street wareroom in 1838: 'I saw here some specimens of elm wood tables (the wood growing within five miles of Edinburgh) which struck me as of surpassing as well as peculiar delicacy.'[10]

The burr, an abnormal growth caused by chance fungal attack or encouraged by severe pollarding, was sliced into irregularly shaped veneers that were carefully pieced together and applied especially to table tops. The result, a richly figured surface achieved by much labour, can be seen on the upper surface of Shillinglaw's table at Abbotsford, which employs the use of several small and large burrs (Fig. 3). Elm, however, was not the only characteristically indigenous timber used in the early nineteenth century. For example, Trotter was asked to make furniture from Scots Laburnum (*Laburnum Alpinum*) for George Home of Paxton, Berwickshire, in 1814.[11] For a job such as this Trotter's

FIGURE 3
Library table by Joseph Shillinglaw, Darnick, Roxburghshire: detail of burr elm top.
(Photograph: David Jones)

journeymen could have used the flexible tables for 'any other kind of hardwood' quoted in *The Edinburgh Book of Prices for Manufacturing Cabinet Work, 1811.*

The Gothic Revival can be seen as an interesting foil to the particular formula of neoclassicism that was found in Scotland's urban architecture. To strike a different tone, Lobbies were sometimes designed as rib-vaulted Gothic chambers, and 'architectural' wallpapers were generally available to enhance this theme. The Edinburgh price books indicate that an enthusiasm for Gothic first emerged around 1805 when specifications are given for case furniture ornamented in this style. But in 1811 the option of Gothic detail was omitted in favour of classical shapes, indicating a brief wane in popularity. However, demand seems to have recovered and the revival was really at its height around 1820. The fashion is reflected in the 1821 price book volume that offers the greatest quantity of Gothic detail.[12] Looking at Joseph Shillinglaw's furniture in relation to these trends, it can be seen that he was clearly aware of the most fashionable Edinburgh cabinet-making practice. His Gothic panels, for example, seen on the cupboard doors of the Library table and on other smaller items in the house, are of the 'sunk field and bead' type that was so characteristic of Edinburgh work. The repeated reel or bobbin pattern of the bead that frames these panels can be observed even on a diminutive stand that he made for a brass-bound box in Scott's Armoury (Fig. 4).

This Gothic furniture at Abbotsford is neither original nor exclusive, but is the product of a talented young cabinet-maker working in the Edinburgh manner. He incorporated signature features, such as the sunk field and bead panel and graduated ring-turned leg, that had been developed as part of a regional Gothic vocabulary before Scott's showhouse had been built. It may not, however, be entirely fanciful to suggest that the success of Abbotsford, and the publicity it received in the capital, provided the spur that restored the fashion for Gothic furniture in Edinburgh during the 1820s and enabled it to move on.

There is no surviving documentation that records Scott's involvement in the design or execution of the Shillinglaw furniture described so far, but correspondence reveals that he did have very specific wants in relation to some pieces. His young Darnick cabinet-maker was able to help realise these requirements. Scott wrote to his friend Terry on 18 June 1823:

> Has an old-fashioned consulting desk ever met your eye in your rambles? I mean one of those which have four faces, each forming an inclined plane, like a writing desk, and made to turn around as well as to rise, and be depressed by a strong iron screw in the centre . . . choicely convenient, as you can keep three or four books, folios if you like, open for reference. If you have not seen one, I can get one made to a model in the Advocates' Library.[13]

This library would have been particularly in his mind at this time because it had been completely furnished in 1822, in the Roman style, by William Trotter of 9 Princes Street, Edinburgh.[14] Shillinglaw duly produced something that is an extraordinary hybrid of an Edinburgh lawyer's desk and Venetian baroque centrepiece (Fig. 5). He reused four elaborate monopodia that are made from boxwood and are very probably Italian. These support a four-sided inclined folio stand as Scott had stipulated, and the whole piece was mounted on castors. Although

FIGURE 4
Box stand by Joseph Shillinglaw, Darnick, Roxburghshire.
(Photograph: David Jones)

the style of this desk is very different from Shillinglaw's other furniture at Abbotsford, the oak-veneered faces of its top display the characteristic geometric dark stringing that seems to identify his work.

Shillinglaw's furniture then, was made to a fashionable Edinburgh standard[15] with, at Scott's request, the occasional adoption of antiquarian personality. But the real antiquarian furniture (that acquired for its specific historical or literary associations and greatly prized by Scott) illustrates a different strand of furniture history that involved the first stirrings of an antiques trade – or rather trade in antiquities – in Scotland.

FIGURE 5
Consulting desk by Joseph Shillinglaw, Darnick, Roxburghshire.
(Photograph: David Jones)

One of Scott's favourite pieces, so much so that he kept it by his desk in the small study where he did most of his writing, was a carved chair made by George Stirling of Kirkintilloch. It is of late seventeenth-century form, the solid central back panel and cresting carved with Scottish emblems of thistle, heather and rocks. The back and front rail are further inlaid with brass, depicting the Harp of the North (Ossian), surrounded by laurels and, below, targets, claymores, Lochaber axes and war horns. Underneath, it has a small drawer let into the back rail and seat, perhaps to keep a weapon – but more likely a pedigree, because this chair was specifically made to commemorate William Wallace (Fig. 6). Wallace was executed in London on 23 August 1305, but had been abducted from a cottage at Robroyston, Lanarkshire, from the remaining roof timbers of which this chair was built. The chair was a deliberately constructed relic that gained further publicity by way of its transport to Abbotsford. It was shipped to the house entirely by water from the maker's workshop in Kirkintilloch, which was on the Forth and Clyde Canal. But perhaps of more interest than the maker or the mode of transport by which the chair reached Abbotsford is the man behind this stunt: an Ayrshire customs officer named Joseph Train.

Born in November 1779, the son of a farm labourer at Gilminscroft outside Ayr, Train was apprenticed as a weaver but, like Robert Burns, became a customs officer.[16]

FIGURE 6
The Wallace chair by George Stirling, Kirkintilloch.
(Photograph: David Jones)

The peripatetic nature of this job was ideal for collecting, and Train had made a very large collection in the west of Scotland before being posted to Cupar, Fife, where he became Excise Supervisor in 1820. The William Wallace chair that Train had made for presentation to Scott has definite connections with a particular type of 'relic' furniture that had developed in Ayrshire during the late eighteenth century. This had originated in the cult of personality that followed the death of Burns in 1796. The ordinary local furniture that Burns had used, such as the chair he sat upon at Newmilns Masonic Lodge, was embellished with symbolic brass plaques. In 1818, a special chair was made, to the design of David Auld, that commemorated Burns in all his works. This was made from 'relic' timber and was inlaid with engraved brass symbols. It was presented to the Earl of Eglinton in 1818. A second version was made for presentation to George IV on the occasion of his state visit to Scotland in 1822.[17] Train's chair belongs firmly in this tradition, being made for presentation, constructed from timber that had personal associations, and ornamented with engraved brass symbols.

Furniture forms an important component of the collection at Abbotsford, but the house was by no means an experimental laboratory for the development of new ideas in this field. As far as the Scottish-made pieces are concerned – those in the Edinburgh Gothic style and antiquarian 'relic' furniture such as the Wallace chair – they did not make their first appearance at the house, but the fashion they represent was both stimulated and prolonged by the celebrity of Scott's country seat.

NOTES

1 *Romantic Interior*, pp. 163–74.
2 Ibid., pp. 179–94.
3 This enigmatic type of chair had been collected in the eighteenth century by Horace Walpole and William Beckford, so Scott was no pioneer collector in this case. But he can claim to have made the type a popular item amongst aspiring connoisseurs in Scotland for nearly a century after their first appearance at Abbotsford. Their antiquarian history is fully surveyed in Clive Wainwright, 'Only the True Black Blood', *Furniture History*, XXI, 1985, pp. 250–5.
4 *Romantic Interior*, fig. 160, p. 193.
5 Represented, for example, by Thomas Chippendale's Library table made for Harewood House, Yorkshire, c. 1771. This table is now in the collection of Leeds City Art Galleries, Temple Newsam House, Leeds.
6 J. G. Lockhart, *Memoirs of Sir Walter Scott* (London 1900 edn), IV, p. 146.
7 *Supplement to the Edinburgh Book of Prices for Manufacturing Cabinet Work, 1825*, p. 43 in David Jones, *The Edinburgh Cabinet and Chair Makers' Books of Prices 1805–25* (Cupar 2000).
8 Wych Elm (*Ulmus Glabra*) was particularly favoured by Scottish makers during the second half of the eighteenth century. Many examples made in this distinctive golden timber were interpretations of Thomas Chippendale the Elder's *Director* designs. There is a good suite of chairs answering to this description at Pollok House, Glasgow.
9 Jones, *The Edinburgh Cabinet and Chair Makers' Books of Prices*, pp. 16, 19.
10 T. F. Dibdin, *A Bibliographical Antiquarian and Picturesque Tour in the Northern Counties of England and in Scotland*, 2 vols (London 1838), II, p. 505.
11 Home of Wedderburn papers, NAS, GD267 4/1, 5/36, 8/5, 10/9, 12/5, 12/6/8, 17/12.
12 *The Edinburgh Book of Prices for Manufacturing Cabinet Work, 1821*. Jones, *The Edinburgh Cabinet and Chair Makers' Books of Prices*.
13 *Letters*, I, p. 19.
14 Francis Bamford, *Dictionary of Edinburgh Furniture Makers 1660–1840*, ed. Christopher Gilbert, 1983, p. 122; and Iain Gordon Brown, *Building for Books: The Architectural Evolution of the Advocates' Library, 1689–1925* (Aberdeen 1989), p. 94.
15 There exists in the collection of Dundee Museums and Art Galleries a pedestal table that is thought to have come from Abbotsford. The quality of the piece is not comparable with Shillinglaw's work for Scott and it seems safe in this case to rule out his authorship.
16 See John Paterson, *Memoir of Joseph Train F.S.A.: The Antiquarian Correspondent of Walter Scott*, 1857.
17 See David Jones, 'Furniture Associated with Robert Burns', *Regional Furniture*, XI, 1997, pp. 8–21.

'A VERY CHOWDER-HEADED PERSON': RAEBURN'S PORTRAITS OF SCOTT

Stephen Lloyd

THE fame of Sir Walter Scott during his own lifetime ensured that he was portrayed in a variety of media and formats: oil paintings, marble busts, watercolours and drawings, medallions and miniatures, as well as silhouettes. Among the artists to whom Scott sat were some of the finest portraitists active during the later Regency period (1806–32): John Henning, Sir Henry Raeburn, William Nicholson, Sir David Wilkie, Andrew Geddes, Sir Francis Chantrey, Sir Thomas Lawrence, Sir William Allan, Sir Edwin Landseer, Colvin Smith, Sir John Watson Gordon, Sir Francis Grant, Auguste Edouart and Bertel Thorvaldsen. Many of these portraits were produced as prints: mezzotint and stipple engravings, in addition to etchings and lithographs, all of which were vital in spreading the image of the celebrated writer to an ever wider public.

Since 1987 any student of this diverse iconography has been well served by Francis Russell's *Portraits of Sir Walter Scott*.[1] The most important collection of Scott's portraiture remains with the Scottish National Portrait Gallery. That institution has made a few highly significant acquisitions in recent years, including the marble bust by Bertel Thorvaldsen (Fig. 1), modelled in Rome during the last year of Scott's life, which was purchased from a private collection in 1993.[2] Five years later the Gallery acquired at auction the important group portrait painted in oil on panel by Sir William Allan during 1819, depicting a *Celebration of James Hogg, the Ettrick Shepherd's Birth Day* (Fig. 2) – which includes the prominent figure of Scott, second from the left and next to Hogg himself.[3]

Unsurprisingly, before he began to achieve celebrity as a writer, Scott was portrayed relatively infrequently. His earliest portrait was a profile miniature painted in watercolour on ivory, attributed to Abraham Daniel, and produced in 1775–6, when Scott visited Bath, aged six.[4] As a young man on the verge of marriage in 1797 to Charlotte Margaret Charpentier, Scott sat to an unknown miniaturist in Edinburgh, who may well have been Alexander Gallaway, for a portrait he presented to his fiancée.[5] During the first few years of the nineteenth century, Scott, then active as a young Edinburgh lawyer and just beginning his literary career, was portrayed only a few times. First, while visiting Oxford in 1803, he had a profile drawing taken by the little-known amateur Edward Berens.[6] Two years later Scott sat to the minor English painter James Saxon, while that artist was visiting Edinburgh, for what was to be the writer's first oil portrait. This uninspiring three-quarter length, painted in the same year as the publication of *The Lay of the Last Minstrel*, showed Scott seated with his bull-terrier Camp crouching on his knee.[7] This image was engraved in stipple by J. Heath and used as the frontispiece for *The Lady of the Lake* (1810). In the following year, during which Scott was appointed a Clerk of Session, he was drawn in a profile portrait by the Paisley-born draughtsman and modeller John Henning, who then had a studio in Edinburgh. This image, which was commissioned by Gilbert Elliot, 1st Earl of Minto, would have been the basis of Henning's profile portrait medallion modelled in wax. Whereas the original drawing is untraced, its austere neoclassical appearance can be gauged from a similar profile made by this artist in 1810.[8]

FIGURE 1
Sir Walter Scott, *by Bertel Thorvaldsen, marble bust, 58cm high (including socle), modelled in Rome 1832, carved in Rome 1833–4.*
(Scottish National Portrait Gallery, Edinburgh. Purchased in 1993 with assistance from the National Heritage Memorial Fund and the National Art Collections Fund)

The year 1808 was not only marked by the publication of the poem *Marmion: A Tale of Flodden Field*, but also by the first outstanding portrait of Scott. This was painted by (Sir) Henry Raeburn, who dominated the market for oil portraiture in Edinburgh from 1787 until his death in 1823 (Fig. 3).[9] In this full-length portrait, Raeburn depicted Scott seated by a ruined building in the sitter's beloved Borders landscape. In the background can be seen Hermitage Castle and the hills of Liddesdale, based on a sketch provided by Scott himself. The foreground is dominated by Camp, the faithful bull-terrier. Scott is shown wearing a green coat and breeches with black Hessian boots. He holds a red notebook in his left hand, and a silver-mounted pencil in his other hand. This portrait, which has come to be seen as the quintessentially romantic image of Scott – the writer inspired by landscape – had been commissioned by Archibald Constable, his friend and publisher. The creation of this portrait marked the close personal and business relationship between the two

FIGURE 2
Celebration of James Hogg, the Ettrick Shepherd's Birth Day, *by Sir William Allan. Oil on wooden panel, 61 × 82.5cm, 1819.*
(Scottish National Portrait Gallery, Edinburgh. Purchased in 1998 with assistance from the National Art Collections Fund)

men. That year Constable had not only published Scott's *Marmion*, but also an eighteen-volume edition of Dryden, edited by Scott.

Initially, Scott seemed pleased by the picture. In a letter to John Christian Schetky, written on 14 August 1808, Scott noted:

> I sate [*sic*] last spring at the request of the bookseller, to Raeburn for a full length portrait, seated under the fragment of an old tower, with Hermitage Castle in the background. Camp is also introduced, *couchant*, as the heralds call it. The connoisseurs think it is the best portrait Raeburn has ever done. I fancy it will be in the next Exhibition.[10]

The painting was first shown publicly in Edinburgh during 1809 at the annual exhibition of the newly founded Associated Society of Artists, and then again at the Royal Academy, London, in 1810. During the Edinburgh display a reviewer in the *Scots Magazine* for April 1809 remarked it was 'an admirable painting with most appropriate scenery'. In the October issue of the same magazine later that year, another critic added: 'To say that

FIGURE 3
Sir Walter Scott, *by Sir Henry Raeburn. Oil on canvas, 182.9 × 147.3cm, 1808.*
(The Duke of Buccleuch and Queensberry KT, Bowhill)

FIGURE 4
Sir Walter Scott, *by Charles Turner after Sir Henry Raeburn. Mezzotint, 45.7 × 35.7cm, 1810.*
(Scottish National Portrait Gallery, Edinburgh)

Mr Raeburn's portraits are admirable likenesses is the least part of the praise they deserve. The figure of Mr Scott is in a meditating posture beside a ruin with a favourite dog.' This reviewer went on to praise Raeburn's colouring, in particular the greenish tones, as original and distinctive. However, after the presentation of the portrait in London, a critic in *The Repository of Arts* in 1810 was less complimentary, both about the painting and the mezzotint after it, that was engraved by Charles Turner and published that year (Fig. 4).

> The last of the minstrels shows how lamentably the race is degenerated, for never was a more unpoetical physiognomy delineated on canvas; we might take him for an auctioneer or a land-surveyor, a travelling dealer or chapman: in short for any character but a bard. As a print by the Scotch Reynolds (falsely so called) is before the public, we merely remark, that the back-ground appears too methodical, and the distance wants medium. The figure, upon the whole, is well drawn and composed.[11]

It does appear that Scott too was neither entirely happy with Raeburn's composition, nor indeed with Raeburn's style as a portraitist. A decade later Charles Scott, 4th Duke of Buccleuch, who had been notoriously critical of Raeburn's 'half-finished' painting style, was looking for a portrait of Scott to hang in the library at Bowhill. Scott wrote to the Duke on 15 April 1819, referring to the picture of 1808 and its replica painted the following year (Fig. 5):

> I hesitate a little about Raeburn, unless your Grace is quite determined. He has very much to do: works just now chiefly for cash, poor fellow, as he can have but a few years to make money; and has twice already made a very chowder-headed person of me, I should like much (always with your approbation) to try Allan, who is a man of real genius and has made one or two glorious portraits though his predeliction is to the historical branch of the art.[12]

After lamenting his block-headed appearance at Raeburn's hands, Scott went on to laud the work of the history painter Sir William Allan, and continued by praising a recent portrait sketch of the Duke by the genre painter Sir David Wilkie. Scott also urged the Duke to sit to Raeburn's great rival in London, namely Sir Thomas Lawrence: 'We should have at least one picture of your Grace from a real good hand.'[13]

Further evidence of dissatisfaction with Raeburn's effort came from a close member of Scott's circle, the writer's friend and correspondent John Morritt of Rokeby Park, who wrote about the 1808 portrayal of Scott to the writer's son-in-law and biographer, John Gibson Lockhart:

> His person at that time may be exactly known from Raeburn's first picture, which had just been executed for his bookseller, Constable, and which was a most faithful likeness of him and his dog Camp. The literal fidelity of the portraiture, however, is its principal merit, The expression is serious and contemplative, very unlike the hilarity and vivacity then habitual to his speaking face, but quite true to what it was in the absence of such

FIGURE 5
Sir Walter Scott, *by Sir Henry Raeburn. Oil on canvas, 182.9 × 147.3cm, 1809.*
(The Abbotsford Collection, Abbotsford, Melrose)

> excitement. His features struck me at first as commonplace and heavy, – but they were almost always lighted up by the flashes of the mind within. This requires a hand more masterly than Raeburn's . . .[14]

Morritt continued by praising the portrait bust of Scott made by Sir Francis Chantrey. This had been modelled in plaster in 1820. The prime marble version, which was also carved that year, is still at Abbotsford: 'And indeed, in my opinion, Chantrey alone has in his bust attained that, in his case, most difficult take of portraying the features faithfully, and yet giving the real and transient expression of the countenance when animated.'

However, after Raeburn's death in 1823, Scott's view of the original painting had become somewhat more sympathetic. In 1826, Constable was forced to sell the portrait, when his business collapsed into bankruptcy. The picture was bought privately for the substantial sum of 350 guineas by Scott's young protégé, Walter Francis, 5th Duke of Buccleuch, and was hung at Dalkeith House. Scott saw it there on 12 December 1826 and noted in his *Journal*, with some evident relief at seeing the painting in such a distinguished and appropriate setting:

> One thing I saw there which pleased me much and that was [my] own picture painted twenty years ago by Raeburn for Constable and which was to have been brought to sale among the rest of the wreck; hanging quietly up in the dining room at Dalkeith. I do not care much about these things yet it would have been annoying to have been knockd down to the best bidder even in effigy and I am obliged to the friendship and delicacy which placed the portrait where it is now.[15]

Scott's general antipathy to this portrait – and indeed towards Raeburn's pictorial style in general – was rectified only when he sat again to the artist in 1823 for the iconic head-and-shoulders portrait (Fig. 6).[16] This portrait had not been commissioned by Scott, but was intended by Raeburn to join his own collection of head-and-shoulders portraits, containing 'most of the celebrated characters in Edinburgh', that were hung in the private picture-gallery above his studio in York Place.[17] This portrait would also appear to encapsulate a deliberate summation by Raeburn of Scott's celebrity and status as a man of letters. This is conveyed in the correspondence, after Raeburn's death on 8 July 1823, between the artist's son Henry and Lord Montagu, the younger brother of the late 4th Duke of Buccleuch. According to the artist's son, Scott had long agreed to sit to Raeburn, so that he could paint a portrait of him for his gallery. Lord Montagu was – with Scott's help – also attempting to extract an equally high-quality simultaneous replica of this portrait of the writer.[18] At the time of Raeburn's death, the prime version for his gallery was complete, but the version for Lord Montagu was unfinished (Fig. 7).

Lord Montagu was attempting to fulfil the desire of his late brother, Charles, 4th Duke of Buccleuch, to commission a portrait of Scott by Raeburn to hang in the new library at Bowhill. According to Lockhart, the 4th Duke's last letter to Scott had stated

FIGURE 6
Sir Walter Scott, *by Sir Henry Raeburn. Oil on canvas, 76.2 × 63.5cm, 1822–3.*
(Scottish National Portrait Gallery, Edinburgh)

FIGURE 7
Sir Walter Scott, *by Sir Henry Raeburn. Oil on canvas, 76.2 x 63.5cm, 1822–3.*
(Private collection)

> My prodigious undertaking of a west wing at Bowhill is begun. A library of forty-one feet by twenty-one is to be added to the present drawing-room. A space for one picture is reserved over the fire-place, and in this warm situation I intend to place the Guardian of Literature. I should be happy to have my friend Maida appear. It is now almost proverbial, 'Walter Scott and his Dog'.[19]

The Duke's praise for Scott was matched by his scepticism about Raeburn's abilities as a portraitist.

> Raeburn should be warned that I am as well acquainted with my friend's hands and arms as with his nose – and Vandyke was of my opinion. Many of his works are shamefully finished – the face is studied, but everything else is neglected . . . Besides Raeburn has really a fair opportunity of producing something worthy of his skill & talents.[20]

Scott himself was also critical of Raeburn's style, as he noted in a letter to Lord Montagu of 7 February 1822: 'I was to charge Reaburn [*sic*] to paint the hands &c with the same accuracy with the face instead of his usual sketchy way of disposing of the person & accessories.'[21]

In a letter of 19 April 1819 to the 4th Duke of Buccleuch, Scott mentioned his willingness to sit to Raeburn with self-deprecating good humour.

> Respecting the portrait I shall be equally proud and happy to sit for it & hope that it may be executed in some degree worthy of the preferment to which it is destined. But neither my late golden hue for I was coverd with jaundice nor my present silver complection looking much more like a spectre than a man will present any idea of my quondam beef-eating physiognomy.[22]

However, as Scott confessed in a letter to Lockhart, he would rather have sat to his favourite artist Sir William Allan, even though he is reluctant to distract him from history-painting for mere portraiture.

> The Duke wants me to sit for him for a picture in his fine new library and names Raeburn – I should like much better to sit to Allan. But it is a sin to take up his time with Chowder-pates.[23]

Just prior to Raeburn's death, Scott and the artist had both joined a touring party of mutual friends visiting historical sites in Fife, during which the two men had got to know and like each other over a period of a few days. In a letter of 17 July 1823 to Lord Montagu, Scott described his sittings to Raeburn for the two versions of the portrait, as well as the artist's recent death.

> My Dear Lord, – Poor Sir Henry Reaburn [*sic*] is no more – He was over in Fife with the Chief Commissioner Chief Baron & myself on a pleasure party about three weeks hence and I never saw a man in better health. But he died of water in the head a hopeless disease which must have been long in the constitution. When he came back from Fife he said

now [that] I am better acquainted with your face than ever I was (having been three or four days in company) I will finish Lord Montagu's picture & my own for I had agreed long since to sit to him on his own account and both pictures were nearly finishd. I went accordingly and sate [*sic*] to him for nearly three hours when he finishd his own head in a masterly manner and did a great deal to that designd to your Lordship but chiefly to the drapery. I upbraided him in jest with having taken best care of himself & he allowd he had but agreed whenever the paint on your copy was dry I should have a finished sitting. All this being the case I think your Lordship should have the finishd picture which is really considerd as the best likeness which ever has been made of so indifferent an original for your Lordship cannot certainly be expected to take the unfinishd picture which would require one long sitting to bring it to the same perfection. In all respects they are quite the same only the dress is different to show that both were originals.[24]

This last 'finishing sitting' for the version of Raeburn's portrait of Scott (intended for Lord Montagu) never took place, owing to the artist's death. In the course of Scott's correspondence with Henry Raeburn the younger, the artist's son referred to the primacy of the portrait destined for his father's gallery. He added that he was unable to send the finished version to Lord Montagu:

I would have cheerfully complied with your, & Lord Montagues wish, by giving him the finished Portrait, had not my Father, from the time he first laid a Brush on it, called that particular one his own. From what I have stated you will at once perceive that a Sale of the picture is out of the question. I shall ever value it, as being one of my beloved & ever to be lamented Fathers last & greatest efforts, and on account of it being the absolute Portrait of the greatest man alive.[25]

Scott regretted Raeburn's death, even though he did not know him well. According to the artist's friend John Morrison, Scott was affected by the memory of his last portrait sitting.

I never knew Raeburn, I may say, till during his painting my last portrait. His conversation was rich, and he told his story well. His manly stride backwards, as he went to contemplate his work at a proper distance, and, when resolved on the necessary point to be touched, his step forward, were magnificent. I see him, in my mind's eye, with his hand under his chin, contemplating his picture: which position always brought me in mind of a Jupiter which I have somewhere seen.[26]

Scott also regretted his delay in arranging his sitting to Raeburn, firstly for the late (4th) Duke of Buccleuch, and secondly for his brother Lord Montagu. This had meant that the portrait destined for Lord Montagu remained unfinished at Raeburn's death, and was most probably completed by the artist's principal studio assistant John Syme. As Scott wrote:

It will be a lesson to me on the subject of procrastination so long as I live. Mr Syme was used to finish the draping of Raeburns portraits but your Lordship will be best judge whether he should be permitted to touch yours. You can see the picture by looking in at 32 York Place.[27]

However, despite its being unfinished, Scott still thought highly of this version of his portrait by Raeburn. He wrote to Lady Louisa Stuart, who had recently seen the work hanging at Lord Montagu's residence, Ditton Court, near Windsor: '. . . it is still a better picture (the subject considered) than any one but Lawrence could at present produce'.[28]

The reputation of this last painting by Raeburn of Scott was greatly increased by its reproduction as a mezzotint engraving by William Walker (published in 1826) (Fig. 8). That year Scott noted in his *Journal* that he had received two impressions of the print, one of which he gave away.

> I got yesterday a present of two engravings from Sir Henry Raeburn's portrait of me which, poor fellow, was the last he ever painted and certainly not his worst. I had the pleasure to give one to young Mr. Davidoff for his uncle the celebrated Black Captain of the Campaign of 1812. Curious that he should be interested in getting the resemblance of [a] person whose mode of attaining some distinction has been very different.[29]

By closely examining the rich documentary material concerning Raeburn's two major portrait compositions of Scott from 1808 and 1822–3, it is possible to establish the writer's ambivalent attitude not only towards Raeburn's 'half-finished' style of painting, but also towards the whole business of sitting for his portrait. To modern eyes Scott's reservations about Raeburn's style appear odd, especially in light of that artist's considerable reputation both in his own lifetime, and especially since his death. However, Scott's critique of Raeburn was in line with other criticisms voiced by some art commentators and certain eminent figures within the writer's circle, including John Morritt and Charles, 4th Duke of Buccleuch. Scott himself clearly preferred the portraits executed by Allan, Wilkie, Lawrence and Chantrey, all of which probably concurred more with his own idea of his appearance and status. Interestingly, despite Scott's disappointment with Raeburn's first portrait of 1808, which he felt revealed him too prosaically, the writer did mollify his opinion of the artist's iconic head-and-shoulders portrait of 1822–3, to the extent that he described the painter as working in 'a masterly manner'.

Perhaps this eventual softening of Scott's attitude may have arisen from his sympathy with Raeburn's financial predicament, or more likely from his appreciation that the prime version of the later portrait was intended to hang in the artist's private picture-gallery of 'most of celebrated characters in Edinburgh'. Ironically, it was only after Raeburn's death in July 1823 that Scott realised the extent of the loss to the art of painting and to Scottish society. He described sympathetically (in a letter to the English artist Benjamin Robert Haydon) the situation 'by which painting is deprived of a votary of genius, our city of an ornament, and society of a most excellent and most innocent member'. In this eulogy Scott could almost have been writing about himself.[30]

FIGURE 8
Sir Walter Scott, *by William Walker after Sir Henry Raeburn. Mezzotint, 28.3 × 25.2cm, 1826.*
(Scottish National Portrait Gallery, Edinburgh)

APPENDIX

A first-hand account of Scott's portrait-sittings to Raeburn in 1823

John Morrison, 'Reminiscences of Sir Walter Scott',
Tait's Edinburgh Magazine, 11 (January 1844), pp. 16–17

Sir Henry Raeburn regretted to me that Sir Walter had declined to sit to him. 'The portrait I have already painted,' he said, 'has a heavy look. There are three; but two are copies, although I wished to sit for them all. But he is a restless sitter.' – 'Not only myself,' said Sir Walter, on the other hand, 'but my very dog growls when he observes a painter preparing his palette.' – 'I will undertake,' said I, to Sir Henry, 'to prevail with him to sit, provided I am to be present with the sitter's leave, and permitted, by way of lesson, to copy the work in certain stages.'

'You shall not only have my leave to be present,' said Sir Henry, 'but I may paint your own head into the bargain.' I mentioned to Sir Walter that it would be conferring on me a most particular favour, as I had conventioned with Sir Henry Raeburn that I should be present at all the sittings, if he was not averse to the arrangement. 'I have been painted so often,' said he, 'that I am sick of the thing; especially since, with the exception of Raeburn's old portrait, I can only see so many old shoemakers or blue-gown beggars.' Even Lawrence, whose portrait is in progress, has been thinking more of the poet than the man.

'*The poet's eye in a fine frenzy rolling* is what he is aiming at; but I anticipate a failure. Raeburn's portrait looks down, and Sir Thomas's too much up. I think that something between the two would be better; I hate attitudes. – My compliments to Sir Henry, and say that I will be glad to see him here to-morrow, to breakfast: it is not a court day. You will accompany him, of course.' This was after dinner. I called at St Bernards on the following morning, and found the artist walking in his garden. He was much gratified with my success, and prepared to go with me to Castle Street.

'His time,' said he, 'as well as my own, is so much taken up, that I seldom see him. I will send an apology to all my sitters to-day.'

'You will do well,' said I, 'for he mentioned that if no unlooked-for thing came in the way, he would accompany you to York Place, and have the first sitting.'

After breakfast, they sat two hours conversing. It was interesting to hear two men, the first and most accomplished in their several departments as poet and painter, discoursing on different effects and departments of their art.

'I wish,' said Sir Walter, 'that you would let us have a little more finishing in the backgrounds. Sir Thomas Lawrence, I understand, employs a landscape painter.' – 'Of that I do not approve,' said Sir Henry. 'Landscape in the background of a portrait ought to be nothing more than a shadow of a landscape: effect is all that is wanted. Nothing ought to divert the eye from the principal object – the face; and it ought to be something in the style of Milton's Death:

> The other shape, if shape it might be call'd
> That shape had none, or substance might be call'd
> That shadow seem'd, for each seem'd either.

I am at present painting an admiral, and had some thought of asking my friend, the minister of Duddingston, to paint me a sea; but, on second thoughts, I am afraid that Mr Thomson's sea might put my picture to the blush.'

'We will proceed to the first sitting,' said Sir Walter, 'and I think that I shall be able to find you a customer for the picture.'– 'You may, for a copy, Sir Walter, but the portrait that I am now painting is for myself, although it may find its way, in time, into your own family.' A copy of this portrait was painted for Lord Montague [*sic*]; but the original is in the possession of the painter's only son, Henry Raeburn, Esq., of St Bernards.

During the painting of the portrait I attended, and throughout its progress made many studies. After two or three sittings, Sir Walter was highly pleased. 'I wish none but your portraits of me were in existence,' said Sir Walter. 'A portrait may be strikingly like, and yet have a very disagreeable effect.' This portrait is the *beau-ideal* of his appearance. The painter has seized the happy moment; and it is, by far, the best likeness that has ever been painted. A small head in wax, by John Henning, done about 1807, of which I have a copy, is also a capital likeness.

I was preparing to go to London; and being anxious to see Sir Thomas Lawrence, both Sir Walter and Sir Henry gave me cards of introduction. I was particularly anxious to see the arrangement of his palette. 'I will,' said Sir Walter, 'desire that favour for you. I think that you will find double the number of tints, as you term it, that are on Raeburn's palette.'

On arriving in London, I delivered Sir Walter's note, and was asked to breakfast next day. Sir Henry Raeburn's card I still retain. 'With respect to the arrangement of my palette,' said Sir Thomas, 'which your friend Sir Walter desires me to exhibit, you shall see it immediately.' He was, in other respects, most polite. He showed me Sir Walter's portrait, which was in progress. I knew it, and that was all; it had an affected cast-up of the eye; in fact, he had determined to make him a poet. He asked my opinion, which I gave him frankly, and which he received with great good nature. 'Sir Walter, when he looks up, half shuts his eyes; yours are too open.' – 'You are quite correct in your remark; and I will endeavour to attend to it.' On leaving, Sir Thomas gave me a card to attend his lecture in the Royal Academy; but I was obliged to leave London soon after, and did not see him again.

In the time of breakfast, Sir Thomas spoke much of Mr Raeburn and his style of painting. – 'He ought to be richer than I can be; for he can paint three pictures for my one. His prices are much too small. His portrait of Highlander McNab, is the best representation of a human being that I ever saw. Mr Raeburn's style is freedom itself.'

NOTES

1 Francis Russell, *Portraits of Sir Walter Scott: A Study of Romantic Portraiture* (London 1987).

2 Tim Knox and Todd Longstaffe-Gowan, 'Thorvaldsen's "Valdrescot": A lost bust of Sir Walter Scott rediscovered', *Apollo*, 138 (February 1993), pp. 75–81.

3 Jeremy Howard *et al.*, *William Allan: Artist Adventurer*, exhibition catalogue, City Art Centre (Edinburgh 2001), pp. 7–8, 50, 87 and fig. 3 (col.).

4 Russell, pp. 36–7, no. 43, pl. 1; NMS, Edinburgh (Society of Antiquaries of Scotland), on long-term loan to SNPG, Edinburgh.

5 Russell, p. 95, no. 231; untraced.

6 Russell, p. 29, no. 20; untraced.

7 Russell, p. 77, no. 168, pl. 3; SNPG, Edinburgh.

8 Russell, pp. 48–9, nos 83 and 85, pl. 2. The profile of 1810 is in a private collection.

9 Russell, pp. 73–74, no. 161, pl. 5; and David Mackie, 'Raeburn, Life and Art', unpublished PhD thesis (University of Edinburgh 1994) 6 vols (4), pp. 785–8, no. 640; and *Raeburn*, exhibition catalogue by Duncan Thomson *et al.*, Royal Scottish Academy, Edinburgh, and National Portrait Gallery, London, 1997–8 (Edinburgh 1997), pp. 132–5, no. 38, col. pls. Another slightly different version of this portrait, which includes one of the sitter's greyhounds (Percy or Douglas) was commissioned by Scott from Raeburn in 1809 to hang in the writer's Castle

Street house in Edinburgh (fig. 5). This version of the portrait was moved to Abbotsford in 1831, where it has hung ever since. The original composition was engraved in mezzotint by Charles Turner in 1810 (fig. 4), a reproduction described as one of the two finest prints after all the portraits of Scott (see Russell, p. 24).

10 Russell, pp. 73–4, n. 1.

11 *The Repository of Arts*, 3 (18 June 1810), p. 36 and William T. Whitley, *Art in England, 1800–1820* (Cambridge 1928), pp. 170–1. Scott sent a copy of this print ('very cleverly engraved') to Dr Leyden in Calcutta (see *Letters*, II, pp. 441–2, letter dated 20 February 1811) and ('prettily engraved and not worth refusing') to Lady Abercorn (*Letters*, II, p. 450, letter dated 25 February 1811).

12 *Letters*, V, p. 349.

13 *Letters*, V, pp. 350–1.

14 *Life*, p. 163.

15 *Journal*, p. 252.

16 Mackie, 4, pp. 789–92, no. 640c; and Thomson *et al.*, pp. 193–5. This was the version of the portrait, which was engraved in line and stipple by William Walker during 1826 (fig. 8).

17 John Morrison, 'Reminiscences of Sir Walter Scott, The Ettrick Shepherd. Sir Henry Raeburn, &c., &c. – No. III', *Tait's Edinburgh Magazine*, 10, December 1843, p. 783 (also see Appendix).

18 This replica portrait of Scott, painted for Lord Montagu, is in a private collection. See Mackie, 4, pp. 792–5, no. 640b. This version is illustrated in *A Descriptive Account of the Portraits, Busts, Published Writings, and Manuscripts, of Sir Walter Scott, Bart., collected and exhibited at Edinburgh on occasion of the Scott Centenary in 1871* (Edinburgh 1874), no XIII, illustrated opposite p. 70.

19 *Life*, p. 391.

20 Ibid.; and *Letters*, V, pp. 307–8, n. 1.

21 *Letters*, VII, p. 55.

22 *Letters*, V, p. 349.

23 *Letters*, V, p. 323, 23 March 1819.

24 *Letters*, V, pp. 45–6.

25 *Letters*, VIII, p. 63, n. 1.

26 'Reminiscences', p. 782 (and see Appendix).

27 *Letters*, VIII, p. 69, 4 August 1823.

28 *Letters*, VIII, p. 245, 4 April 1824.

29 *Journal*, p. 159, entry for 16 June 1826.

30 *Letters*, VIII, p. 32, 8 July 1823.

'HE WAS A GENTLEMAN, EVEN TO HIS DOGS': PORTRAITS OF SCOTT AND HIS CANINE COMPANIONS

Jeanne Cannizzo

ANYONE walking along Princes Street in Edinburgh must be aware of the huge, neo-Gothic monument towards the east end. Inside the memorial is a sculpture, twice life-size, of a man and his dog. Sometimes described as the first marble statue commissioned from a native artist in Scotland, it is Sir John Steell's tribute to Sir Walter Scott and Maida. According to the first public guidebook to the monument, published in 1852: 'The Minstrel has been engaged in writing, and seems pleased with the result of his labours. The dog Maida, who has been reposing by his side, appears to have been startled by the shutting of the book in the hand of the master, and seems participating in the pleasure which is spread over his benign countenance'[1] (Fig. 1).

However, before discussing status, locality, a sense of place, and the promotion of a certain image of himself, it should be noted that Sir Walter Scott was a genuine lover of animals. At one time his household included not only many dogs and a cat, but a talking raven known as Ralph, which was said to have died from immoderate imbibing of alcohol. Scott's family and friends used the word tail – the same word used for the followers of a Highland chief – to talk about the immense posse of animals, not only dogs but also a pig which thought it was a dog, as well as a hen and a donkey, which followed their master around on his perambulations. In 1830 a visitor witnessed Scott taking one of his dogs (which had a cough) into his carriage rather than let it ford swollen streams, and wrote

> His tenderness to his brute dependants was a striking point in the general benignity of his character. He seemed to consult not only their bodily welfare, but their feelings, in the human sense. He was a gentleman, even to his dogs.[2]

Scott famously complained in 1822 in a letter to Maria Edgeworth that 'I have sometimes thought of the final cause of dogs having such short lives, and I am quite satisfied it is in compassion to the human race; for if we suffer so much in losing a dog after an acquaintance of ten or twelve years, what would it be if they were to live double that time?'[3] Scott was said to have been thrilled by the founding in 1824 of what we know as the Royal Society for the Prevention of Cruelty to Animals: this was well before

FIGURE 1
A small porcelain model from about 1850 of Sir John Steell's sculpture of Scott and Maida for the Scott Monument.
(Scottish National Portrait Gallery, SNPG 1302)

Queen Victoria's own sentimentality in reference to her pets is said to have transformed middle-class Britons, by emulation, into a nation of animal-lovers. Apparently this fellow feeling was reciprocated: one Blenheim cocker spaniel, notorious in Edinburgh for his extreme shyness, always rushed to Scott, licked his shoes and generally fawned on him whenever they passed each other in Princes Street.[4]

Many of Scott's distinguished visitors, numerous correspondents, and members of his family, record again and again the bond between Scott and his dogs.[5] The well-known American chronicler of life on the Hudson, Washington Irving, visited Scott in 1817 and left this description of an expedition to the hills:

> As we sallied forth, every dog in the establishment turned out to attend us. There was the old staghound Maida, . . . a noble animal, and Hamlet, the black greyhound, a wild thoughtless youngster, not yet arrived at the years of discretion; and Finette, a beautiful setter, with soft, silken hair, long pendant ears, and a mild eye, the parlour favourite. When in front of the house, we were joined by a superannuated greyhound, who came from the kitchen wagging his tail; and was cheered by Scott as an old friend and comrade. In our walks, he would frequently pause in conversation, to notice his dogs, and speak to them as if rational companions; and indeed, there appears to be a vast deal of rationality in these faithful attendants on man, derived from their close intimacy with him.[6]

Even when weighted down with fears of financial ruin, in 1825, Scott wrote in his *Journal*: '. . . it is foolish – but the thoughts of parting from these dumb creatures have moved me more than any of the painful reflections I have put down – poor things, I must get them kind masters. There may be yet those who loving me may love my dog because it has been mine. I must end this, or I shall lose the tone of mind with which men should meet distress.'[7]

Dogs' noted loyalty and want of human company obviously appealed to a man described by his son-in-law as one who lived on love. As a child Scott kept a dog called Snap, said to have been at least part bulldog, which was allowed to sleep in his bedroom.[8] There is no known portrait of the young Scott with what seems to have been his first dog. There is at Abbotsford a portrait of Scott's cat, named Hinse of Hinsefeldt after a character in a German folktale, and another by Sir John Watson Gordon of Scott in his study at his Edinburgh house in Castle Street (Fig. 2). Painted sometime after 1840, this features the cat stretched out on Scott's desk. But portraits of the Scott pets, other than dogs, are rare. And, indeed, not all of Scott's dogs regularly accompany him in his portraits. On his visit in 1817, Washington Irving had noted what he called 'a whole garrison of dogs' betraying 'Scott's catholic taste in canine types'.[9] But only certain breeds and individual animals are so frequently portrayed with the older Scott that they have come down to us as part of our image of 'the wizard of the north'.

One of the earliest portraits of Scott before he became the laird of Abbotsford, and, indeed, before he wrote the *Waverley* novels, is by James Saxon. Dating from 1805, it features his dog Camp, and was used, as an engraving, as the frontispiece for the first edition, in 1810, of *The Lady of the Lake*. It is said to have been his wife's favourite

FIGURE 2
Sir Walter Scott *(with Hinse), by Sir John Watson Gordon.*
(Scottish National Portrait Gallery, SNPG 1249)

portrait of her husband; Camp himself had been acquired about the time of their marriage and lived with the family for about twelve years. Scott's son-in-law considered Camp to be particularly well painted in Saxon's portrait – although one has to say that Scott himself is not.

Camp's ancestry was described by Scott in a letter of 11 March 1828 to John Stevenson, an Edinburgh bookseller who once received a painting of the dog by James Howe from Scott (Fig. 3). 'Camp was got by a black and tan English terrier called Doctor, the property of Mr Storie, farrier in Rose Street, about 1800, out of a thoroughbred English brindled bull-bitch, the property of Mr John Adams of the Riding School, Adjutant of the Royal Edinburgh Volunteer Cavalry.'[10] In the nineteenth century, bull-terriers were used for dog-fighting and bull-baiting, which was made illegal in Great Britain in 1835, three years after Scott's death. Camp was known for his fighting abilities and bellicose nature with other dogs, which Scott called 'an excessive ferocity towards his own species, which sometimes brought his master and himself into dangerous scrapes'.[11]

Sir Henry Raeburn's 1808 full-length portrait of the author with Camp seems to reveal another side of the dog's character, at least as described by Scott: 'He was of great strength and very handsome, extremely sagacious, faithful and affectionate to the human species and possessed of a great turn for gaiety and drollery.'[12] Archibald Constable, the publisher, commissioned the portrait, but sold it in 1826 to the Duke of Buccleuch. A second version, commissioned by Scott in 1809 after he fell out with Constable, hangs today in the Dining Room at Abbotsford. Here Camp has been given a canine companion, a greyhound named Percy. The contrast between the two dogs was pointed to in 1805 by Scott's lifelong friend, James Skene of Rubislaw, in the following way:

> [Camp] was very handsome, very intelligent and naturally very fierce, but gentle as a lamb among the children. As for the more locomotive Douglas and Percy, he kept one window of his study open, whatever might be the state of the weather, that they might leap out and in as the fancy moved them. He always talked to Camp as if he understood what was said – and the animal certainly did understand not a little of it; in particular, it seemed as if he perfectly comprehended on all occasions that his master considered him as a sensible and steady friend – the greyhounds as volatile young creatures whose freaks must be born with.[13]

Certainly Scott was very fond of Camp, having once saved his life by force-feeding the dog with milk in a teaspoon. He often jokingly described Camp in human terms, suggesting to Richard Heber, the MP and book collector, that Camp sent his love, and writing to George Ellis that 'Camp has been regularly wedded to a fair dame in the neighbourhood . . .'[14] He also accompanied the poet on his trip to London in 1803. Camp, like Scott, was fond of hare coursing, and on the rare occasions when Scott went duck hunting acted as his retriever.

Camp died in 1809, his owner noting that he 'might have lived longer but for the severe exercises which he had taken when young and a considerable disposition to voracity, especially where animal food was to be come by . . .'[15] He was buried one moonlit night, with the weeping family in attendance. Scott himself patted down the

FIGURE 3
Sir Walter Scott *(with Camp), by James Saxon.*
(Scottish National Portrait Gallery, SNPG 628)

turf in the garden of his house in Castle Street. The grave was sited so that Scott could gaze upon it when sitting at his writing desk.

Even after his death Camp often featured in Scott's correspondence. The antiquary and artist Charles Kirkpatrick Sharpe once told Scott

> I find something uncomfortable in the decease of poor Camp. He was a wag-tail acquaintance only, but I entertained a great deal of respect for him; and, had we possessed opportunities, I am certain that we should have become very intimate. When a dog dies we are sure that he will never come alive again in other regions, and that always adds greatly to my affliction, . . . However, it is perhaps as well that poor Camp has now departed, before the evils of age fell sorely upon him. A superannuated favourite of the canine species (I speak from experience) is a sad burden, both to himself and his friends.[16]

Scott sent engravings by Charles Turner of the Raeburn portrait of himself and Camp to his old friend the Scottish orientalist Dr John Leyden of Calcutta and to Lady Abercorn, writing to the latter that

> It is prettily engraved and not worth refusing – the dog is my *poor deceased Camp* whom your Ladyship has often heard me mention: my friends wrote as many elegies for him in different languages as ever were poured forth by Oxford or Cambridge on the death of a crowned head. I have Latin, French, Italian, Greek, Hebrew, German, Arabic, and Hindostanee poems to his memory . . .[17]

The poet finished by asking her to put the engraving in her boudoir.

Scott replaced Camp with a terrier. These so-called 'earth dogs' are recorded in Argyll in the sixteenth century. Of particular interest here are the Border terriers, which, as a group, are said to have descended from the dogs bred by itinerant musicians and tinkers who lived in the Borders and used their dogs in poaching and sometimes for badger-baiting as well as for general fieldwork. However, Scott's terrier was of more genteel origin. Writing to his friend George Ellis on 8 July 1809, Scott notes:

> I have supplied the vacancy occasioned by the death of poor old Camp with a terrier puppy of the old shaggy Celtic breed. He is of high pedigree; so I have christened him Wallace, as the donor is a descendant of the Guardian of Scotland.[18]

Wallace died in October 1812, but not before providing sterling service, according to the poet and journalist Robert Pearse Gillies, by waking the author each morning at six o'clock. Later, their next ritual seemed to begin with Wallace upright in a chair beside Scott who gave him a newspaper which he took firmly in his mouth. Only then was Scott ready to write. A painting or drawing of this charming tableau is not recorded, and it is hard to know what kind of terrier Wallace was, or if his appearance on the scene was in response to advice from a criminal. At least one historian of terriers claims that as a young lawyer Scott was advised by the burglar he was defending to keep a small dog with a bark rather than a larger pet which might sleep,[19] an episode that was alleged to be the start of his dedication to terriers.

It is, of course, the Dandie Dinmont with which Scott is most associated, the one breed known certainly to have been named from literature, in this case Scott's own novel *Guy Mannering* (1814). The book features, among other characters, a bluff and hearty farmer whose name was Dandie Dinmont. Scott himself makes it clear the figure was a composite creation.

> The author may here remark that the character of Dandie Dinmont was drawn from no individual. A dozen, at least, of stout Liddesdale yeomen with whom he has been acquainted, and whose hospitality he has shared in his rambles through that wild country, at a time when it was totally inaccessible save in the manner described in the text, might lay claim to be the prototype of the rough, but faithful, hospitable, and generous farmer. But one circumstance occasioned the name to be fixed upon a most respectable individual of this class, now no more. Mr James Davidson of Hindlee, a tenant of Lord Douglas, besides the points of blunt honesty, personal strength, and hardihood, designed to be expressed in the character of Dandie Dinmont, had the humour of naming a celebrated race of terriers which he possessed, by the generic names of Mustard and Pepper (according as their colour was yellow or greyish-black), without any other individual distinction, except as according to the nomenclature in the text.[20]

It is not surprising that his dogs would become known as Dandie Dinmont's terriers. Davidson, a well-known breeder, used his terriers for fox-hunting and a huge popular demand for his dogs was generated by Scott's novel, which had made the animals fashionable. Scott described them thus: 'the race of Pepper and Mustard are in the highest estimation at this day, not only for vermin-killing, but for intelligence and fidelity. Those who, like the author, possess a brace of them, consider them as very desirable companions.'[21] Some of his dogs came from Davidson and at least one was a present from Lord Montagu at Dalkeith House, who sent him a Dandie Dinmont, 'a real pepper which I take as a piece of great attention'.[22]

Scott owned not only a brace, but a whole 'cruet set' of Dandie Dinmonts which he called Spice, Pepper, Mustard, Ginger, Catchup and Soy. However, most of the anecdotes relating to this breed are about the adventures of Ginger and Spice, the latter given a carriage ride because of her cough which developed after having had distemper as a puppy. Later dogs were inoculated against it. The tale of Spice, the 'little spit fire', getting stuck in a garden wall flue when chasing a cat was often re-told.[23] Ginger was once referred to as the 'Liddesdale devil' when she attacked Ourisk, the Kintail terrier, usually described as one of Mrs Scott's devoted pets. These terriers were allowed to eat the leftovers of cold meat from the poet's breakfast table and were not only his constant companions, but earned these rewards by killing rats and vermin. Ginger and Spice are said to be the two terriers in Sir William Allan's portrait of Scott entitled *The Minstrel of the Scottish Border*. It dates from the 1830s, but recalls Scott's early career as a poet and collector of Border ballads (Fig. 4). A brace of terriers also appears in Allan's painting *The Author of Waverley in his Study* (1828).

Like monarchs of ages past, Scott also presented dogs bred on his estate as gifts to friends and acquaintances, and records the safe delivery of the puppies of both

FIGURE 4
Minstrel of the Scottish Border *(with Ginger and Spice), by Sir William Allan.*
(Scottish National Portrait Gallery, SNPG 1366)

Ginger and Spice. For example, his *Journal* entry for 8 April 1827 notes that 'Ginger, being in my room, was safely delivered in own basket of four puppies – the mother and children all doing well – faith! That is as important an entry as my journal could desire.'[24]

Among the recipients of these canine gifts were his publisher Archibald Constable, the Dundas family of Arniston, the Duchess of Buckingham and Chandos, Lord Polwarth of Mertoun, and the sculptor Sir Francis Chantrey, who had presented Scott with a portrait bust of himself. In 1825 Scott gave Chantrey a puppy which originally had been destined for the brother-in-law of Maria Edgeworth. In a letter of March 1825 he explained to the Irish novelist his breeding policy.

> I did not send you one or indeed keep any of the first litter which is seldom good for much but she will have a family this spring and as the sire is of high fame and she herself one of the best-bred terriers in Scotland I wish to know whether you still wish me to keep a whelp and whether it should be male or female or if you would prefer a brace.[25]

Her tardy reply to this letter meant that the puppy, called Mustard, was eventually despatched to the sculptor. In 1835, Chantry, who 'fell in high fancy'[26] with the dog, commissioned Landseer to paint his pet in the setting of his studio which also featured a bust of Scott. Exhibited at the Royal Academy in 1836 and admired by Queen Victoria, it now hangs in Balmoral.[27]

Spice featured in a silhouette by Augustin Edouart of 1831, but Ginger was painted much earlier, in 1824 (without her master) by Landseer. However, both men undoubtedly shared Landseer's feeling that '. . . the companionship of a dog seemed almost as necessary as a hat or a stick. A man was not complete without a dog, and a dog was scarcely complete without a man'.[28] In his *Journal* entry for 13 February 1826 Scott praised Landseer's dogs as 'the most magnificent things I ever saw – leaping and bounding, and grinning on the canvas'[29] thus fulfilling the prediction of C. R. Leslie, the American artist who visited Abbotsford the same year, that Landseer 'would make himself very popular, both with the master and mistress of the house, by sketching their doggies'.[30] Ruskin once said of Landseer that 'It was not by study of Raphael that he attained his eminent success, but by healthy love of a Scotch terrier.'[31]

The terriers, particularly the Dandie Dinmonts, clearly acted as a cipher of his literary fame. They are often pictured when locality and a sense of place are important, for these dogs are distinctively of the Borders. Scott's identity as a Border laird was central to his sense of self as well as part of the public image of the famous author; it established him for his English readers, for whom he hoped to interpret Scotland, as an authentic authority by virtue of ancestry and residence, as well as historical and literary knowledge.

The other element in his title of laird of Abbotsford is associated with another breed, the greyhound. His son-in-law wrote of how, in 1811, 'Scott fixed his eyes on a small farm . . . which it was understood would presently be in the market, and resolved to place himself by its acquisition in the situation to which he had probably from his earliest days looked forward as the highest object of ambition, that of a Tweedside Laird.'[32]

Scott himself wrote to his brother-in-law in August 1811 about the purchase of land along the River Tweed: 'This is the greatest incident which has lately taken place in our domestic concerns, and I assure you we are not a little proud of being greeted as *laird* and *lady* of *Abbotsford*.'[33]

Indeed, the Ettrick Shepherd, James Hogg, was to say that, 'The only foible I ever could discover in the character of Sir Walter was a too strong leaning to the old aristocracy of the country. His devotion for titled rank was prodigious . . .'[34]

For many centuries, perhaps thousands of years, the greyhound has been associated with the nobility. Perhaps first domesticated in Egypt, it is said that Cleopatra presented a miniature greyhound to Caesar. Portraits abound of European monarchs and aristocrats with their greyhounds. In an association which would have appealed to the author of *Ivanhoe*, the greyhound was brought back by Crusaders returning from the Holy Land. This breed then enters Christian iconography and is sometimes presented as a manifestation of chivalry. An unfinished oil sketch by Sir William Allan, usually called

FIGURE 5
Gala Day at Abbotsford, *by Sir William Allan. Oil on panel.*
(Scottish National Portrait Gallery, SNPG 1193)

Gala Day at Abbotsford, shows Scott as the laird at home in the Borders. At Abbotsford, Scott founded, at least in theory, an ideal community of family, friends and retainers in a quasi-feudal idyll, complete with greyhound (Fig. 5).

Scott is especially associated with a particular kind of rough-coated greyhound, the Scottish staghound, known since the sixteenth or seventeenth century when it was reputed to be the best of its kind for deer hunting. In his novel *The Talisman*, the northern greyhound is referred to as 'a most perfect creature of heaven' with the 'strength to pull down a bull' and the 'swiftness to catch an antelope'. However, the breed was much diminished by the end of the eighteenth century. 'The Jacobite Rebellion of 1745 brought an end to Highland life as it had been lived through the Middle Ages. In the grim times that followed, deerhounds became very scarce. However, the end of the Napoleonic Wars brought peace and some stability to the new landowners and to those families that had survived the Forty-Five.'[35] Archibald McNeill of Colonsay believed, early in the nineteenth century, that only a dozen or so pure-bred deerhounds were left. In 1825 he initiated, with his brother Duncan McNeill, later Lord Colonsay and Oronsay, a breeding programme which saved the breed, so renowned for its pursuit of the wild red deer, from extinction.

Over the years Scott owned several Scottish deerhounds and greyhounds which appear with him in various portraits. In general, according to those who have studied the long intertwining of human and canine history, hounds represent freedom and, through their association with hunting, virility.[36] Interestingly enough, although he owned greyhound bitches, all those with which he is painted seem to have been dogs. There appears to be, for example, no portrait which includes a gift from his fellow author George Ellis in 1810, a bitch called Lady Juliana Berners, presumably the namesake of the Prioress of Sopwell who wrote a medieval treatise on dogs. Scott clearly appreciated the animal's quality, but was not depicted in her company.

Scott, who was lame since early childhood, often wrote of how unencumbered – how whole – he felt when riding, free of his handicap. There may be some association here between hunting with hounds, in his case mostly hare-coursing, and a sense of well-being. Francis Russell, in his study of portraits of Scott, has noted that 'dogs were Scott's most regular aesthetic standbys, tangible link that they were with the out of door existence he relished'.[37]

Ownership of such animals were also part of his own family history, or so Scott wrote, in 1813, of his 'ancient pedigree' to George Ellis, an editor of medieval romances, as including 'one or two half-starved lairds, who rode a lean horse, and were followed by leaner greyhounds'.[38]

Two of the greyhounds who followed Scott were given the good Border names of Douglas and Percy, bred by Scott's friend and benefactor, William Laidlaw, with whom he often went coursing for hare. This seems to have been Scott's favourite sport, which in the early part of the nineteenth century in Scotland was enjoyed by all classes. Scott also regularly went coursing with the Duke of Buccleuch. However, by the end of 1809 he is complaining that Douglas and Percy 'wax old and *unfeary*'.[39] Percy, who died in 1812, was honoured by a monument inscribed in Gothic letters: Cy gist li preux Percie [Here lies the brave Percy]. Scott, himself a noted antiquary, wrote to Daniel Terry that 'I hope future antiquaries will debate which hero of the house of Northumberland has left his bones in Teviotdale'.[40] The visiting American novelist Washington Irving fell for the joke, although by this time, some four or five years later, Scott dismissed it as one of his 'nonsense things'.

Another greyhound, Hamlet, was presented to Scott in 1816, through Daniel Terry, as a gift from a noted breeder and sportsman in Cornwall. Mr St Aubyn originally had called the dog Marmion after Scott's poem, but Scott renamed him, with St Aubyn's permission, Hamlet, because of his 'inky coat'. Writing to Terry in September 1817, Scott kept him informed of the dog's hare-catching abilities and his developing personality: '. . . he is moreover a very funny & amiable fellow & is at this moment gnawing my shoe latchets, so you see he is in full possession of the fire side'.[41] In a letter to his son Walter two years later, he described how canine illness was treated in the absence of professional veterinarians: 'Hamlet had an inflammatory attack, and I began to think he was going mad, after the example [of] his great namesake, but Mr Laidlaw bled him and he has recovered.'[42]

Hamlet had recovered sufficiently for the American artist Charles Robert Leslie to report, during his 1824 visit, that Scott

> always liked to have a dog with him in his walk, if for nothing else but to furnish a living object in the foreground of the picture; and he noticed to me, when we were among the hills, how much interest was given to the scene by the occasional appearance of his black greyhound, Hamlet, at unexpected points.[43]

However, Scott was dismayed and probably embarrassed when Hamlet killed a sheep and stood with blood dripping from its mouth for all to see. Scott took the blame himself, suggesting that since he had given up hare-coursing Hamlet had not been chasing game for some time. Luckily, he never sinned again.

Yet another of Scott's greyhounds, Nimrod, was named after the great biblical hunter. Out walking at Huntly Burn, Scott's friend J. L. Adolphus observed that

> Several times we paused to admire the good taste, as it seemed, with which his great Highland staghound Nimrod always displayed himself on those prominent points of the little glen, where his figure, in combination with the scenery, had the most picturesque effect. Sir Walter accounted for this by observing that the situations were of that kind which the dog's instinct would probably draw him to if looking out for game.[44]

Nimrod much distressed Scott and his daughter by killing a young girl's cat and then his own feline companion, 'my acquaintance and in some sort my friend of fifteen years',[45] Hinse of Hinsefeldt. This animal was not a favourite with Andrew Shortreed, who sometimes acted as Scott's amanuensis. He was constantly losing his hat to the dog and clearly disapproved of the author's frequent caressing and occasionally kissing his canine friends.[46]

FIGURE 6
Sir Walter Scott *(with two staghounds, the grey-and-white staghound is Bran, the brown one lying by Scott's chair is Nimrod), by Sir Francis Grant.*
(Scottish National Portrait Gallery, SNPG 103)

Nimrod acquired a companion when Bran arrived in early 1830, the gift of Macpherson of Cluny, a great Highland chief whom Scott describes thus: 'He is a fine spirited boy, fond of his people, and kind to them, and the best dancer of a Highland reel now living.'[47] Bran was Fingal's giant hound in the Ossian cycle so much imbued with Celtic myth. His appearance generated some tension in the canine entourage in that 'Nim was disposed at first to savage him a little. But as Bran is young they were soon reconciled by the mediation of a pocket whip which I have got for the occasions'.[48] Scott was upset when Bran disappeared on a walk to see Newark Castle, fearing he had been stolen by 'Gypsies', and was immensely relieved when it transpired that the dog had spent a few hours in the kennels of a neighbour, John Pringle, the Member of Parliament for Selkirk, who was known for his menagerie.[49] Bran appears in, among several others, Sir John Watson Gordon's 1830 portrait of Scott, painted for Robert Cadell. The two dogs appear together in the aptly named *Sir Walter Scott with two Staghounds* by Sir Francis Grant (Fig. 6). Scott liked the picture, noting in his *Journal* that

> Frank Grant is still with me, and is well pleased, I think very deservedly so, with a cabinet picture of myself, armour and so forth, together with my two noble Staghounds . . . The dogs sate [sic] charmingly but the picture took up some time.[50]

However, Scott's most frequent and certainly most famous fellow sitter was Maida, who shares his plinth in the monument on Princes Street. They were stared at in life as well, in the streets of Edinburgh, probably because of the dog's great size. Maida's sire was said to have been a mountain dog from the Pyrenees or as the new owner put it, 'He is descended of the Blue Spanish wolf-dog, and the real deer grey-hound.'[51]

A gift to Scott from Colonel Alexander Ranaldson Macdonell of Glengarry, who is said to have been the original of Fergus McIvor, the wild Jacobite in *Waverley*, the dog was named in honour of the chieftain's brother, James, who led the 78th Highlanders to victory against the French at Maida in Calabria in 1806. Suggesting that he had added 'a most romantic inmate to my family', Scott bragged to his fellow poet Joanna Baillie that Glengarry had refused to present others of the breed 'to people of the very first rank', and described how the dog sat beside his chair during dinner but was rather afraid of the cat who regularly scratched him on his nose.[52]

Scott described his new acquisition to the Irish author Matthew Weld Hartstonge in 1816 as a being 'such as you see in the Boar hunts of Reubens and Schneiders'.[53] In the same month, in a letter to the actor Daniel Terry, he wrote

> I have got from my friend Glengarry the noblest dog ever seen on the Border since Johnnie Armstrong's time. He is between the wolf and deer greyhound, about six feet long from the tip of the nose to the tail, and high and strong in proportion: he is quite gentle, and a great favourite . . .[54] (Fig. 7)

Scott was very interested in the breeding of Maida and complained to John Wilson Croker, the Irish politician and Secretary to the Admiralty, that he had not yet found 'a suitable wife' for Maida:

FIGURE 7
Sir Walter Scott *(with Maida), by William Nicholson.*
(Scottish National Portrait Gallery, SNPG 1188)

The breed of the large greyhound, certainly one of the noblest animals which Britain has to boast, is now almost extinguished among us, although in my remembrance every gentleman in the mountains who loved sport was proud to have one. I intend to go or to send to Liddesdale in this month and I trust to find a proper female for my dog; and I

FIGURE 8
The Abbotsford Family, *by David Wilkie (including Maida and Ourisk). Oil on panel.*
(Scottish National Portrait Gallery, SNPG 1303)

> hope I shall play the part of Sir Pandarus of Troy with good success. I will keep the puppies till they are of a proper size and appearance to run with a carriage for nothing is so ugly as they are before they attain their shape. If they prove at all like their father they may be in some degree worthy to be sent to Carleton House.[55]

He must have been successful, as a son of Maida, named Gary, was sent to Lord and Lady Compton (afterwards Northampton) in 1818, and another of Maida's puppies went to Lord Hertford.

Luckily, Maida did not succeed in beheading himself in Scott's sawmill, an incident he reported on to the Duke of Buccleuch in 1818, as this dog became Scott's most frequent companion in art. The young Maida is featured in 1817 with Mrs Scott's Kintail terrier in Sir David Wilkie's *The Abbotsford Family* in which the human sitters are costumed in rustic dress (Fig. 8). During the same visit Wilkie did a sketch of Maida alone which much pleased Scott, who wrote to him:

> There is a certain old proverb which said Love me love my dog, and I feel very much flattered indeed to judge of your regard by the honour which you have done Maida. The picture is most beautiful and expresses the form and character of the animal perfectly.[56]

However, the dog grew to dislike artists. Scott wrote about Maida's loathing for the artistic set to several of his correspondents. For example, he told Lady Abercorn

> I have a very large wolf-greyhound I think the finest dog I ever saw but he has sate [*sic*] to so many artists that whenever he sees brushes & a pallet he gets up and leaves the room being sufficiently tired of the constraint.[57]

Bribes of cold beef bones from his master's hand were necessary when Maida sat as a figure in a landscape for Nasmyth.[58] Such behaviour was understandable; there were, for example, five different artists at Abbotsford for sittings in 1824. J. L. Adolphus, who visited in that year, noted that

> . . . old Maida was still alive, and now and then raised a majestic bark from behind the house. It was one of the little scenes of Abbotsford life which should have been preserved by a painter, when Sir Walter strolled out in a sunny morning to caress poor Maida, and condole with him upon being so 'very frail'; the aged hound dragging his gaunt limbs forward, painfully, with some remains of dignity, to meet the hand and catch the deep affectionate tones of his master.[59]

The voice that shook the Eildon Hills with its roar, as Scott had poetically put it in 1817, fell silent in October 1824, soon after Landseer had sketched him. In a letter to his son Charles, then an undergraduate at Oxford, he records that 'Old Maida died quietly on his straw last week after a good supper. This, considering his weak state, was a deliverance . . .'[60] Sir Thomas Lawrence had planned to include Maida in his painting of Scott (now in the Royal Collection), but the dog died during the lengthy periods between sittings which began in 1821: the picture was completed not until 1826.

Maida's grave is in the forecourt of Abbotsford. A monument, in the form of a recumbent canine, was made in advance of the dog's demise by a local stone-mason. The block is said to have begun life as a louping-on-stane which Scott, because of his lameness, used in mounting his horse. It is engraved in Latin 'Beneath the sculptured form which late you wore,/Sleep soundly, Maida, at your master's door.' Notice of his death appeared on the back page of the *Caledonian Mercury* of 28 October: 'Sir Walter Scott's fine old stag-hound, Maida, which has been introduced into several portraits of that distinguished person, died a few days since . . .'

Maria Edgeworth, whose Irish historical novels were much admired by Scott, wrote in 1830 offering him, as a replacement for Maida, an Irish wolfhound or staghound. Now seriously ill and no longer coursing for hare, Scott reluctantly refused the gift.

Early in 1832 Scott was travelling in Italy. He confessed to one of his companions, the archaeologist Sir William Gell, that 'I have got at home two very fine favourite dogs – so large, that I am almost afraid they look too handsome and too feudal for my

FIGURE 9
The Façade of Abbotsford *(the two greyhounds are probably Bran and Nimrod), by Sir William Allan.*
(National Gallery of Scotland, D 2071)

diminished income . . .'[61] Sir William Allan's 1832 watercolour of the façade of Abbotsford with two elegant greyhounds, probably Bran and Nimrod, presents just such a vision (Fig. 9). Such meditative conversation suggests that Scott was conscious of the power of the greyhound as a cipher of lairdship, as a kind of badge of his status as a member of the landed gentry.

On his return, when he was put to bed in the Dining Room where he was to die, 'His dogs assembled about his chair – they began to fawn upon him and lick his hands, and he alternately sobbed and smiled over them, until sleep oppressed him.'[62]

In 1819 Scott had suggested to the Duke of Buccleuch that Maida be included in a portrait he had commissioned. In reply, which was the last letter Scott was to receive from his chief, the Duke agrees, noting that 'It is now almost proverbial, "Walter Scott, and his Dog"'.[63] In 1821 Scott insisted that Maida be included in his portrait being undertaken by Thomas Lawrence for the King, joking that 'I want to have in Maida that there may be one handsome fellow of the party'.[64] An examination of these portraits, and his *Journal* entries and letters about these animals, clearly reveal Scott at work carefully nurturing his public image, promoting a particular view of himself as romantic poet of the Borders, and the best-selling author of the *Waverley* novels presented as the epitome of a Scottish gentleman, the genial laird of Abbotsford. However, these same sources have revealed not only the public man but also, in their warmth and intensity of affection for his dogs, the intimate Scott, the private personality behind the man of letters.

NOTES

1 *Guidebook to the Scott Memorial* (Edinburgh 1852).
2 Lockhart, *Life*, IX, p. 321.
3 *Letters*, VII, p. 141.
4 Thomas Carlyle, *Critical and Miscellaneous Essays*, 5 vols (London 1899), IV, p. 70.
5 This paper relies on Francis Russell, *Portraits of Sir Walter Scott* (London 1987) and should not be regarded as a complete list either of portraits of Scott which feature dogs or of pet portraits without Scott. It is not a study of the literary manifestations of Scott's various animals. For such an analysis see E. Thornton Cook, *Sir Walter Scott's Dogs* (Edinburgh 1931).
6 *Life*, V, p. 223.
7 *Journal*, p. 39.
8 Percy Stevenson, 'Sir Walter Scott and his Dogs', *Cornhill Magazine*, XLVII (1919), pp. 584–94.
9 Ibid., p. 589.
10 *Letters*, X, pp. 398–9.
11 Ibid.
12 *Letters*, X, p. 398.
13 *Life*, II, p. 228.
14 *Letters*, I, p. 203.
15 *Letters*, X, p. 389.
16 Wilfred Partington, *The Private Letter Books of Sir Walter Scott* (London 1930), p. 12.
17 *Letters*, II, p. 450.
18 *Letters*, II, p. 205.

19 Carson Ritchie, *The British Dog: its history from earliest times* (London 1981).
20 Author's note in *Guy Mannering*, Magnum Opus Edition, 1829, vol. 3, p. 241.
21 Ibid., p. 243.
22 *Letters*, VIII, p. 69.
23 *Letters*, IX, p. 357.
24 *Journal*, p. 294.
25 *Letters*, IX, p. 44.
26 *Letters*, IX, p. 175.
27 Sir Oliver Millar, *The Victorian Pictures in the Collection of Her Majesty The Queen* (Cambridge 1992), p. 151.
28 W. Cosmo Monkhouse, *Landseer's Animal Illustrations* (Alton 1990), p. 139.
29 *Journal*, p. 88.
30 Russell, p. 11.
31 Katharine MacDonogh, *Reigning Cats and Dogs* (London 1999), p. 22.
32 *Life*, III, p. 292.
33 *Letters*, II, p. 537.
34 James Hogg, *Domestic Manners of Sir Walter Scott* (Stirling 1909 edn), p. 62.
35 Kenneth Cassels, *A Most Perfect Creature of Heaven: The Scottish Deerhound* (Saffron Walden 1997), p. 10.
36 See MacDonogh.
37 Russell, p. 22.
38 *Letters*, III, p. 221.
39 *Letters*, II, p. 269.
40 *Letters*, III, p. 182.
41 *Letters*, IV, p. 529.
42 *Letters*, V, p. 451.
43 Russell, p. 11.
44 *Life*, IX, p. 18.
45 *Letters*, XI, p. 59.
46 *Journal*, p. 288.
47 *Letters*, XI, p. 366.
48 *Letters*, XI, p. 309.
49 *Letters*, XI, p. 327.
50 *Journal*, p. 643.
51 *Letters*, IV, p. 180.
52 *Letters*, IV, pp. 206–7.
53 *Letters*, IV, p. 226.
54 *Letters*, IV, p. 218.
55 *Letters*, V, p. 124.
56 *Letters*, V, p. 10.
57 *Letters*, VI, p. 252.
58 *Letters*, IV, p. 329.
59 *Life*, IX, p. 117.
60 *Letters*, VIII, p. 413.
61 *Life*, X, p. 140.
62 *Life*, X, p. 184.
63 Partington, p. 287.
64 *Letters*, VI, p. 368.

SCOTT, ABBOTSFORD AND THE RUSSIAN GOTHIC REVIVAL: INFLUENCE AND COINCIDENCE

Jeremy Howard

'Before you lie the ocean deeps.
Behind you Grief in anguish weeps.
On one side is the barren heath
On t'other is the groan of death.'

Answer of a Russian peasant to Peter the Great who had asked his opinion of his new Capital Saint Petersburg[1]

THE rhyme noted in Walter Scott's *Journal* was full of implication about the oppressive, inhumane and artificial appearance of the capital conceived as the centre of a new world empire. It was the product of the Minstrel of the Borders' meeting with Vladimir Davydov that same day. As if in response to the verse's latent observation on the autocratic vision that was evident in St Petersburg, the young Russian count, motivated by his prolonged immersion in the world of Scott and Abbotsford, published his own ideas for the humanisation of the built environment.

> I am certain that architecture, in comparison to painting, excites such little interest just because its art is considered more mathematical than moral. In my opinion this is the greatest mistake. The essence of human life and nature always bears many relations to the proportions of construction. So the architect who genuinely understands his purpose must first learn to draw not only the human body but also animals, plants and everything that has life.[2]

Simultaneously, Davydov, together with Alexander Bryullov, the architect most completely identifiable with the former's concerns for a moral architecture, engaged in their diverse realisation of his humanist thought. They were far from being alone. Here then, the focus is on how, in relation to Scott and Abbotsford, Davydov, Bryullov and several key writers, artists and patrons developed a Russian romantic aesthetic.

GOGOL, SCOTT AND THE EMERGENCE OF GOTHIC REVIVAL DESIGN

In 1831 the young Nikolai Gogol, author of *Dead Souls* and *The Government Inspector*, wrote an essay entitled 'Concerning the Architecture of our Times'. In it he attributed the contemporary Russian mode for the Gothic Revival style to the fundamental influence of Scott:

> Walter Scott was the first who shook the dust off Gothic architecture and showed its value to the world. From that day it has rapidly spread . . . Through the powerful words of Walter Scott taste for the Gothic has extended everywhere and penetrated everything. Even before appearing grand it has appeared in the small and fine: country cottages, cabinets, screens, tables and chairs – all have been converted to the Gothic.[3]

When the article was published in 1835 Gogol added a footnote in which he particularly praised Alexander Bryullov [Brulleau], designer of the new Gothic Revival SS Peter and Paul Church at Pargolovo, as the unique, genuine Russian architectural talent-in-waiting.[4] Anticipating the monumental imperial commissions that Bryullov was shortly afterwards to receive, Gogol's appreciation was written in the wake of the First All-Russian Manufactory Exhibition. This show, which had opened in St Petersburg in 1829, had been particularly notable for its display of furniture, applied art and domestic utensils in the 'Gothic' style, or, at least, with Gothic motifs. Exhibitors had included Heinrich Gambs & Sons, the court cabinet-maker, Russia's most prolific Gothic Revivalist, who contributed a series of small screens and variety of chairs in local birch finished with walnut; and August Montferrand, then designing the gigantic Alexander Column for Palace Square, who presented a stained-glass window. While the exhibition ran, Bryullov, then in Paris, received a letter from his brother, Fyodor [Friedrich], who was assisting Montferrand with the reliefs on the column's pedestal:

> In Petersburg everything Gothic has become greatly fashionable. In Peterhof a small palace has been built for Empress Alexandra in the Gothic taste; in Tsarskoye Selo there is a farm; now Count Potocki has already made his dining room Gothic, together with all the furniture, and, as a result, the whole of society is straining to be Gothic . . . Montferrand has mounted one stained glass window and people coming to look at it stare with mouths agape, as if at some miracle. He's valued it at 1,300 roubles so you can well imagine what a foothold 'Gotiqe' [*sic*] has now.[5]

Fyodor Bryullov's observation of the St Petersburg court's Gothic rage is illustrated by Princess Maria Baryatinskaya's Gothic 'study' in her new two-storey mansion at 46–48 St Sergey (now Tchaikovsky) Street. This was created in 1837. The architect was George Dimmert,[6] designer of numerous tenements as well as the picturesque neo-baroque Church of the Exaltation of the Cross in the Russian capital during the second quarter of the nineteenth century. A surviving watercolour gives the impression of a dark room whose quasi-spiritual environment is effected by tall ogival windows. The geometrical tracery of these contain stained-glass panels, the principal ones apparently adorned with chivalric figures. The quality of light is enhanced by the high ceiling's dark, heavily ribbed fan vault. Foils and ogives are the dominant decorative motifs and forms of the room, these being found in the chairs, tables, windows, door panels, flooring, vault and at least one of the visible pictures. Such resonant interplay of colour, light and shape contrasts with the clear bright ambience of the neoclassical music salon and nursery seen through the open door of the study.[7]

AROUND THE SCOTT-RUSSIA AFFAIR: NICHOLAS I, ALLAN AND BRYULLOV

Walter Scott was revered in Russian circles. It is worth recalling here that his poems and books were translated into Russian very quickly after they had appeared in Great Britain. They were published both in periodicals and as separate volumes. By the mid-1820s, *Kenilworth* was out, as were, for example, *A Legend of Montrose*, *Old Mortality*, *Guy Mannering*, *Waverley*, *The Heart of Midlothian*, *The Antiquary*, *The Abbot* and *Ivanhoe*. The last had even been adapted for the stage by Prince Alexander Shakhovskoy, its St Petersburg premiere occurring in 1821, less than two years after the novel had first been published. There followed performances of *The Pirate* (1823) and *The House of Aspen* (1832). These were accompanied by a wave of *tableaux vivants* 'on subjects from Walter Scott, in appropriate historical costumes, in the salons of the artistocracy'.[8]

The literary side of the Scott phenomenon in Russia is well known and has been substantially researched.[9] His impact in spheres other than literature has been relatively little explored. Likewise, given that he considered 'the Russians had been the saviours of Europe' for their heroic successes in the Napoleonic wars, the respectful impact Russia had on Scott's thought and persuasions has received scant attention.[10] Here, then, although Scott's influence in Russia takes precedence, the Scott-Russia relationship is treated as a two-way affair. This entails partial focus being given to specific, mainly artistic, stimuli that one side provided (or is perceived as having provided) for the other's development.

One of the leading translators of Scott's verse was the romantic poet Vasily Zhukovsky, who was simultaneously employed as tutor of Russian language and literature in the 'German' household of Tsar Nicholas I and his wife Alexandra (former Princess Charlotte of Prussia). Yet it was neither Zhukovsky, nor indeed untranslated Scott, that were the principal conduits for Tsar Nicholas and his court's acquaintance with the writer. Rather, there were distinct alternatives, most of them lesser-known aspects of the Scott relationship with Russia, and it is these that this paper explores. In particular, by selecting for discussion examples from a distinct range of fields, and within them some individual peculiarities, the focus is turned upon what can be considered as Scott's impact on approaches to architecture, interior design, collecting and history. How much may be perceived as his influence and how much may be attributed simply to parallel cultural inclinations remains, of course, open to question. What cannot be denied, however, is that the images both of Abbotsford and of Scott himself had, and continue to have, immense power and attraction in Russian art and thought.

The taste of Tsar Nicholas I played a key role in fostering the Russian court's Scott vogue. Following the allied victory over Napoleon and the successful conclusion of the Congress of Vienna, he had visited Britain to cement relationships. With his elder brother Alexander still on the Russian throne, he arrived in Edinburgh as Grand Duke Nicholas in December 1816. Accompanying him was Baron Paul von Nicolai (1777–1866), a German in the Russian diplomatic service in Britain and a close follower of British fashions. Within five years of the visit von Nicolai employed Charles Heathcote Tatham to design a 'Saxon Gothic tower', known as the Ludwigstein Chapel (Fig. 1) in remembrance of his father Ludwig von Nicolai, atop an island in his Finnish estate of Mon Repos. In fact, the estate, which ran along the northern Baltic shore of the Karelian isthmus, made use of the natural landscape, with its granite rocks, cliffs, pine trees and undulating coastline, to establish a very effective, romantic, 'Ossianic' park. Whereas it would be difficult to construe Scott's 'atmospheric' influence as either direct or determinant, the fact that von Nicolai was in Nicholas' entourage during the Edinburgh visit in the role of 'mentor' is significant since it means he played a principal part in forming the young prince's taste.[11]

FIGURE 1
Ludwigstein Chapel ('Ludwigsberg'), Mon Repos, Vyborg. Charles Heathcote Tatham, 1821.
(Photograph: Jeremy Howard, 1999)

Another important companion on Nicholas' trip was his physician, Dr Alexander Crichton, a native of Edinburgh. It was almost certainly through Crichton's agency that Nicholas became the first major patron of the young painter William Allan, himself recently returned from a decade in Russia. Before his departure for eastern Europe, Allan had worked as a painter of armorial bearings on carriage panels for Crichton & Field, an eminent Edinburgh coachmaking company owned by Lieutenant-Colonel Patrick Crichton, brother of Alexander. Upon his arrival in St Petersburg in 1805 it had been Crichton who had introduced him in fashionable social circles. Now, the royal patronage, and the publicity it received, brought Allan to the attention of Scott's circle. A particular chord was struck on 25 January 1817, when the founding issue of *The Scotsman* devoted its first attempt at art criticism to an extensive review of Allan's contemporary exhibition and the purchase of his works by Nicholas. Excerpts are worth citing.

> Mr Allan seems to delight most in local history and heroic landscape. His fable is always well managed, and is either interesting or humorous, or both. His subjects are adapted to his style of painting, and his style to his subject. Harshness is always avoided in both; for his anxiety is to gratify, not to astonish. And yet, after feasting the eye for some time on any of his best pieces, and attending to all its merits, one feels astonished by reflection . . .
>
> His great propriety in the representation of character could be attained only by an observer endowed with equal industry and genius. For the truth of this we need only refer to the figure of the robber who leans upon his sword, and endeavours to prevent himself from being over-reached; to the musicians and the dancer in *The Jewish Wedding*; and to the pampered, despotic Turk who lolls on his cushions, and amuses himself with buying Circassian beauties . . .
>
> We cannot leave . . . his great picture of *The Circassians* without taking notice of . . . the hatred which it excites generally against tyranny, and the pathos of many of the subordinate circumstances. It is impossible to look at the female who is seen embracing her child, or the agony of the mother who is deprived of hers, without being touched; and the infant which is thus torn from the breast of its mother may be considered as a chef d'oeuvre, for drawing, attitude and expression.
>
> Mr Allan is, indeed, a master in representing the characteristic. His pictures abound with figures of an expression so true and natural, that even their foreign costume does not prevent us from recognising what we have frequently met with in real life . . . In saying that Mr Allan excells in delineating what is characteristic, we are far from intending to insinuate anything against his ideas of grace and beauty. The figures, so lately before us in *Haslan Gheray*, and that of the Young Boy in No. I, furnished ample proofs that he is also master of this important branch of his art. In the last mentioned picture there was an enlivening clearness, which had an excellent effect when compared with the more rich, tempered, and qualified colouring and lights of No. II. We regret exceedingly that Scotland has been deprived of the small picture, *The Sale of Circassian Boys*, No. I, *Haslan Gheray*, No. XI, and *The Bashkirs*, No. III, all now despatched to London, to the purchaser, the Grand Duke Nicholas of Russia. It is a reflection, we cannot help thinking, on our national taste, that it is left to a foreign Prince to be most forward in affording encouragement to Mr Allan.

> *Haslan*, one of Mr Allan's most recent performances, possessed great breadth, and was painted in a tone considerably different from his other pictures. The figures were surrounded with high rocks, and a low light indicating morning; and produced a suitably cool effect; the whole picture exhibiting that liquid juicy appearance produced by the trees, shrubs, and other surrounding accessories. The river, in perfect unison with the rest of the picture, was made to lave its banks, and sparkle on the leaves of the bordering plants in a very beautiful manner. But we regret still more the loss of *The Bashkirs*. In poetical conception it perhaps surpassed all the rest. A boundless desert spread off at one side; and on the foreground we saw the exhausted exiles lying down in despair. One of them kneeled, and seemed to beg that an end might be put to his existence; the rest were represented in attitudes strongly expressive both of physical and mental suffering.[12]

Within a year the artist and Scott had begun a friendly collaboration that was to bear fruit right up to Allan's death in 1850. First signs involved Allan's drawing the Sword of State from the rediscovered Honours of Scotland and Scott assisting in the acquisition by the Earl of Wemyss of Allan's *Circassian Captives*. If this represented indirect Russian influence on Scott's artistic patronage and taste, Scott's interest in Russia was simultaneously to be crystallised in literature. For, most significantly, Nicholas had also met Scott during his stay in Edinburgh. On 19 December 1816, the day after Nicholas had visited Allan's studio and had his portrait drawn by the artist, a banquet in his honour was given by the Lord Provost, William Arbuthnott. Scott wrote an ode for the occasion. It bore much in common with the themes and sentiments evident or implicit in the Allan pictures bought by Nicholas and Lord Wemyss. Set to Haydn's air 'God Save the Emperor Francis', it pandered to Nicholas' vanity by praising his brother's role in liberating Europe from Napoleonic tyranny:

> God protect brave Alexander!
> Heaven defend the noble Czar!
> Mighty Russia's high commander,
> First in Europe's banded war.
> For the realms he did deliver
> From the Tyrant overthrown,
> Thou, of every good the Giver,
> Grant him long to bless his own.
>
> Bless him! 'mid his land's disaster,
> For her rights who battled brave;
> Of the land of foemen master,
> Bless him, who their wrongs forgave.
> O'er his just resentment victor,
> Victor over Europe's foes,
> Late and long, Supreme Director,
> Grant in peace his reign may close.

Hail! then, hail! illustrious stranger!
Welcome to our mountain strand;
Mutual interests, hopes, and dangers,
Link us with thy native land.
Foemen's force, or false beguiling,
Shall that union ne'er divide;
Hand in hand, while peace is smiling,
And, in battle, side by side.[13]

From this point on, if indeed he had not been before, Nicholas was a committed and fervent admirer of Scott. Scott, on the other hand, as his *Journal* was later to show,

FIGURE 2
Walter Scott. Alexander Bryullov. 1826. Engraving.

remained alert to the dangers of the despotic and expansionist politics of Nicholas as Tsar. And while the sympathies expressed in the ode undoubtedly coincided with Scott's own, he dismissed it (in a contemporary letter to John Ballantyne) as 'a trumpery thing'.[14]

FIGURE 3
Ss Peter and Paul Church, Pargolovo, St Petersburg. Alexander Bryullov.
(Photograph: Jeremy Howard, 1987)

The Russian court and high society rapidly followed Nicholas' suit in terms of Scott admiration. Ten years after the Edinburgh visit, on 6 November 1826, an evening at which Scott was guest of honour was held by Princess Praskovya Golitsyna (née Shuvalova), while Scott was in Paris for the production of Rossini's opera *Ivanhoe*. The salon bore witness to Scott's great influence and renown in Russian circles. It was regarded as one of *the* events of the winter season: 'all Parisian society was there . . . All the women wore Scottish plaids, scarfs, ribbons etc etc.' Scott himself noted in his diary that there was a 'whole covey of princesses of Russia arrayd in tartan with music and singing to boot'.[15] One of those present was also a Russian artist: Aleksandr Bryullov, the brilliant young architect and painter discovered by Gogol, a graduate of the St Petersburg Academy, then on his Grand Tour and having recently returned to Paris from London. He drew Scott's portrait for the elderly Princess Golitsyna; she had it engraved and it was then widely reproduced in Russia – in the *Moscow Messenger* (1827) and in various Scott publications, e.g. *Anne of Geierstein* (St Petersburg 1830) (Fig. 2).

The appearance of Bryullov's portrait of Scott presaged the architect's return to St Petersburg and emergence as a leading exponent of the Gothic Revival. His first commission was a picturesque church atop a small hillock and above a pond on the (now late) Princess Golitsyna's Shuvalov family estate at Pargolovo to the north of the city. This was the Church of SS Peter and Paul, the building of which began in 1831 and which was consecrated in 1840 (Fig. 3). It was commissioned by Countess Varvara Polier, the widow of Golitsyna's brother and niece of Shakovskoy, the first interpreter of Scott (in the play *Ivanhoe*) for the Russian stage. As the church was to be a memorial to her recently deceased second husband Count Adolphe Polier, a French explorer and master of ceremonies at Nicholas' court, it was constructed on the slope above his ogival-shaped burial vault. Bryullov completed it as a restrained, symmetrical Gothic basilica with a fine coppered openwork spire and crown surmounting the western portal, and stained-glass windows by the local master Ryabkov. The Pargolovo church was to prove a signpost for the new Russian Gothic Revival movement, yet Bryullov rejected the slavish following of style. Instead he followed the project with the neo-Romanesque Lutheran St Peter's Church on Nevsky Prospekt (1832–8). Then, after a disastrous fire, which lasted three days (17–19 December 1837), he was employed by Nicholas to redesign the destroyed interiors of the Winter Palace. The Gothicised Imperial Alexander Hall, Malachite Room, Pompeii Dining Room, White Hall, Moorish Bathroom, Greek Rotonda, etc. showed him as an eclectic connoisseur of style. These qualities reappeared in the interiors of the Marble Palace, which he designed for Nicholas' son Konstantin on his marriage (1844–51). Perhaps, as suggested by some of the other examples given below, a significant coincidence with Scott can be found in the range and exploration of antiquity present in these commissions from Tsar Nicholas.

ABBOTSFORD AND RUSSIA: THE DAVYDOV EFFECT

Significantly, both Bryullov and Scott had a connection with Davydov. From the early 1820s numerous articles began to appear in the Russian press devoted not only to Scott but also to Abbotsford. These studied Scott's medievalism and surveyed his collection of antiquities.[16] They also encouraged Russian tourists to visit the laird. Foremost among them were the historian and chronicler of European life Alexander Turgenev who spent several days at Abbotsford in August 1828 (unfortunately at a time when Scott was not keeping his *Journal*); Aleksey Olenin, son of the president of the St Petersburg Academy of Arts, who arrived in November 1825;[17] in the same year, Vladimir Davydov [later Count Orlov-Davydov, 1809–82], a student at Edinburgh University and grandson of Count Vladimir Orlov, director of the St Petersburg Academy of Science. Davydov stands out as the Russian who established the most intimate contact with Scott and Abbotsford. A particular means for the dissemination of his impressions within his homeland appears to have been the interior design of his family residences.

Davydov and Scott got on excellently, the young Russian visiting Abbotsford on several occasions until 1828, and accompanying Scott to the Selkirk elections in 1826. He also put Scott in touch with his uncle, Denis Davydov, the partisan-hero of the Napoleonic Wars, a poet, and thereafter a source of some items of armour for the Abbotsford collection. Vladimir Davydov later recalled:

> I was very glad about the choice of Edinburgh, not so much for my study of philosophy, as in that city was living Walter Scott, in whom we had all begun to get a suspicion of *The Great Unknown* – the author of *Waverley*, *Rob Roy*, *Ivanhoe* and so many other novels that are known throughout the world . . . Scotland has long been renowned for its hospitality,

> a trait which is characteristic of all those who live in mountainous countries. In those days Russians were welcomed particularly graciously. I quickly got an opportunity to get acquainted with Walter Scott. Together with my tutor [August Colyer] I set out with a letter of recommendation for Abbotsford, a castle in a mixed Gothic style, erected by the poet on the shore of the rapidly flowing River Tweed, so famous in history and verse. A powdered servant informed us that the laird had left with his guest Thomas Moore the Irish poet, for the ruins of Melrose Abbey but would return in a couple of hours. We awaited the poet in the tall entrance hall, decorated right up to the ceiling with armour of various ages and dimly lit by windows on which were stained glass coats-of-arms. Scott arrived just before dinner time and received us with great civility, which soon took the form of a very friendly disposition . . . The poet so marvelled at the elevated role of Russia in 1812 that I, the Russian student, was beside myself with feelings of pride and rapture.[18]

While Scott's own *Journal* and correspondence indicate the warmth and respect he felt for Davydov, the effects of their relationship were to find telling material expression. Presents were exchanged. The young Russian received a signed copy of *The Talisman* and, to present to his uncle, an engraving of the portrait Raeburn had painted of Scott in 1822–3. Davydov, in turn, gave Scott a steel snuff-box, presumably of Russian manufacture: 'wrought and lined with gold, having my arms on the top and on the sides various scenes from the environs and principal public buildings of Saint Petersburgh – a *joli cadeau*'.[19] He was also one of the most generous contributors to the 'Abbotsford subscription', being recognised by J. G. Lockhart, George Cranstoun and Alexander Young for the key part he played thereby in the preservation of the estate.[20]

If Davydov helped to secure Abbotsford, his acquaintance with it and its laird affected profoundly the cultivation of his own views and surroundings. After leaving Scotland he removed to London, where he worked in the Russian Embassy. Quite probably encouraged by his exposure to Sir William Hamilton's cosmopolitan philosophy, he travelled to Paris to attend lectures by Francois Guizot and Victor Cousin before visiting various German universities on his way back to Russia.[21] Through inheritance and marriage he became extremely rich. In 1832 he married Princess Olga Baryatinskaya, the eldest child of Maria Baryatinskaya. Having been brought up in Italy, Davydov took his young family there in 1833. Though he missed Scott's visit by a few months, the circle in which he moved had shared that episode of Scott's life. Most significantly, Karl Bryullov, the greatest Russian romantic painter, and brother of Alexander, had met Scott. During his four weeks in Rome in April–May 1832, Scott had requested and been granted a visit to the artist's studio in order to view his great *The Last Day of Pompeii*, then nearing completion after six years' work. By this time Scott was no longer strong enough to keep his *Journal*. Nevertheless, it is known that he spent a while studying the enormous (4.5 × 6.5m) canvas and was greatly moved by its Vulcanian comment on the history of civilisation. His recorded response was that it was 'an epic', 'an entire, veritable poem'. Bryullov observed that 'Walter Scott sat before the picture the whole morning. He penetrated its every aspect, its meaning'.[22]

Scott had gained a rare preview of *The Last Day of Pompeii*. Davydov arrived in Rome as the picture went on public show for the first time and caused a sensation. Its acclaim meant that Bryullov's contemporary celebrity status was without parallel. He was fêted by European society. His most loyal and loving admirer was Countess Julia Samoilova who featured in the foreground of the painting as the figure of the mother embracing her daughters.[23] Davydov's support was barely less ardent. He had Bryullov paint a group portrait of his family in Rome in 1834 and then, following up Russian interests in the Greek War of Independence, took him on his expedition to the eastern Mediterranean. As Britain vied with Russia for political control over liberated Greece, it was hardly coincidence that Davydov should embark on this expedition not long after Scott had been forced to abandon ideas of a Greek sojourn of his own. Encouraged by his acquaintance with Sir Frederick Adam, the British High Commissioner in Corfu and a key figure in the British campaign, Scott had planned to visit the Ionian Islands and Greece with a new tale of chivalry in mind. It was to be one of his last unfulfilled wishes. It would be for Davydov to make an expedition. He took with him Bryullov, the architect Nikolay Yefimov (who made many drawings of the historical sites) and the archaeologist Dr Kramer. The result, rather than the Aegean romance envisaged by Scott, was to be Davydov's more serious and factual *Travel Notes taken during a sojourn to the Ionian Islands, Greece, Asia Minor and Turkey in 1835* (St Petersburg 1839–40) with an accompanying *Atlas* illustrated with Bryullov's and Yefimov's drawings. No sooner had it appeared than Davydov sent a copy to Lockhart. Within a year or so, on the merits of this work, a doctorate was conferred upon him by the University of Edinburgh.[24] Bryullov made many images of the sites and peoples encountered, not all of which were published. Had Scott lived, what he would probably have appreciated most was the special attention the artist paid to Greek soldiers, depicting them in dramatic poses in the mountains wearing their pleated kilt-like fustanellas. These even included a portrait study of the klephtic leader Theodore Kolokotronis in proud, pensive mood.

Upon settling in his homeland after the Greek expedition Davydov began work for the Ministry of the Interior and published his travel notes. Bringing with him a large quantity of editions of the classics, including Herodotus' *History* and Pausanias' *Description of Greece* he became an ardent bibliophile, adding to the library left him by his grandfather and buying whole collections of books. Simultaneously, he and his family became involved in the redesign of their houses. The alterations to the style of decoration and the treatment of space introduced a new, enlivening intimacy and variety. This accorded with Davydov's stated concern for a humane, arousing approach to architecture. His *Travel Notes* contained further thoughts on this.

> The secret of ancient architecture, which we have completely lost, is this: how, in constructions that demand symmetry, to observe some picturesque disorder which forces the eye to turn with pleasure from one object to another. We can see this very well in the remains found in Rome. If, on the basis of the unearthed foundations, we were now to rebuild and restore all the former edifices then they would be arranged in extreme disorder in relation to one another. One pediment would protrude at an angle over another. From

> a certain viewpoint it would appear that the structures were assembled without any order, as if one had been raised upon another. From this we would see a considerably greater degree of chance, and hence more variety, than in the rectangular systems that presently define our main squares.[25]

It would seem reasonable to suggest that Davydov's eclectic taste can be felt in the Sotira watercolour of his mother-in-law's Gothic study. Are those his children playing in the neo-classical nursery-music room beyond? They seem to be of the right age and gender. Did he bring the mysterious Sotira with him from Greece? In any case the two appear connected again for Sotira was to make at least five interior views of Pavlino, a country house ten miles along the Peterhof road from St Petersburg. This had been built for Davydov's in-laws in the early 1830s. The views, made between 1835 and 1838, show great stylistic variety. At the same time they reveal a predilection for Gothic Revival furnishings and for walls covered with romantic paintings of ruins, moonlit nights, seascapes, Italian scenes, knights and even a life-size *Anne Boleyn taking leave of the infant Princess Elizabeth*.[26] Coincidentally, Davydov's principal excursion into art criticism was dedicated to the Catholic revivalist Friedrich Overbeck: in 1865 he published an essay on the Nazarene leader's huge *Sacrament of Penance* (now in the State Hermitage Museum, St Petersburg).

Although the interior design of Davydov's St Petersburg mansion remains a mystery due to its subsequent turbulent history, what is known is that he occupied the family house on St Sergei Street, opposite that of Princess Baryatinskaya, and that in the 1860s he had it rebuilt by Karl Kolmann, an architect renowned for his experimentation with historical styles. Most significantly, however, after inheriting the Otrada [literally: Joy] estate near Moscow he made it his principal residence and had its essentially neoclassical palace transformed by Mikhail Bykovsky. In the late 1840s and early 1850s Bykovsky 'romanticised' the complex in keeping with Davydov's ideas. Corner terrace-rotundas with external staircases were added to the main block, these allowing extensive views of the surrounding *jardin anglais*. Individualised red brick wings, pavilions and conservatories, joined by a variety of internal and external links, were added. Karl Bryullov painted a ceiling and Bykovsky also planned a Gothic rib-vaulted spiral stairwell to the rear.[27] Davydov made Otrada home to his extensive library and broadened the repertoire of his estate theatre, introducing, for example, a gypsy chorus.

THREE ESTATES

If the stamp of Davydov upon Russian material and intellectual culture bears at least some imprint of Scott's approach to Antiquity and the Middle Ages, it also reflects the wider Russian appeal of Abbotsford and Scott. As Pushkin, Lermontov, Gogol, Zhukovsky and others started to develop a distinctive Russian romantic literature in which the fate of the individual, and individual choice, was paramount, so were many Russian estates transformed. In the post-Napoleonic era imperial, classical, ordered regularity began to be considered inappropriate for the home. Three projects stand out

FIGURE 4
The Arsenal, Alexandrovka, Tsarskoye Selo. Adam Menelaws. 1819–34.
(Early photograph)

as having particular 'Scott' resonance in their novel historicising. The first two, at Tsarskoye Selo and Peterhof, are in the environs of St Petersburg; the third, in Alupka, is on the southern, Black Sea coast of the Crimea.

The 'Alexandrovka' project at Tsarskoye Selo was the joint creation of the brothers Alexander I and Nicholas I. It was begun by Tsar Alexander in 1818 and completed by Tsar Nicholas in 1834. As such its creation roughly coincides with that of Abbotsford. If one can surmise that Scott, because he had elicited Allan's help in arranging his Armoury in 1818, had been impressed by the seventy-two-piece collection of Near-Eastern costume and armour exhibited by William Allan at Marnoch's Gallery on Princes Street in 1817, it seems likely that he would also have approved of the Arsenal, designed by a fellow citizen of Edinburgh, Adam Menelaws. Ostensibly, the Arsenal (Fig. 4) copied the symmetrical castellate form with polygonal corner towers of Isaac Ware's belvedere, Cranbourne Tower, in Windsor Great Park (Shrub Hill, c. 1756, for the Duke of Cumberland).[28] Yet, instead of being triangular in plan, with three crenellated towers surrounding a hexagonal central space, the Arsenal is quadrangular, with four towers flanking an octagonal mass. It was sited at the centre of Alexandrovka's radiating paths as a symbol of the strength and historic place of Russia in the world family of nations. In fact, it replaced and used the materials of a rococo pavilion known as Mon Bijou. Built (by Rastrelli) seventy years earlier for Empress Elizabeth, this was now regarded as too feminine and too French.

The new Arsenal was garrisoned by twenty veterans of the Napoleonic Wars. There were two main floors. On the ground floor was located the library, study, chancellery and great hall lit by large Venetian-style windows with seventy-two sixteenth-century and seventeenth-century stained-glass lights. The first floor was dominated by the so-called Hall of Knights, a tall, octagonal chamber decorated at the base of its vaults with shields representing the separate provinces of the Russian empire: the coats of arms of the provincial governors appeared on each. Distributed around the hall, up the stairs and over the walls of the ground floor was Nicholas' 5,000-piece collection of arms. The acquisition, arrangement and curating of the works was the responsibility of the Arsenal's keeper, Charles Sayger [Sager], apparently a philosopher from Lancashire, who had arrived in Russia in 1813 to become Nicholas' first English teacher. Indeed, in 1829, Nicholas sent Sager off with General Diebitsch's troops on the Balkan campaign that resulted in Greek independence, his mission being, first and foremost, to collect foreign arms for the Arsenal. Among those he brought back were Turkish and Albanian weapons. In fact, Nicholas' collecting habits seem to bear much in common with Scott's, particularly with regard to the commemoration of recent historical events.[29] He had begun to collect as early as 1811, when he acquired the sabre of a Turkish pasha, taken during Kutuzov's Danubian campaign against the Turks that year. Other exhibits destined for the Arsenal were those of other 'vanquished' opponents of Russia: there was Tadeusz Kosciuszko's sabre; Imam Shamil's pole-axe and cudgel; Cossack Hetman Ivan Mazepa's sword and mace; and some of Napoleon's personal belongings. Sager's *Rare, Ancient and Eastern Arms in the Imperial Arsenal*, a two-part catalogue of the Arsenal's collection published in 1840, gives an indication of its breadth. As keeper he took special care in the display of the collection: grouping specific weapons; picturesquely posing the antique suits of armour; and having special glass cabinets made in the chancellery for the guns, swords, daggers and war trophies which were decorated with gems and valuable metals. In addition, Scott-like *tableaux vivants* were organised in and around the Arsenal. On 3 May 1842, for example, thirty-two members of the royal family and court took part in a chivalric pageant known as a 'Carousel': the sixteen ladies wore sixteenth-century costumes. The men dressed up in the Arsenal's armour and became cavaliers, these including Nicholas and his son Alexander who wore armour of 'Emperor Maximilian's time'. The occasion was celebrated in a painting of the same year by Horace Vernet (now in the collection of Tsarskoye Selo Palace Museum). Clearly Nicholas' love of chivalry was akin to Scott's. Further, like Scott, he was no ordinary collector: he crammed his Arsenal with numerous other historical and exotic curiosities – Catherine the Great's walking stick, rare Eastern saddle-cloths, ethnographic and archaeological artefacts, monies.

In fact the Arsenal was just the central part of an exotic ensemble created at Alexandrovka by Menelaws. Other elements included a castellated Llama House; an 'Indian-style' Elephant pavilion with elephants from the Emir of Bukhara and Negus of Abyssinia; a Gothic farm and Pensioners' Stables; the White, or Heirs, Tower; and the Chapel. The cuboid Gothic White Tower (1821–7) rose to 38m in height. It was approached via an artificial ruin, earth ramparts and a moat that were built using the material of the old walls of the estate. On the terrace in front of it were sited two sculpted lions, as if obstructing the approach to this 'House of Knights'. On either side of the entrance and apertures on the ground floor were lancet niches, eight in all, which housed statues of Russian warriors [*vityazei*] and medieval knights (by the sculptor Vasily Demut-Malinovsky). In reality, the tower was a fancy, six-storey residence for

Nicholas' sons, hence its alternative name. On the ground floor was the dining hall with pantry. The walls were appropriately painted with polychrome bouquets of flowers and cereals in baskets as well as perspectival Gothic ornaments and columns in grisaille. The reception hall on the second floor, with its balcony, was the most elaborate room. It was decorated by an Italian artist, named (appropriately enough) Giovanni Battista Scotti. On the stuccoed ceiling he painted 'Glories holding chivalric coats of arms with military trophies', and on the walls 'Battles from the Crusades' in which medieval Christian knights engaged the infidel (102 figures in all). The reference to Nicholas' ongoing and current Russian campaign against the Turks (also known as a Holy War) was clear. For the study on the floor above, Scotti also painted Gothic architectural motifs and twelve medallions containing groups of knights with coats of arms and trophies. Surely, the inspiration of Scott's *Ivanhoe* and *The Talisman* played a part in all of this.

FIGURE 5
The Chapel, Alexandrovka, Tsarskoye Selo. Adam Menelaws. 1825–28.
(Photograph: Jeremy Howard, 1994)

The other principal structure in the picturesque Alexandrovka park was the artificially ruined Chapel which Menelaws built between 1825 and 1828 (Fig. 5). This is another quadrangular tower; but now, with its squat pyramidal spire and pinnacles, ogival windows with lancet and rose tracery, it has become more reminiscent of a Scottish church, more particularly Dunkeld Cathedral as it appeared (after a drawing by Paul Sandby) on a round compotier in the famous Green Frog Dinner Service. It was to be Nicholas' private house of prayer. As such it was com-pleted with stained-glass depicting biblical subjects, sculpted angels by Demut-Malinovsky, a weather-cock atop the spire, and a beau-tiful two-metre white Carrara marble crucifix executed in Stuttgart by the German sculptor Johann von Dannecker.

The Gothic spirituality of the Chapel set among the slender

FIGURE 6
St Alexander Nevsky Chapel, Alexandria, Peterhof. Karl Friedrich Schinkel, Adam Menelaws, 1829–33.
(Photograph: Jeremy Howard, 1994)

tree trunks of the wooded park was to find echoes in Menelaws' next project for Nicholas: another picturesque palace and park complex, known as Alexandria. This time the estate was named after his wife, Alexandra, and comprised extensive (116ha) wooded land on the southern Baltic coast west of St Petersburg that had been given to Nicholas by his brother Tsar Alexander. It was to be the favourite family retreat, particularly following the suppression of the 1825 Decembrist Uprising. There, between 1829 and 1833, Menelaws built the Alexander Nevsky Chapel (Fig. 6) to designs by Schinkel, and, most important, the Cottage Palace (1826–9). The latter, a belvedere overlooking the Gulf of Finland, was inspired by the contemporary taste for *cottages ornées* among the British gentry and by a medievalist vision akin to that of Abbotsford. Yet, since it fused Gothic, oriental and marine elements and was again dedicated to victory over the Turks, there are differences.

Essentially, the Cottage Palace is a two-storey villa, with a garret for Nicholas' naval study and attic (Fig. 7). On the exterior the Gothic detailing is restrained and light, restricted to the thicket-like white ironwork with its floriate ogee arches (created at Charles Baird's ironworks in St Petersburg); the limited quatrefoil tracery of the windows,

FIGURE 7
Cottage Palace, Alexandria, Peterhof. Adam Menelaws. 1826–9. Northern façade.
(Photograph: Jeremy Howard, 1994)

FIGURE 8
Cottage Palace, Alexandria, Peterhof. Adam Menelaws. 1826–9. Painted stairwell.
(Photograph: Jeremy Howard, 1994)

only a few of which are lancet-shaped; and the cornice and window mouldings. In addition, the estate's own coat of arms appears: an azure shield with argent knight's sword piercing a wreath of argent roses, symbolising the union of Nicholas and Alexandra. The motto of the estate, 'For Faith The Tsar and Loyalty', was sometimes inscribed around the edge of the shield. In addition trophies from the 'Holy War' with Turkey were incorporated into the building and its gardens, these including a cannon and a stone with an inscription venerating Sultan Mahmut II, taken from the Turkish forts at Isanchi and Varna. The picturesque massing, variety of roofing and gabling, and almost exaggerated interactive play of internal and external space with extended loggias, verandahs, balconies, galleries and porches, is compact. Inside, however, the space feels relatively confined and circulates essentially around the central drawing room of the ground floor. The homely concept and absence of great suites of halls and corridors was quite revolutionary as far as a residence for Russian royalty was concerned. Gothic took over, and it was for this reason that the palace was mentioned in Bryullov's letter as one of the initial sparks of the Gothic Revival in contemporary Russia. Scotti was again employed for the painted decoration, his most important contribution (completed by his assistants) being the covering of the staircase hall and the stoves with perspectival painting of Gothic architectural features (Fig. 8). The Gambs company produced most of the furnishings and fittings, again using Gothic forms, for screens, chairs, cabinets and tables. These were complemented by Gothic light fixtures and stuccowork, a Gothic spiral staircase, Gothic cathedral clocks and caskets, Gothic inkwells and a Gothicised piano, many of which items were displayed at the 1829 Manufactory Exhibition.

Significantly, the furniture in Nicholas' study used wood taken from trees in Peter the Great's famous Summer Garden that had been uprooted during a storm and flood in 1824. It is also worth noting that the Wedgwood Green Frog Dinner Service with its British views was displayed in the Cottage Palace and that the walls of Nicholas' study were adorned with *Harbour at Night* and *On a Sailing Ship* by Caspar David Friedrich; works that had been purchased by the Tsar from the artist in 1820. Undoubtedly influenced by Zhukovsky's friendship with Friedrich, both works can be seen as emblematic of Nicholas' Alexandria vision: they feature tenuously touching couples seen from behind, gazing across stretches of water towards a panoply of Gothic spires and masts. The aspiring diagonals and verticals of these are, at various levels, linked hermetically with the depersonalised young figures.

The sense of communion and recognition of a new destiny in Friedrich's painting coincide with the Romanov vision of Russian mission, particularly as embodied by Nicholas, his wife, court and government. Simultaneously this was to find another, exceptional form of expression, with different Scott connections, in Count Mikhail Vorontsov's Alupka palace estate in the Crimea (Fig. 9). One of the principal points of contact is Edward Blore. Just as he was acting as Scott's consultant and architect at Abbotsford, Blore was commissioned by Vorontsov to design his residence on land, recently acquired on Russia's new southern seaboard. This land had long been a Turkish dominion, having been governed for centuries by the Tatar khanate. In 1823 it was transferred to Vorontsov as governor of Southern Russia and Bessarabia. Vorontsov's

FIGURE 9
Alupka Palace, Crimea. Edward Blore, William Hunt, 1831–48. Northern façade.
(Photograph: Jeremy Howard, 1997)

appointment followed his achievements as a military commander in the Napoleonic Wars. The period of building on the estate coincided with the prominent part he was to play in Nicholas' 'Holy War' with Turkey during 1828–9, and the subsequent Caucasian campaign against Shamil. Significantly, he was the son of Semyon Vorontsov, the long-serving, Anglophile, Russian Ambassador to Britain. Until he settled in Russia in 1801, at the age of 19, he had spent virtually the whole of his life in England. Furthermore, his sister was married to the Earl of Pembroke, for whom Blore was working at Wilton in 1831 when Vorontsov arrived looking for an architect to employ at his new property. By that time, an incredible landscaped park had already been laid out by the gardener Karl Kebach. It included a great variety of trees, waterfalls, fountains, rocky crags, grottoes, lakes and glades. Blore was given drawings of some of its buildings, which included an 'Indian mosque', 'Asian pavilion' and various fountains.

Scott had employed Blore to blend medievalist styles and to 'Scottify' Abbotsford by means of the addition of characteristic elements of the 'old-fashioned Scotch stile which delighted in notch'd Gable ends & all manner of Bartizans'.[30] For Vorontsov he produced

FIGURE 10
Alupka Palace, Crimea. Edward Blore, William Hunt, 1831–48. Southern portal.
(Photograph: Jeremy Howard, 1997)

an alternative medievalist-'native' synthesis. Blore began work in 1831, sending to the Crimea his assistant William Hunt, to supervise construction and entrusting him with making the necessary adjust-ments for the site and taste. Building continued into early 1848, and Hunt remained in Alupka until 1852.

There are five main buildings in the complex, these being linked by narrow walled passages, an iron bridge, flights of stairs, terraces, courtyards, verandahs and corridors. The asymmetry of the planning, the spreading horizontality and the use of local, dark dolerite stone all added to the feel of the 'swelling feudal castle', as Scott had described Horace Walpole's Strawberry Hill in his introduction to the 1821 edition of *The Castle of Otranto*. The main central block and dining hall were completed by 1837. The motivation to finish these seems to have been the visit of Nicholas and his family, with Zhukovsky, on a royal tour of the new Russian province. In November the following year Vorontsov was in Scotland, admiring (as he wrote to his wife Elizabeth) the hilly landscapes, recalling the sad novels of Walter Scott, and being surprised at a first impression by the associations with the Crimea.[31] Subsequently he sets in motion a further phase of building at Alupka, which included the library wing, the Bakhchisarai and Georgian courts and the southern terraces with their Italian marble lions. Antique marble from the Greek colonies in the Crimea, then being excavated, was used to make flowerbed surrounds, fountains and 'sarcophagus' ornaments in the gardens. A Venetian cannon given to Vorontsov by Nicholas was also displayed.

The element of surprise, synthesis and change that was valued as life-enhancing by both Scott and Davydov is everywhere to be felt. The northern façade is Tudor, the southern, with its iwan-style portal, Moorish (Fig. 10). There are roundels and square towers; discrete dark corners and light open spaces; onion domes and ogival apertures; a small Chinese study and a large Blue Salon; a Turkish room and a Chintz drawing room; wainscoting, coffered ceilings and English wallpapers; an oriental tiled fountain instead of a fireplace (Fig. 11); roofs at various levels and of differing pitch. Individually the dining hall and the Gothic library are most reminiscent of Abbotsford.

FIGURE 11
Alupka Palace, Crimea. Edward Blore, William Hunt, 1831–48. Fountain in the Dining Hall.
(Photograph: Jeremy Howard, 1997)

Yet behind the whole of Alupka, and the rest of the Russian creations discussed here, lies the shadow of Scott. Paramount is the suggestion of 'roots', of compatibility with place and country; the evocation of the medieval, the antique and the individual. Such fusion of assemblage, location and idea may be seen as part of the legitimisation of a quasi-history for political purpose. [32] It is also a materialisation of Scott's romance.

NOTES

1 *Journal*, p. 167. Scott spent 2–5 July 1826 in the company of the 17-year-old Russian count Vladimir Davydov. The rhyme surely derives from this meeting. The encounter was to signify a new breadth and vision to the burgeoning Russian romanticist movement: its concern with personal, political and artistic freedoms (and persuasions) henceforth reaching new heights in both the literary and plastic arts.

2 V. Davydov, *Putevye zapiski, vedennye vo vremya prebyvaniya na Ionicheskikh ostrovakh, v Gretsii, Maloy Azii I Turtsii v 1835 godu* (St Petersburg 1839) (trans., as all the citations from the Russian below, by JH).

3 N. Gogol, 'Ob arkhitekture nyneshnego vremeni', in *Arabeski. Raznye sochineniya N. Gogolya*, part 1 (St Petersburg 1835), pp. 229–71, as republished in N. V. Gogol *Sobranie sochineniy*. vol. 6 (Moscow 1978), pp. 78–9.

4 Ibid., p. 87.

5 Cited in G. A. Ol', *Aleksandr Bryullov* (Leningrad 1983), p. 44. It is worth noting that several members of the 'St Petersburg' branch of the Potocki family resided in Edinburgh in the early nineteenth century.

6 Dimmert was the interior designer. The house had recently been built by the prolific Joseph Charlemagne I, who had begun his career as a student of Charles Cameron. Charlemagne, like Bryullov, belonged to a family of French artists settled in modern Russia.

7 The watercolour is by Viktor Sotira (1803–39), apparently from Vienna, an architect and academician of the St Petersburg Academy. Princess Baryatinskaya (c. 1793–1858), like her architect Dimmert, was German. Her father was the Swabian Count Christophor Keller, her mother was a Sayn-Wittgenstein. Widowed in the late 1820s, her new St Petersburg mansion was to be a refuge for young children and widows. It is perhaps significant that it was created at the time that her eldest son Alexander, future field marshal, having returned from war in the Caucasus, had joined the retinue of the Grand Duke Alexander, heir to the throne, and was in the process of travelling to France and Britain where he studied and mixed in the circles associated with 'high' culture. The watercolour, accompanied by an inaccurate and confused text, is reproduced in C. Gere, *Nineteenth-Century Interiors: An Album of Watercolours* (London 1992), p. 136. The house passed to the Russian royal family (Grand Princess Olga) in 1901 and, following the 1917 revolution, became the local Chamber of Commerce. Very little has survived of the interiors.

8 A. L. Punin, *Arkhitektura Peterburga serediny XIX veka* (Leningrad 1990), p. 31.

9 See, for example, G. P. Berdnikov *et al.*, eds, *Russko-Angliiskie literaturnye svyazi (18 vek – pervaya polovina 19 veka)* (Moscow 1982), pp. 247–393; and M. G. Al'tshuller, *Epokha Val'tera Skotta v Rossii* (St Petersburg 1996).

10 See R. F. Christian's slight study 'Sir Walter Scott, Russia and Tolstoy', *Scottish Slavonic Review*, Spring 1988, pp. 75–91. The only detailed account is in *Russko-Angliiskie literaturnye svyazi*.

11 Von Nicolai was adviser and secretary to Count Semyon Vorontsov, Russian Ambassador to London, whose own celebration of Scott is described below. Nicolai further employed Tatham to design an obelisk in memory of his French emigré brothers-in-law, the Princes Auguste and Carl de Broglie who had been killed while serving in the Russian army against Napoleon, at Austerlitz and Kulm.

12 Anon. 'Mr Allan's Pictures', *The Scotsman*, no. 1, 25 January 1817, p. 7. The paintings mentioned in the review were reunited and brought back to Edinburgh for the first time since 1816 for the 'Sir William Allan: Artist Adventurer' exhibition, at the City Art Centre, June–October 2001. See Jeremy Howard, *William Allan: Artist Adventurer* (Edinburgh 2001).

13 Originally printed on 19 December 1816, shortly afterwards the ode was reproduced together with a detailed account of the Nicholas' visit to Allan in *The Scots Magazine* (vol. 79, 1817), p. 75.

14 See *Letters*, vol. 1, p. 512.

15 This and the foregoing quote from Susanna (Fenimore) Cooper is cited in *Russko-Angliiskie literaturnye svyazi*, p. 366; see *Journal*, p. 233.

16 See *Russko-Angliiskie literaturnye svyazi*, pp. 261f and 376f.

17 'November 24 [1825] . . . Count Olonym (Olonyne – that's it), son of the President of the Royal Society and a captain in the Imperial Guards. He is mean-looking and sickly, but has much sense, candour, and general information', *The Journal of Sir Walter Scott* (Edinburgh 1998), p. 14. Neither W. E. K. Anderson nor J. G. Tait (Edinburgh 1939), successive editors of Scott's journal, identified Olenin.

18 Cited in *Russko-Angliiskie literaturnye svyazi*, p. 265.

19 *Journal*, p. 380 (entry for 18 November 1827).

20 See *Russko-Angliiskie literaturnye svyazi*, pp. 313–19. Staying at 42 York Place, Davydov's integration into Edinburgh society was remarkable. He was taught and became highly respected by his professors: William Hamilton, James Pillans and John Wilson. He graduated with an arts degree in 1828 and was subsequently awarded a doctorate through the agency of his former tutors (see below).

21 It is possible to conjecture, given the healthy mutual regard expressed in their contemporary correspondence, that Hamilton's historical concerns, combined with his advance of a critique of Cousin and Kant in his ideas concerning the relativity of perception and the ineffibility of God, comprised a type of synthetic metaphysics attractive to Davydov.

22 See, for example, *Russko-Angliiskie literaturnye svyazi*, p. 367. The painting is in the State Russian Museum in St Petersburg.

23 Samoilova was also prominent among those taken up by the contemporary Russian vogue for the Gothic Revival. She adorned her spacious Milan villa with Gothic furniture made by Gambs in St Petersburg in 1835. Alexander Bryullov designed her summer house near St Petersburg in the early 1830s.

24 See *Russko-Angliiskie literaturnye svyazi*, pp. 316–21.

25 *Putevye zapiski*, part one, p. 220. Significantly, in an appendix to the *Travel Notes*, Karl Friedrich Schinkel echoed Davydov's ideas and noted how he had been helped in his recent Greek projects by the use of Yefimov's and Bryullov's site drawings and plans. Schinkel had been engaged by Tsar Nicholas in the construction of a Gothic Revival chapel at Peterhof and the planning of a Greek Revival palace at Orianda in the Crimea.

26 Pavlino was built by the young architect Alexander Kudinov. The Sotira interiors, together with two from the Davydov property at Ivanovski, are reproduced as part of the 'Wittgenstein Album' in *Nineteenth-Century Interiors*. Davydov was connected through his marriage to the Sayn-Wittgensteins, an immensely wealthy family, originally from Westphalia, whose younger

members also adopted the Gothic Revival style for several of their houses. In 1834 they also employed Alexander Bryullov to design a church and pavilions for their Druzhnosel'ye estate south of St Petersburg.

27 Concerning Otrada and Bykovsky, a leading Moscow architect of the period and organiser of the first Moscow art school, see E. I. Kirichenko, *Mikhail Bykovskii* (Moscow 1988).

28 As viewed in Thomas Sandby's picture on a piece of the Wedgwood Frog Service for Catherine the Great; and an engraving hung in the nearby Tsarskoye Selo Admiralty.

29 See *Romantic Interior*, p. 201f.

30 *Letters*, IV, pp. 333–4, to Daniel Terry, 28 December 1816.

31 See A. Galichenko, *Alupka. Dvorets i park* (Kiev 1992), p. 25.

32 In fact the oriental appearance of the southern façade, the coastal location and some of the internal details, bring to mind the colonial romanticism of Nash's Royal Pavilion in Brighton (1815–22).

I am grateful to the British Academy for its support of fieldwork concerned with the gathering of material presented here. JH

RUSKIN ON SCOTT'S ABBOTSFORD

Julie Lawson

THE year 2000 was marked by a number of events designed to celebrate the life and legacy of John Ruskin (1819–1900). An impressive exhibition held at the Tate Gallery in London reminded us not only of Ruskin's skill as a painter and draughtsman but also of his importance as an art critic: his eloquence and descriptive powers, when applied to paintings, have probably never been surpassed. Ruskin was the champion of Turner whose greatness he quite literally taught us to see. He also defended the Pre-Raphaelite painters against their critics, particularly commending the religious and high moral character of their subject-matter, and, most importantly, the fact that their work insisted upon close scrutiny of Nature which Ruskin asserted was the basis of all great art.

A conference held at Ruskin's own college, Christ Church, Oxford, served in turn as a reminder of his equally important contribution to the economic and political thinking of his day. There was his opposition to John Stuart Mill's Utilitarianism, his proto-Marxist opposition to the factory system and the capitalist mode of production, and his influence on political thinkers including William Morris, Tolstoy, the Fabians, and Gandhi.

At the Oxford conference was one speaker, however, who, somewhat apologetically, introduced a discordant note into the proceedings. The historian Simon Schama had elected to speak about Ruskin and Dutch art. His paper contained a seemingly relentless and somewhat mystifying barrage of quotations from Ruskin castigating the Dutch School of painters for their insincerity, inferiority and immorality. It was disconcerting to hear such criticism of some of the greatest and best-loved landscape painters, such as Ruisdael and Hobbema, particularly as they had been so much admired and emulated by Ruskin's own idol, Turner. The paper reminded us sharply that Ruskin's pronouncements on art were based upon very complex, passionately held beliefs about art and its place in society. Schama demonstrated that Ruskin's aesthetic was an emphatic denial of the autonomy of crafts and genres. Ruskin's social and moral views drove his aesthetic judgements, resulting in violent dislike of some artists and some styles of art and architecture as well as great enthusiasms and adulation of others. In fact, the strong negative responses Ruskin displayed to some kinds of painting and building should be seen as the inevitable result of his positive responses to others. They are mutually defining, inextricably bound together, two sides of the same coin.

If our admiration for Dutch painting must coexist with our appreciation of Ruskin's thought, something similar must apply at Abbotsford. An apologia for Ruskin's negativity, on the grounds that an attempt to understand the reasons for it will lead to a greater understanding of his thinking in general, can also serve as a warning when it comes to a consideration of Ruskin's views on Abbotsford. To say that Ruskin disliked the building would be to understate the case. Being Ruskin, and not given to moderation when it came to his aesthetic feelings, it would be more accurate to say that he hated it. Our task is to discover the reasons for this strength of feeling and dislike of the building, never fully articulated by Ruskin himself.

It is important to note that Sir Walter Scott was one of John Ruskin's heroes. If he disliked Abbotsford, he worshipped its begetter. As a child in the 1820s Ruskin had eagerly awaited the appearance of each of the novels, which his Scottish father would read aloud to him. 'The series of Waverley novels was,' he wrote, 'the chief source of delight in all households caring for literature; and I can no more recollect the time when I did not know them than when I did not know the Bible.'[1] Indeed, Scott, and the dramatic world that his novels opened up for the young Ruskin, must have been a welcome relief from the passages of the Bible that his pious Scots mother, who had dedicated him to God before he was born, made him learn by heart every day.

Ruskin continued to read and re-read the works of Scott throughout his life. He always took them with him on his travels, and they were his constant bedside reading.[2] The reason for Scott's presiding presence in Ruskin's imagination, I believe, is that he found that it was Scott, more than any other writer, who had the power to transport him into another time and place. Scott's exciting romances epitomised a literature that met a popular appetite which Ruskin shared, but which he had to an intense degree. Ruskin was constantly in search of self-forgetting experience. This experience of loss of a sense of 'self' was one that he found again in sublime landscape. The value of distraction from self-absorption to this highly sensitive only child was enormous. He was to seek and find the experience again when looking at great painting.

As champion of the Pre-Raphaelite painters, Ruskin favoured a kind of painting that deliberately set itself apart from familiar academic values. He preferred the sincere naïvety, as he thought it, of the Italian Primitives over the insouciant mastery of their sophisticated successors. In Scott, Ruskin found the perfect writer. Scott could paint in words in the Pre-Raphaelite manner, paying attention to the smallest details of the natural world, or equally with the breadth and sweep of Turner, firing the imagination of the reader. It was this Prospero-like power of Scott's appeal to the imagination that was, when it came to its manifestation in architecture, part of the problem Ruskin had with Abbotsford.

Ruskin first visited the house in 1838 as a young man, and found it to be a bitter disappointment.[3] At first, this may come as something of a surprise. It is certainly the case that we can readily list those aspects of the house that we should expect to have met with Ruskin's approval. Most obviously, there is the fact that Abbotsford is an example of Gothic Revival. The medievalism of Scott was, after all, one of the influences on both Ruskin and Pugin as admirers and advocates of Gothic architecture. Ruskin effectively acknowledged this in his first 'Edinburgh Lecture' on 'Gothic Architecture' delivered at the Edinburgh Philosophical Institution in November 1853. In seeking to demonstrate the superiority of the Gothic over the bland and repetitive Classical style, he cited examples of Scott's use of evocative architectural terms such as 'turret' and 'spire' in preference to more pedestrian lacklustre vocabulary. Scott's writings reveal his appreciation of the effect on the reader of the language of Gothic architecture. This matter of 'effect', when it comes to the actual building, is something that also gives a clue as to why Ruskin disliked Abbotsford so much. Ruskin was forced to confront, in Scott the builder, something of the mountebank.

Like Pugin, Ruskin advocated the use of Gothic in secular as well as religious buildings; so we need not suppose that he would have disapproved of the incorporation of carved saints and Latin inscriptions into the fabric at Abbotsford. Much has been written, not least by Ruskin himself, acknowledging the fact that, when he responded negatively to works of art or a particular style of architecture or building – particularly in his youth – this was often because of certain 'Protestant' prejudices on his part. At the more practical level, Ruskin would undoubtedly have approved of Scott's use of local stone at Abbotsford. He believed that architects should build with the materials that were to hand rather than import from further afield.

It is to Ruskin's own analysis of Gothic architecture that we must turn in order to understand his disapproval of Abbotsford. In *The Seven Lamps of Architecture* he gives the most complete statement of his interpretation of Gothic. The seven lamps referred to in the title are the lamps of Sacrifice, Truth, Power, Beauty, Life, Memory and Obedience. Under these different headings, Ruskin amplifies and elaborates his passionately held belief that Gothic architecture was essentially an expression of the highest moral values. Architecture, for Ruskin, was a language that spoke clearly and eloquently of the society that produced it. Gothic is, of course, set up in opposition to Classicism, which Ruskin berated as a style based on pride and tyranny. If the classical craftsman is a slave, obliged to repeat *ad infinitum* the established forms and motifs of the 'orders', the medieval mason is at liberty to express his love of nature, and through that his worship of God, in the free exercise of his skills and his imagination.

In *Modern Painters,* Ruskin has the following harsh words to say of the man whom he admired so much as a writer.

> More than any age that had preceded it, ours had been ignorant of the meaning of the word Art. It had not a single fixed principle, and what unfixed principles it worked upon were all wrong. It was necessary that Scott should know nothing of art. He neither cared for painting nor sculpture, and was totally incapable of forming a judgement about them. He has some confused love of Gothic architecture, because it was dark, picturesque, old and like nature; but he could not tell the worst from the best and built for himself perhaps the most incongruous and ugly pile that gentlemanly modernism ever designed.[4]

What, then, for Ruskin made Abbotsford an 'incongruous and ugly pile'? In order to attempt an answer, we might first of all adopt a 'Pre-Raphaelite' method of close examination of the details. In, for example, the carving of the foliated panels in the frieze of the garden arcade (Fig. 1), each one is different, according to the Gothic principle of variety and 'freedom'. It might be assumed, therefore, that Ruskin would have delighted in this detail executed by craftsmen who have clearly looked closely at individual plant forms. However, the fact that each one of these carved plants is circumscribed or confined within a square, so that the overriding impression is one of order and uniformity, means that it would fail to meet Ruskin's criteria. He would have condemned it because the insistently imposed pattern and the regimented character of this architectural feature dominates the sculptor's art. In fact, this is a kind of Gothic – Tudor or Perpendicular Gothic – that Ruskin particularly disliked, considering it to be a regulated and therefore debased form of Gothic.

Inside Abbotsford we might suppose that the Library, a handsome panelled room full of light, and pleasing in its proportions, should have impressed Ruskin. But on closer observation (and few people can ever have observed more closely than Ruskin) he would have noticed that here was an example of something else he loathed. In his chapter entitled 'The Lamp of Truth' in *The Seven Lamps of Architecture*, Ruskin asserted that: 'The violation of truth which dishonour poetry and painting are . . . for the most part . . . confined to the treatment of their subjects. But in architecture another and a

FIGURE 1
Frieze of the garden arcade.
(Photograph: Julie Lawson)

less subtle, more contemptible, violation of truth is possible; a direct falsity of assertion respecting the nature of material, or the quantity of labour.'[5] One of the ways in which this architectural deceit manifests itself – he goes on to say – is in 'the painting of surfaces to represent some other material than that of which they actually consist (as in the marbling of wood) or the deceptive representation of sculptured ornament upon them'.[6] In the Library what at first glance we take to be wooden panelling and ornamentation – the carved ceiling bosses – is, in fact, wood-grained plaster. In that case, the structural material is not all it seems.

Also in the Library there is an example of something Ruskin considered an unforgivable breach of architectural decorum. That is, the use of a 'quotation' from a medieval building in a modern domestic interior for an inappropriate or incongruous function. Ruskin actually cites the fireplace in the Library as an example of an error he regarded as typical of the age. He wrote that Scott '. . . reverences Melrose Abbey yet casts one of its piscinas, puts a modern steel grate into it, and makes it his fireplace'.[7] At worst, this 'mingling of reverence and irreverence' was sacrilege, and at best, bad taste.

Elsewhere, we might speculate on what would have displeased the critic. Scott had a collection of casts of 'grotesque' medieval carvings on display at Abbotsford. While the spirit of 'the grotesque' in Gothic ornament was praised by Ruskin as an embodiment of the freedom and exuberance of the medieval masons, and even the very coarsest of sculpted figures were proof, for him, of noble vitality, here the type is of a debased and degenerate kind. The casts are vulgar rather than grotesque in the sense of untrammelled and untamed. This was, for Ruskin, quite a different thing. When we examine these carvings at Abbotsford we are obliged to acknowledge that there is something formulaic in their 'freedom'.

Ruskin may well have known that Scott's original intention had been to build himself a modest house on the River Tweed at Abbotsford. The ostentation evident in what Abbotsford evolved into may have saddened Ruskin. He would have thought such materialism unworthy of as great a man as Scott. Ruskin would have agreed with his friend and mentor, Thomas Carlyle, who wrote:

> Alas, Scott, with all his health, was infected; sick of the fearfulest malady, that of Ambition! To such length had the King's baronetcy, the world's favour and 'sixteen parties a-day', brought it with him. So the inane racket must be kept up, and rise even higher. So masons labour, ditchers delve; and there is endless, altogether deplorable correspondence about marble slabs for tables, wainscoting of room, curtains and the trimmings of curtains, orange-coloured or fawn-coloured: Walter Scott, one of the gifted of the world, whom his admirers call the most gifted, must kill himself that he may be a country gentleman, the founder of a race of Scottish lairds.
>
> It is one of the strangest, most tragical histories ever enacted under the sun. So poor a passion can lead so strong a man into such extremes. Surely, were not man a fool always, one might say there was something eminently distracted in this, end as it would, of a Walter Scott writing daily with the ardour of a steam-engine, that he might make £15,000 a year, and buy upholstery with it.[8]

We could go on to enumerate details of the ornamentation and furnishing at Abbotsford which may have met with Ruskin's disapproval: the suits of armour, the relics, the walls covered with weaponry – all the trappings and show that denote an ancient lineage. However, it is equally important to consider the more general aspect of the building. The façade of the house gives the impression of having grown over time rather than having been pre-planned by an architect. It is an architectural idea that we later expect from Edwin Lutyens or Norman Shaw, in houses designed to give the impression of being not new but of having grown by accretion over the centuries. This, in turn, created the impression that the inhabitants could trace their forebears back to the Elizabethans if not the Normans. It was presumably in the interests of speed of construction that standard sash-and-case windows, familiar to Ruskin from his walk along Queen Street in Edinburgh in 1853, were used on the river façade at Abbotsford (Fig. 2). It would not have escaped Ruskin's notice that the building is not so varied as it might at first seem. Ruskin in fact wrote of Scott: '. . . he supposes the Gothic barbarous, notwithstanding his love of it; admires, in an equally ignorant way, totally opposite styles; is delighted with the new town of Edinburgh; [and] mistakes its dullness for purity of taste.'[9]

FIGURE 2
Windows on the River Tweed side of the building.
(Photograph: Julie Lawson)

Whereas for Ruskin, the admiration of Gothic architecture was based on analytical study of its underlying principles and its detail, Scott's concern was with effect. It was to do with the impact – at a glance one might say – of the whole building on the senses and, thence, on the imagination. Notions of 'integrity' and 'honesty' in architecture, so important to Ruskin, would have meant little or nothing to Scott. We should recall that it was Scott who exhorted us to see Melrose Abbey by moonlight. While Ruskin was far from impervious to the Romantic effects of buildings, he did not stop there. For him, they were sermons in stones. For Scott, who, as Ruskin says, 'gathered what little knowledge of architecture he possessed, in wanderings among the rocky walls of Crichtoun, Lochleven, and Linlithgow and among the delicate pillars of Holyrood, Roslin and Melrose'[10] buildings were primarily an access to the past and a trigger to the imagination.

The small tower at Abbotsford epitomises Scott's medievalism as characterised by Ruskin (Fig. 3). Its miniature, 'domestic' scale renders it so clearly pointless. Its purpose is decorative rather than defensive. It is, in short, theatrical. The theatricality of much of Abbotsford is what Ruskin would have found impossible to stomach. Scott has provided himself with a kind of stage-set for a scene from *Ivanhoe* – a place where he could imagine that he was going to meet a knight in armour, or a damsel in distress. The tower is a folly within a folly. This is a building eminently suited to the great impresario who stage-managed the biggest fancy dress party or piece of amateur theatricals in Scottish history – the visit of George IV to Edinburgh. The 'Wizard of the North' could pretend to be Merlin at Abbotsford. Ruskin himself sums it up: 'Scott's romance and antiquarianism, his knighthood and monkery, are all false – and he knows them to be false.'[11]

Ruskin allows himself a rare public statement about Scott and Abbotsford in the Appendix to *The Seven Lamps of Architecture*. Summing up what he describes as 'The four modes of admiration', Ruskin identifies a common mode of admiration of Gothic architecture. This he calls:

> Sentimental Admiration: the kind of feeling which most travellers experience on first entering a cathedral by torchlight and hearing a chant from concealed choristers; or in visiting a ruined abbey by moonlight, or any building with which interesting associations are connected, at any time when they can hardly see it.[12]

He goes on to say:

> This kind of feeling is instinctive and simple . . . excitable in nearly all persons, by a certain amount of darkness and slow music in a minor key . . . on the whole . . . apt to rest in theatrical effect, and to be as well satisfied with the incantation scene from 'Robert le Diable', provided there were enough gauze and feux-follets, as by the Cathedral of Rheims . . . Even in its highest manifestation, in the great mind of Scott, while it indeed led him to lay his scenes in Melrose Abbey and Glasgow Cathedral, rather than in St Paul's or St Peter's, it did not enable him to see the difference between true Gothic at Glasgow, and false Gothic at Abbotsford.[13]

FIGURE 3
Tower at Abbotsford.
(Photograph: Julie Lawson)

NOTES

When quotations from John Ruskin are taken from the Library Edition, *The Works of John Ruskin*, ed. E. T. Cook and Alexander Wedderburn, 39 vols (London 1903–12), references will be given by volume and page, e.g. C&W, XXXIV, p. 700.

1 John Ruskin, *Praeterita*, (Oxford University Press 1978 edn), p. 30.
2 C&W, XXXIV, p. 700.
3 C&W, I, p. 163.
4 C&W, V, p. 338.
5 John Ruskin, *The Seven Lamps of Architecture* (London 1891), p. 60.
6 Ibid., p. 62.
7 Loc. cit.
8 Thomas Carlyle, *Scottish and other Miscellanies* (London, 1967), I, p. 98.
9 John Ruskin, *Modern Painters* (London 1888), IV, p. 272.
10 Ibid., p. 316.
11 Ibid., p. 271.
12 John Ruskin, *The Seven Lamps of Architecture* (London 1891), p. 390.
13 Loc. cit.

INDEX

References to illustrations are in **bold** type